Club George

Club George

THE DIARY

OF A CENTRAL PARK

BIRDWATCHER

Bob Levy

THOMAS DUNNE BOOKS
St. Martin's Press
New York

THOMAS DUNNE BOOKS.
An imprint of St. Martin's Press.

www.stmartins.com

Design by Kathryn Parise

Library of Congress Cataloging-in-Publication Data
Levy, Bob.
    Club George : the diary of a Central Park birdwatcher / Bob
Levy.
       p. cm.
    ISBN 0-312-34167-9
    EAN 978-0-312-34167-1
    1. Red-winged blackbird—New York (State)—New York
Anecdotes. 2. Bird watching—New York (State)—New York—
Anecdotes. 3. Central Park (New York, N.Y.) I. Title.

QL696.P2475 L48 2006
598'.07'2347471—dc22

                                                    2005051887

First Edition: March 2006

10   9   8   7   6   5   4   3   2   1

Contents

Preface

A Mentor I Was Meant For

Many of us have had the good fortune to find a mentor who took us under her or his wing at just the right moment in our lives. We found someone who provided the guidance, support and encouragement without which we might never have succeeded or even attempted a new endeavor. My book is about a most unexpected mentor in the form of a wild, 8.75 inch long, 2 ounce Redwinged Blackbird named George who inspired me with a new awareness and appreciation of his kind. Rather than taking place in a rural landscape or remote wilderness, the setting for my trans-

Here's my favorite photo of George. I have no way to know if it's his favorite or not. In fact, I have shown him a few pictures of himself, but he always seemed completely disinterested. That's not so unusual. Many humans I know don't like to see pictures of themselves. I'm one of them.

formation into a bird-watcher is New York City's Central Park. The other characters in the text are mostly birds though humans do pop into and out of the story. The book is partly beginning bird-watchers' primer, partly inspirational, partly amateur naturalist's journal, partly photographic essay, partly Central Park tribute and, if I have been able to put the reader into the right mood, partly humorous. It is in the form of a journal beginning with George's arrival in his Central Park breeding ground during the spring migration and ending with his departure during the fall migration. I tell tales about George and many of the other birds I encountered during that four-month interval.

Central Park had long been a favorite place to relax but having recently been downsized out of my corporate career it became a place to seek solace during a period of involuntary unemployment. As self-prescribed therapy I started to keep a journal about my increasingly frequent and lengthening visits to the park. What began as a private diary became a public account of my evolution into a bird-watcher. Sometimes it may read like a detective story as I try to understand an observation whose meaning is at first a mystery to me. However, it is not a reference book or a scientific study though I do report others' research about birds where academic explanations may be needed. I am delighted to have had the advice and encouragement of Ken Yasukawa, Professor and Chair, Beloit College Department of Biology, whose concise and insightful explanations of Red-winged Blackbird behavior and review of portions of the text kept my enthusiastic interpretations about George anchored in the world of science fact and, due to my lack of scientific expertise, not into the world of science fiction. That being said, please be advised that I will volunteer personal insights and commentary that you will not find in reference books.

Central Park is also central to my story as many readers will be surprised to learn how many birds are permanent, part-time residents or transient visitors there. Finally, I hope to demonstrate that anyone can have similar experiences if she or he would only open themselves up to them when the opportunity arrives.

I do not offer this story to suggest Central Park is a virtual peaceable kingdom where one may see the "lion lay down with the lamb" but it does illustrate my point that some birds have adjusted their behaviors to accommodate the presence of people in their environment. I have evidence that not only have birds' behaviors been altered but so have human beings'. I offer myself as living proof that this is so. My behavior changed in significant ways as a direct result of my first interactions with George. I believe that is all the more remarkable because he initiated those interactions.

One would expect a wild Red-winged Blackbird to be either in constant conflict with human intruders or to seek out a territory where it could hope to avoid them. Apparently George, and others of his species in the park, have chosen a third course. These birds have decided if they cannot "beat 'em" they can "join 'em." They return here year after year to successfully reproduce and not only coexist with us but, in George's case, use us as a natural resource. George has come to recognize that people can provide nourishment for himself and his offspring and he has taken deliberate and effective steps to act on his discovery. This ability to do this demonstrates a kind of intelligence at work that I would not have suspected this songbird and others possess. Birds are much smarter than most of us think.

A review of the table of contents will reveal that there are more than seventy chapters in *Club George*. Do not despair. That may seem like an alarming number but remember this is a journal covering a four-month period. Most chapters relate the events of a single day and are very short. I promise.

Even though I freely reveal that all events described in *Club George* took place in New York's Central Park there are no maps or precise directions to enable the reader to literally follow in my footsteps. I have thinly disguised some geographical locations in Central Park because I would not want to encourage a flood of people to deluge these sites. I am well aware that in putting these tales in writing I encourage visitors but at the same I want to protect the birds and their habitat. So, I thought a little bit of judicious obfuscation would be useful. For those readers familiar with Central Park the locations will be transparent. For others consulting a map or someone knowledgeable with the park's geography would be necessary to pinpoint every location. I trust that those who are determined to make an effort to visit these spots are the sorts of people who are likely to share a passion for birds and will act responsibly and respectfully. As a consequence of their close proximity within the finite borders of this refuge nonhuman and human species coexist and interact in a variety of ways. Oddly the birds are much more aware of this relationship than are the majority of people; the birds know we are here; the people more often than not are oblivious to the birds.

The birds are not the only ones in need of special consideration. Many names of the people in *Club George* have been changed in accordance with their wishes to protect their privacy. The birds, however, did not express sensitivity in this area and therefore their names remain unchanged.

Acknowledgments

I am grateful to my brother Walter Levy and Gene Moncrief, his wife, for their encouragement and suggestions when I first told them that I wanted to write a book. There are several Central Park bird-watchers who generously shared their knowledge and camaraderie before, during, and after the events described in this text. I might have listed them but then so many of them have never revealed their full names to me. Sigh. Instead I will single out one among them who gave me the most assistance when I most needed it. I express my gratitude to Ben Cacace for his invaluable advice when I first began bird-watching. I could not possibly fail to single out Tony Outhwaite my friend, fellow jazz fan, and business associate who made this project a reality and to Ms. Marcia Markland at St. Martin's for her faith, enthusiasm, and hard work on the project. No less praise goes to Diana Szu at St. Martin's, as well. Of course, Ken Yasukawa's expertise, patience, and generosity were invaluable in helping me understand and explain the behaviors of the birds I have observed.

None of these acknowledgments would have been forthcoming if I had not had the incredibly good fortune to make the acquaintance of the guiding force and source of inspiration that made the manuscript possible. Thank you George wherever you may be. I will be looking for you at the pond next year. Please do not be late.

Chapter 1

Welcome to the Club

The second of June was a cozily warm, gloriously sunny, summer New York City Sunday. It was the kind of day when the brilliant sunlight makes the scrawniest trees and sootiest buildings glisten. Even the gloomiest people seem to glow. Somehow the intense light brings out the beauty in the natural and unnatural worlds when logic says it should throw a spotlight on their faults.

I was in one of the best possible places to enjoy such a day in the Big Apple. In Central Park I stood on a wooden dock that juts out into a small hourglass shaped pond. It is surrounded by lush plantings of shrubs, grasses, flowers and trees. A fifty-five acre meadow that accommodates eight softball fields with ample space to spare

The song and display of any Red-winged Blackbird may or may not get the attention of the casual observer. However, there was no way I could fail to notice George's energetic and theatrical rendition.

1

for a multitude of picnickers opens on its northern shore. A stone castle set on top of a sheer cliff is the second highest point in the park. It overlooks a tiny island that dominates the southwest corner. By any standards it's one of the most picturesque spots in the park and had been one of my favorites long before the events described in my tale transpired.

On this particular day I was having a chat with Michael, a new acquaintance. He is an accountant by profession and a naturalist and arts enthusiast by inclination. Michael enjoys sharing his knowledge. He was in the midst of explaining to me that the most common turtles inhabiting the pond, the Mississippi Red-eared Sliders, are not native residents but instead are abandoned pets, when a male Red-winged Blackbird landed on the top of the wooden fence, a bird-blind, to our right. This bird perched, on a two-by-six plank, a foot and one-half above our heads and two feet in front of us. As Michael went on to tell me what he knew of the large Snapping Turtles that hunt and breed here, the Red-winged Blackbird began to loudly call "chek" repeatedly and then to sing "konk-la-ree" in an even louder voice. Still vocalizing, the bird raised his wings away from his body. This posture accentuated the display of his scarlet wing patches edged with pale yellow. The patches themselves appeared to literally stand up as if being raised by a charge of static electricity. The theatrical bird was distracting us from our conversation, but we persisted. So did the Red-winged Blackbird. He began to run back and forth still keeping his wings up and away from his torso flaunting his flaming red epaulets and singing passionately. Michael and I kept talking to each other but our eyes became fixed on the bird. After a while I realized that we had begun shouting so we could hear each other over the raucous Red-winged Blackbird.

The bird's singing became so insistent that I began asking Michael to repeat every word he said. I was a bit annoyed, a bit amused and more than a bit surprised by the bird's behavior. When I felt I could no longer act nonchalantly about the situation I said to Michael, using an appropriate New Yorkese expression, "What is it with this bird, anyway?" To which Michael matter-of-factly replied,

"Oh, that's George" as if that was all the explanation required for my understanding of the creature's behavior. "What do you mean, oh that's George?" I said. "Are you telling me you know this wild bird and that you call him George?" Michael did not offer detailed verbal clarification. Instead he gave a practical demonstration. "Watch this," he said, as he tore off a piece of a roll he had in his hand. He held the bread up to the top of the fence and said, "Come on, George." The Red-winged Blackbird immediately fell silent, let his wings fall to his sides and rapidly walked along the top of the fence toward Michael's hand. The bird gingerly took the bread from Michael's fingers and flew off to the nearby island where he landed on a rock and ate his food.

This was how George introduced himself to me.

I do not remember what I said next, but I do remember laughing and feeling more than a little astonished. "George is famous," Michael explained. "He will be back soon." In ten minutes George was back stridently singing his "konk-la-ree" Red-winged Blackbird tune and flaunting those scarlet epaulets. I asked Michael if he thought George might take food from my hand. He saw no reason why he would not. I got a bit of Michael's roll and held it up for the bird. In an instant George rushed toward me and took the bread in his beak and sped off to the island again. This put a smile on my face that I could not wipe off for the next hour. I did not know it at the time, but it marked the beginning of a relationship and a heightening of my awareness of the natural world. Gradually, I would come to understand that I had been given an invitation to join a special club and by giving George an offering I had unconsciously accepted the invitation. I had become a charter member of Club George without knowing it.

What is it about this encounter that affected me so? Unquestionably, I was astounded that a wild animal had interacted and communicated with me. His dramatic audiovisual display had commandeered my attention. Once he had it, he delivered not so much a message, as a demand. George did not offer a timid, "Polly wants a cracker," but a forceful, "Hey buddy, feed me" instead.

The location of this encounter intensified the impact it had on me. The fact that it happened in a city park in the middle of one of the most densely populated and developed areas in the world made it all the more startling. Though still implausible, it seemed to me that this would have been more likely to happen in a sparsely inhabited area where one would have expectations to come into contact with wild animals. But then Central Park does have relatively more wildlife than its immediate surroundings. It is a virtual lifeboat for creatures of the natural world that are surrounded by a man-made sea of concrete and steel. It is home for numerous species of birds, mammals, insects, reptiles, amphibians and spiders that have few places as hospitable to inhabit. It is also the temporary home to dozens more bird species during their spring and fall migration. Though it was not its creators' principal intention, Central Park is a strategically placed haven for birds to rest, feed and even raise offspring as they move along the Atlantic migratory route stretching from Canada to South America.

Because its geography attracts migrating birds Central Park is known as a "migrant trap" to birders around the world. The Central Park Conservancy boasts that the park is "one of the top fifteen bird-watching sites in the entire United States."[1] Marie Winn, science writer for the *Wall Street Journal*, author, translator and birdwatcher, quotes bird expert Roger F. Pasquier as having named the park "one of America's fourteen great bird-watching locales."[2] Marie is pretty fond of it herself. David Allen Sibley, author and artist of several avian works, ranks the park along with Cape May, New Jersey, and the Monterey Peninsula in California as one of the three top bird-watching spots in North America.[3] Other experts might argue that there are geographical sites that offer many more species, rare species or larger numbers of a specific species. Some say ranking locations is inherently futile because the results can vary depending on which of those different criteria I mentioned

[1] www.centralparknyc.org. Virtual Park link for the Central Park Ramble.
[2] Marie Winn, *Red-Tails in Love*, p. 23.
[3] David Allen Sibley, *Sibley's Birding Basics*, p. 17.

are used. Perhaps the issue is best put into perspective by the American Bird Conservancy, which has this to say on the subject.

> Urban green areas—such as city parks and cemeteries—are often the only spots for migrant birds to alight for miles around. Surrounded by roads and buildings, they offer at least temporary respite during the long journey north or south, and birds head for them by the thousands. Resident species tend to be few, but at two seasons of the year a sharp observer can find scores of species in a single morning. Every birder has a few favorite spots like this, but some are justifiably famous for the number and variety of birds they attract—some far outside their normal ranges. These include Central Park in Manhattan; Prospect Park in Brooklyn; Mt. Auburn Cemetery in Cambridge, Massachusetts; Rock Creek in Washington, D.C.; the Magic Hedge on Chicago's Lakefront; the "Migrant Trap" in nearby Hammond, Indiana; and Golden Gate Park in San Francisco.[4]

The number of permanent resident bird species in Central Park is arguably twenty-four. I say "arguably" because at times a few individuals of a species spend a winter there while the majority does not. The total number soars to roughly two hundred when migratory birds visit in the fall and spring.[5] Some species included in this count can be seen flying over the park though they do not usually land there. Birders who track these "flyovers" report hundreds and even thousands of individuals of a particular species traveling in flocks. There is irony in the realization that this haven for wild birds is the product of labors to alter the natural environment with the prodigious application of technologies such as hydraulics, architecture, construction, landscaping, and horticulture among others.

[4]Robert M. Chipley, George H. Fenwick, Michael J. Parr, and David N. Pashley, *The American Bird Conservancy Guide to the 500 Most Important Bird Areas in the United States, Key Sites for Birds and Birding in All 50 States*, p. 322.
[5]The Central Park Conservancy Web site says there are as many as 212 different species over the course of a year. Refer to their Web site at www.centralparknyc.org. for details.

Central Park is a complete fabrication down to the last imported ounce of topsoil covering its 843 acres, which by the way came from New Jersey.

Before meeting George I had never been what you could describe as a nature enthusiast and certainly not a bird-watcher but I always thought of myself as one who was concerned about the state of the environment. I considered myself a person who took time to "smell the roses." I appreciated the beauty of the physical world and was curious about the creatures in it. When George "spoke to me" he asked me to enter into his world where I would also be introduced to other members of his club, but it was going to be up to me to get to know and understand them.

There were so many different kinds of birds in George's territory that I started to make lists of them on my calendar so I could later look up essential facts about each one. Many of these birds were already familiar to me. Even a self-absorbed New Yorker must notice the ubiquitous Rock Pigeon, House Sparrow, and European Starling nearly every day. Others were entirely new to me. For example, the Black-crowned Night Heron, Cedar Waxwing, Belted Kingfisher, Great Egret, Great Blue Heron and Barn Swallow were some of George's neighbors that I had inexplicably missed during my "Pre-George" existence. The lists I made on my calendar gradually became notes. The notes evolved into journal entries I typed into my computer several days a week. The journal grew until it became a story about how my incremental discoveries about George and his neighbors led to my admiration of all birds and their environment.

While watching the birds around George's Pond my powers of observation increased as I exercised them. Trying to make sense of what I saw obliged me to do research. It was not long before I found the two reference books I owned were not sufficient. In a short time I collected a dozen texts each having its strengths and weaknesses, but all of them complementing each other. For example, the *Peterson Field Guide*, which many consider to be the archetypal bird "field guide," is excellent for highlighting the key features that most readily identify a species. Fred J. Alsop III's *Birds of North America: Eastern Region* has a concise one-page summary for each bird that provides not just physical descriptions but facts about behavior, breeding, nesting, songs, calls, size, wingspan, and weight. Most other field guides do not pull all this information together but focus mainly on physiognomy and vocalizations. For an overview of the world of birds and detailed information about each bird family *The Sibley Guide to Bird Life & Behavior*, by David Allen Sibley proved to be indispensable, as did his *Guide to Birds* with its comprehensive descriptions of North American bird species. I found the condensed version, the *Sibley Field Guide to Birds*, was a convenient size to bring along on birding excursions and *Sibley's Birding Basics* was a superior how-to-bird-watch primer. Sibley, Alsop and Peterson's works are among the most helpful a birder can find but I can strongly recommend other texts also. They are too numerous to describe here but I feel duty-bound to make special mention of two books that should benefit novice birders. Kenn Kaufman's *A New Focus on the Field Birds of North America* and Donald and Lillian Stokes' *Stokes Field Guide to Birds* may be more user-friendly to the beginner but no less comprehensive than some other texts. A staple for many is Robbins, Brunn and Zim's *Birds of North America: A Guide to Field Identification*. The *Club George* bibliography lists still more volumes I unequivocally recommend.

There is one thing I urge you to do no matter what books or authors you select: read the introduction you were planning to skip over. Most introductions must of necessity be short and therefore in theory should concentrate a substantial dose of information into a mercifully small capsule that will not overtax your attention span. I believe you will thank me for suggesting this though it may not be for some time after you have waded through the material.

My dwelling on reference books may lead you to believe I only developed an intellectual curiosity about birds. To the contrary, after meeting George all succeeding birds looked to me like works of art. Even those commonly seen birds that I thought of as the "usual suspects" became gorgeous creatures in my eyes. "Post-George," when I looked at a Rock Pigeon I became aware of the iridescent green, purple and bronze on its neck. I looked beyond the American Robin's red breast to see the subtle white highlights on its tail, belly and eye ring. I noticed that the European Starling's black beak turns bright yellow and the white dots on its breast wear away by the time mating season arrives leaving black shiny feathers with shimmering iridescent highlights. The House Sparrow's plumage was not drab as so many describe it but instead it was subtle and refined. Before long I felt self-conscious when I offered a description of any bird at all because I caught myself piling on the superlatives to an embarrassing extent.

Another consequence of Club George membership was making the acquaintance of people who shared mutual interests. Spending long periods with George I met bird-watchers at the pond and when I expanded my bird-watching area, I met more. Park birders proved to be enthusiastic, knowledgeable or both. Though it may seem strange, however, I soon learned that many of them frequently speak to each other without ever knowing or asking one another's names. One such encounter with a resolutely anonymous bird-watcher typifies this New York birder behavior. Together this unidentified bird-watcher and I spied a flock of nearly two hundred birds flying over George's Pond. Taking only a cursory glance my companion concluded they were European Starlings but I, taking a harder look, recognized them as a migrating assemblage of George's Red-winged Blackbird relatives. The mention of Red-winged Blackbirds struck a chord with her. She turned and said, "You're 'George' aren't you?" I corrected her saying, "I'm Bob, but I am a fan of George if that's what you mean." She explained she did not mean to say my name was George, but that she knew me to be one of George's admirers. We never did learn each other's names even after a few subsequent chance meetings. Of course there are Central Park bird-watchers who actually do know each other's names. They even gather on a regular basis not just to bird-watch but to hobnob, consort and otherwise socialize with one another.

Though individual birders' names may or may not be of critical importance there are issues that are. One near continuous topic of conversation, and e-mail via birding networks like eBirds, is the controversy about when human observations in the field become interaction or even intervention in the lives of birds in general and in the feeding of birds in particular. Whether by hand or through the use of a bird feeder some folks argue that it creates problems. I understand these differing opinions. I feel that moderation is the right course. When I see a Red-winged Blackbird or a Northern Cardinal, for two favorite examples, a voice in my head says, "Eat birdie, eat." No doubt this is an unconscious echo of a paternal instinct that my mother instilled in a juvenile me when she would say, "Eat Bobaluh, eat." It is the sociable, noisy, bold species that bring out this behavior in me. I do not attempt to feed shy or unapproachable birds that hide in the brush or perch in the treetops. They are not interested in what edibles I might offer them so I leave them to their own culinary devices.

I am not alone as a bird feeding bird-watcher. Other bird-watchers are obvious about it and, trust me I know what I am talking about, some are closet bird feeders. They do not want it to become public knowledge that they indulge in the practice for fear they will be criticized. In *Red-Tails in Love,* however, Marie Winn points out that most of the Central Park bird-watchers she knows, whom she calls the "Regulars," cannot resist feeding wild birds.

> Sarah unscrewed a small black plastic film canister, removed a peanut fragment, and held it out on her hand. One of the titmice promptly landed and snatched the peanut away. She provided another peanut tidbit for me to do the same. I'm embarrassed to find in my notes that a bird's feet on the palm of the hand feel like "fairy wings." In years to come I was to see this little drama many times for most of the Regulars hand-feed the resident birds on occasion. Chickadees, blue jays, and cardinals are others that yammer to be fed when the Regulars walk by, though they only come close: titmice and chickadees alone actually come to the outstretched hand, with a downy woodpecker taking the plunge once in a blue moon.[6]

[6]Marie Winn, *Red-Tails in Love,* pp. 12–13.

Since she makes no mention of Red-winged Blackbird feet planted on her hand I conclude that Marie was not aware of George when she wrote this passage.

I have mentioned that there are about twenty-four resident bird species in the park but precisely what are they? According to the Central Park Conservancy list, these are the birds living in Central Park all year long: Great Blue Heron, Canada Goose, Mute Swan, Mallard, Red-tailed Hawk, American Kestrel, Peregrine Falcon, Ring-necked Pheasant, Eastern Screech-owl, Northern Mocking-bird, Ring-billed Gull, Herring Gull, Great Black-backed Gull, Rock Pigeon, Mourning Dove, Red-bellied Woodpecker, Downy Wood-pecker, Blue Jay, American Crow, Tufted Titmouse, European Star-ling, Northern Cardinal, House Finch, and House Sparrow. I have succeeded in becoming familiar to varying degrees with all except the American Kestrel and Peregrine Falcon. Frustratingly those two species continue to elude me and consequently are absent from my journal. The rest of this group of species that I refer to as the "usual suspects" will make appearances throughout my story.

The winter after first meeting George was particularly severe and it put tremendous stress on both the usual suspects and visiting migrant birds. It was so cold for such an extended period that al-most all the bodies of water in the park were completely frozen. There was one spot on Central Park Lake (hereafter called the Lake) that remained accessible. According to one widely dissemi-nated though unsubstantiated theory, the constant flow of water into the Lake from Tanner's Spring as it is popularly known, sup-posedly the only natural stream in the park, kept a portion of it from freezing. Here hundreds of waterbirds were able to find food and liquid water, as opposed to frozen water, to drink. Joining the ample Mallard population were some Black Ducks, two dozen Northern Shovelers, one dozen Wood Ducks, some Buffleheads, precisely two American Coots, numerous Ring-billed Gulls, one Great Blue Heron, one escaped domestic Long Island Duck and one domestic Muskovy Duck.

I cannot tell if I stood by a female or a male Great Blue Heron because the sexes look so much alike. I might add that these birds never really look blue to me in or out of a picture or water. Personally, I would have named the species the Great Bluish-Gray Heron, but that is a subjective opinion. What is indisputably objective is how this bird could remain nearly motionless for hours in the nearly frozen water exploiting people's largesse to its own personal advantage. This opportunistic heron would deliberately stand close to those who came to toss bread to the assorted hungry birds on the water. The Great Blue Heron had learned that the bread not only attracted birds but it also attracted fish. When a fish nibbled on a piece of bread within its reach the heron lunged at it. On one particularly freezing day the Great Blue Heron stood so close that I could see ice crystals clinging to its feathers. From that vantage point I watched the Blue Heron catch more than one fish. You might appreciate this scene a bit more knowing that the Great Blue Heron is not a little bird. It is between forty-six and fifty-two inches long from the tip of its beak to the end of its tail with a wingspan from seventy-seven to eighty-two inches.[7] Its stature, I presume, is why these herons are called "Great" and I have no quarrel with that description.

It was here on this same wintry Lake that I met a Mallard that aroused my latent paternal instincts in a big way. Sadly, this bird had a severe diagonal break across his beak. His beak was so mutilated that his pink tongue was visible even when the beak was closed. I felt sorry for him because of his injury and because the other Mallards constantly pecked him and he could not retaliate in kind. One day I brought some seeds especially for him. After I threw a few to him where he floated on the Lake, he paddled straight toward me, climbed out of the water slipping and sliding on the ice until he stood at my feet. His neck was stretched as far as it could be and his eyes stared into mine. I lowered my hand with the food and the Mallard unhesitatingly pressed his beak into it. He ate the seeds so furiously and with such abandon that half of them flew into the air. Five

---

[7]Author's note: Most field guides use average measurements of preserved specimens because there is often variation among populations. The length measures the distance from the tip of the beak to the end of the tail.

of the other Mallards and the escaped domestic Long Island Duck that had been watching from a distance came out of the water to snatch the spilled food lying on the icy ground. I was so amused by the boldness and frenzied eating habits of the beak-challenged Mallard that I decided to name him Daffy after the wildly exaggerated cartoon character. I returned nearly every day to feed this Daffy during the rest of the winter. Some of the other ducks continued to cash in on Daffy's good fortune as they shoved and pushed each other out of the way to get the food he dropped. It made me feel good to help Daffy and it looked to me that he felt pretty good about it too. Some birders said that I should not have fed him; that I should let nature take its course; that I should never intervene in the outcome of the survival of the fittest. I just could not bring myself to accept that.

In the heavily wooded thirty-eight acres known as the Ramble I found another spot where birds found some relief during that harsh winter. Zoe and a number of dedicated bird-watchers maintain a dozen bird feeders in a particular spot called Evodia Field, in the Ramble during the winter. Several different species of birds coexist here, at times begrudgingly, to get their share of the free breakfast, lunch and dinner. The first time I came to watch the birds at these feeders I thought I saw undulating waves on the ground. With the aid of binocular magnification I found I was actually watching fifty foraging White-throated Sparrows turning over fallen leaves to find bugs, seeds and who knows what else to eat. House Sparrows, House Finches, Northern Cardinals, Tufted Titmice, one White-breasted Nuthatch, Mourning Doves, Dark-eyed Juncos and a few contrarian Red-winged Blackbirds that had not migrated like the majority of their kind were feasting on the seeds above them. Noshing mainly on suet were two Red-bellied Woodpeckers and three Downy Woodpeckers. For any winter bird-watcher this would be a satisfying scene but for a beginner like myself it was absolutely fabulous.

When spring approached, my observations increased in length and frequency in direct proportion to the moderating weather. In April, I made my first attempt to study the annual spring migration. I became familiar with colorful birds I never imagined visited these latitudes. I used to think that colorful birds were only seen on television programs about the Amazon, the South Pacific or Equatorial Africa. I discovered that I could find some amazing beauties if I looked for them in the right places at the right time of year. I learned firsthand that some birds like the Northern Waterthrush or Ovenbird remain long enough in the park to rest, find water and food and then move on farther north in the spring migration. Others like George's Red-winged Blackbird cousins or the Baltimore Orioles stay the season to raise a family. In the fall migration these visitors move south while birds like the White-throated Sparrows or Dark-eyed Juncos come to the park to enjoy a milder winter than they could expect to find in their breeding grounds. As peculiar as it may sound some birds find it easier to feed in Central Park during the winter than in territories more northern. "What kinds of food do they find here?" I hear you ask. Seeds, nuts, dried fruit and insect larvae are examples.

When George left the pond after our first season together I decided that I would record my visits with him from the moment he returned during the spring migration until his departure in the following fall migration. At the time of my decision I could not be absolutely sure George would return, but based on my assessment of his resourcefulness, determination and the habits of his species I had faith that he would be back. If any Red-winged Blackbird would survive the stress of winter or a northward migration of hundreds of miles surely it would be one of the pluckiest and sharpest, right? When and if George did come back I could have no idea where his story would lead me but I was confident that by following George a compelling tale would unquestionably unfold. All I had to do, I assumed, was watch, listen and then write it all down. The Club George leader would do the rest.

Chapter 2 · April 21

I Only Had Eyes for George

For the past few days I have watched three male Red-winged Blackbirds at George's Pond. One of the three is demonstrably more aggressive than the other two and chases the others relentlessly. I wondered if this tough guy might not be "the guy." Had George returned? None of these birds came to the dock or approached people so I was skeptical that any of them could be the one I have waited eight months to see. That was until yesterday when one of the three repeatedly landed on the top of the fence where George used to perch so often. On one occasion this fellow called to me and took a bit of food that I threw to him but he came no closer than six feet. That surely was not George's style. Still I had the feeling if it were George his shyness could be explained.

George the consummate performer is in the act of singing for his supper.

He might not yet have acclimated himself to being around New York or New Yorkers again. I supposed that he needed time to feel at home. Or, more likely, he had other priorities to address at this stage of the breeding season. Maybe the answer to that question would be revealed during the course of my own observations. It surely would be something I was hoping to see.

I anxiously returned to the dock on George's Pond today to decide if I had not been correct or mistaken yesterday. There was no mistake. George really was back. He was patrolling his old territory as if he had never left it. Within an hour I watched him circle the western half of the pond, stopping at his usual perches to call "chek" or sing his "konk-la-ree" song and occasionally make a display of his scarlet epaulets. There were many other birds at the pond, but I can't remember much about them. Today, I only had eyes for George.

As I watched him my mind filled with theories and imagined scenarios about what George has been doing and where he has been for the last eight months. Most East Coast North American Red-winged Blackbirds migrate south for the winter. The *Agelaius phoeniceus* usually hightails it about 500 to 600 miles from their breeding ground and as far as south Texas, south Louisiana, and south Mississippi and all over Florida. It is also true that some hardy souls stay in the Northeast all year. In fact a few remained in Central Park last year. I saw them at the bird feeders in the Ramble and in the dormant reeds in two places on the Lake throughout the fall and winter. I cannot know where George went after he left his breeding territory last season but I think it would be just like plucky George to venture south. In my daydreams it is easy to imagine George wearing flip-flops and sunglasses while perched on a lifeguard station on a white sandy beach. Are you getting a visual image of this? But seriously folks, I do know that Red-winged Blackbirds leave their breeding grounds at the end of summer eventually forming flocks segregated by sex and age. Ken Yasukawa says it is not certain if those segregated flocks are created immediately following the breeding season or if they form during or after migration. Maybe the answer to that question will be revealed during the course of my own observations. It surely will be something I will be hoping to see.

The farther north Red-wing Blackbirds are the earlier they migrate. Some leave for their winter grounds from July through September. Most leave in October. George quit his breeding territory on or about last July 24, but it is possible that he did not leave the Northeast or even Central Park. He might have stayed on to molt or joined with other Red-winged Blackbirds in another area of the park, a few miles or even one hundred miles away.[1]

I think it very likely at this point that you are asking yourself, "Why do birds migrate anyway?" Well, it may not be for the reason many assume. Most folks think birds migrate solely to escape cold weather. That is only part of the story. After all, birds wear a down coat, which is one of the best insulating materials ever created. Bernd Heinrich, author of *Winter World: The Ingenuity of Animal Survival*, points out that man-made materials do not hold a candle to the insulating properties of the familiar feather.

> Bird's insulation is, per weight, even better. The chickadees get up on even the coldest morning at first dawn to search for food. Their body core temperatures are slightly higher than ours, and the insulating layer of feathers is less than an inch thick. Heat loss through the feathers is reduced by raising them, which is why many small birds look rounder and fatter as the winter drags on.[2]

It also helps explain to the attentive new bird-watcher why wintering birds may look a bit odd standing on one leg or hiding their beaks under a wing. That is because exposed legs and beaks are not insulated but can be warmed by temporarily stashing them under their feathers. Also, despite their often spindly appearance birds' legs have a remarkably efficient arterial system that aids in keeping these appendages warm. Simply put, many species are

[1] Ken Yasukawa and William A. Searcy, *Red-winged Blackbird*, p. 2.
[2] Bernd Heinrich, Hibernation, Insulation and Caffeination, *New York Times*, January 31, 2004. Op-Ed page.

amply prepared to deal with the cold. The primary reason birds migrate is to find an adequate supply of foods essential for their particular species.[3] In cold weather the majority of insects and spiders disappear from view and seeds, fruits and nuts that were not consumed in the growing season are available, but in dwindling supply. Birds that survive primarily on insects and spiders have to move to warmer climates because that is where the bugs are, at the risk of paraphrasing what John Dillinger said about money. Birds that survive primarily on seeds, fruits and nuts and cannot find enough of the types they require also move to warmer climates where they are more likely to be available. Some birds that can modify their diet may not have to migrate. One insect-eating species, for example, might be able to substitute a diet of nuts and berries that others, due to dietary or physical limitations, cannot utilize.

In the breeding season insects and spiders are nearly two-thirds of the Red-winged Blackbird diet. Adults and nestlings alike need the high concentrations of protein they provide. In the nonbreeding season they tend to eat more seeds, but Red-winged Blackbirds are adaptable and will change their diet to take advantage of the foods at hand, or rather, at beak. Though they are bug aficionados, Red-winged Blackbirds are known, for example, to eat so much commercially grown grain that the local human populations consider them a serious problem. In agricultural areas winter flocks of tens or hundreds of thousands of hungry Red-winged Blackbirds, often with like numbers of their Common Grackle close relations, can find themselves the object of numerous schemes to alter their gastronomic selections or their lives.

Those may include a variety of poisonous substances and the use of firearms. In the fall and winter, however, both cultivated and wild foods are often not in sufficient supply to support the Red-winged Blackbirds in northern habitats. There may be types of seeds and nuts available, but the Red-winged Blackbirds' beaks may not be strong enough to break them into bite size pieces. So

[3]David Allen Sibley, *The Sibley Guide to Bird Life & Behavior,* p. 60.

they go to areas where their slender pointy beaks can process the foods that are in profusion. Western and central Red-winged Blackbird populations do not migrate at least in part because they find the foods they need in the same territory all year. Other birds like the House Sparrows, for example, have no need to migrate at all mainly because their stout powerful beaks enable them to feed on seeds other birds cannot open. Then again the House Sparrow will eat nearly anything up to and including tidbits lodged in other animals' droppings but I shall not delve into that here. Aren't you relieved?

I trust that this digression proved to be edifying but it is time to get back to George's Pond where spring temperatures are climbing and breeding season has commenced. George kept to a basic routine as he reconnoitered for food, mates and enemies. His preferred lookout spots were the top of the birch tree on his island, the wooden bird blind on the dock, the short spruce tree to the north, the willow and metal mesh fence toward the northeast, another birch across the water to the south and a boulder at the base of the cliff to the southwest. It seems to this observer that a disproportionate part of his rounds were taken up watching and pursuing those two other male Red-winged Blackbirds. These uninvited visitors were trying to slip in unnoticed with the intention of stealing his lady friends' attentions or taking over his domain.

This leads us to a point about Red-winged Blackbird behavior that we need to discuss even though some readers may find it a tad distasteful. The males are notoriously polygynous: they take more than one mate at the same time.[4] It is important to point out that one should not label this behavior as promiscuous because that term implies pair bonds are not formed, which they most definitely are even if it is often more than one bond at a time. If you are shocked by this arrangement it may console you to know that only a small percentage of bird species engage in this kind of hanky-panky. Nevertheless Red-winged Blackbirds are so blatant about it

[4]Author's Note: Before you dive into the dictionary I must point out that "polygynous" is the correct spelling and the correct terminology. Look it up if you don't believe it, like I did.

that many reference books cite them as the principal example of polygynous bird behavior. The males are not as active in their parental caregiving roles but rather in their parental creating roles with one or more females. Some researchers suggest that this arrangement works as an effective division of labor. The male spends most of his energy defending the breeding territory and advertising for more mates and the female spends a lot of her energy building nests and raising offspring. However, that is not the whole X-rated story. Studying the genetic makeup of offspring, researchers discovered that a quantity of females chose to surreptitiously mate with other males and vice versa. Hence George truly has an added motivation to be relentlessly on guard against the influx of male Red-winged Blackbirds in his territory.[5]

There are other theories proposed to explain polygynous behavior. One that has wide acceptance in the scientific community may seem counterintuitive to you as it did to me at first. The theory suggests that males do not select females with which to breed but rather the females are the ones that do the selecting. The female Red-winged Blackbird's top priority, it is said, is to acquire the best available breeding territory. How's that? Doesn't the female want the strongest, bravest, healthiest, smartest and best-looking guy she can find? Many ornithologists believe "it ain't necessarily so." Instead, they say, to insure the survival of her chicks the female searches for a location with sufficient sources of food and water, suitable nest sites, numerous hiding places, and strategically placed perches. The females top priority is not try to attract the male, but rather as Ken Yasukawa put it, "She makes the male attract them."[6] It may not matter to her if the male already has one or more mates. She will tolerate the presence of other females in the male's harem, the theory says, as the price to pay for a desirable breeding ground as long as the male can do an adequate job of protecting her and their offspring. Yasukawa asserts that his research and that of others demonstrate it is more crucial for the female to make mating

[5]David Allen Sibley, *The Sibley Guide to Bird Life & Behavior,* pp. 75, 546–47.
[6]Ken Yasukawa, e-mail message, November 11, 2004.

choices than it is for the males. That is because it is more "costly" for the female, as the behaviorists say, because she puts the success of her brood at risk if she should choose a poor mate and nest site but the male can have one or more mates, and potentially more than one brood to make up for his errors or deficiencies should disaster befall a clutch. Yasukawa explains it this way:

> I would say the evidence is very clear that females choose both territories and males, and that males are not very choosy. The reason is that it is costly to a female to choose badly, but not to a male.[7]

Even females that lose their mates will remain on his former territory in hopes of being accepted by the next male to take control of that territory because it is the location, not necessarily the quality of the mate, that counts.[8] Nero offers additional information to help us understand this theory. First year females breed while most first year males do not. The young males are physically able to breed but fierce competition from more mature and experienced males for territories discourages them. This creates a situation in which there is a surplus of breeding females as compared to males. The older males, or those holding territories, get to reproduce with the surplus of available females and the first year males, with a few exceptions, get to flock together and wait for the next season when they will have a better chance of winning and holding a territory. These first year males are sometimes referred to as floaters because that is what they do until they are mature enough to win a breeding ground.[9]

When she is ready to raise a family the female builds the nest. The males may help her find a suitable spot and possibly engage in the symbolic act of manipulating a few twigs in an apparent effort to motivate the female to begin construction. She may have one or possibly two broods in one breeding season. However she will replace

[7]Ken Yasukawa, e-mail message, November 11, 2004.
[8]Les Beletsky, *The Red-winged Blackbird: The Biology of a Strongly Polygynous Songbird,* pp. 131–42.
[9]Robert W. Nero, *Redwings,* p. 77.

failed clutches as many as four or five times. A clutch that hatches will take about a month of intensive care to raise. Once a brood leaves, or fledges, the nest will not be reused. If she attempts another brood the female will build a new nest. It takes three or more days, depending on environmental conditions, but in a pinch the female can construct it in a single day. Used nests become soiled by nestlings and consequently laden with bacteria, parasites and even bugs. You would move too under those circumstances, wouldn't you?

In territories where there are great quantities of insects and spiders, a male might have three to six mates. Bugs are not an aphrodisiac. They provide a higher protein diet than seeds and fruit, which newborn offspring require in profusion. A pond-based territory though modest in size where water, insects and seeds are plentiful, like George's, will attract at least two or three females each season. According to one expert, however, some Red-winged Blackbird males may have considerably more mates. A male was observed to have fifteen females in his breeding territory.[10] That male must have had one terrific territory. In the Red-winged Blackbird world the three top criteria for breeding are location, location and location.

During George's patrols he often perches on the metal mesh fence at the northern peninsula jutting out into the middle of the pond. It is here that a boundary line divides the pond in two. Though invisible, this boundary is very real. There are only two male Red-winged Blackbird territory owners and two that are persistent interlopers that challenge them. Each territory owner rules one half of the water's surface and its immediate surroundings. George has the western half. His oft-singing neighbor, whom I have named Mel after an arguably better-known and better-sounding jazz singer, has the eastern half. The pond is roughly in the shape of an hourglass. Opposing peninsulas pinch in its center where the invisible border stretches between two Weeping Willow Trees on the northern peninsula, crosses the water, proceeds through the middle of the southern peninsula that is thick with phragmites, cat-

[10]Ken Yasukawa and William A. Searcy, *Red-winged Blackbird,* p. 10.

tails and other aquatic vegetation and finally through a line of trees and shrubs behind it. As far as I can tell, neither George, nor Mel, ventures into the other bird's half of the pond. They appear to have made a "gentle-bird's agreement" concerning territorial rights but, knowing the breed's penchant for clandestine meetings of the sexes, crossings likely do occur. I just have not been able to catch them in the act.

As I did today, I often see George perched in one Weeping Willow Tree on the western side of the northern peninsula while Mel sits in the adjacent Weeping Willow Tree to the east. At times they perch nearly side by side on the wire fence or even in the same tree: George always on the western side and Mel on the eastern side of that invisible boundary. One bird will sing out his "konk-la-ree" territorial song or make his "chek" call as a reminder that he will not abide trespassing. The other bird responds by singing his "konk-la-ree" song or making his "chek" call. Sometimes they tilt their beaks at one another signaling their independent if not defiant natures. The two male Red-winged Blackbirds do not have to be sitting close to each other to carry on this call-and-response routine. Their vocalizations can be heard as they go about a variety of daily activities. As yet I have never seen any hostility between them, but I have heard lots of soulful "konk-la-ree" singing, forceful "chek" calling and bill-tilting.

Red-winged Blackbirds are also often cited in the textbooks as practitioners of a more dramatic behavior. I experienced firsthand-close-up-and-personal-proof of this in my youth. For a while I walked to school when budget cuts eliminated our suburban school-bus service. I did not complain much because on fair weather days my route of choice passed through a vacant field filled with dense shrubbery, wildflowers and birds. In the breeding season, the local Red-winged Blackbird population hid their nests and chicks in those bushes. On one occasion, I unwittingly came too close to a nest site. That flushed two male Red-winged Blackbirds out of hiding and into attack mode. They screamed at me. They flew directly at the top of my head, missing it by an inch or two. They zipped by so closely decades later I still remember hearing the sounds of their wings and feeling the rush of air as they barnstormed me.

The reference books say adult Red-winged Blackbirds will respond this way to man, bird or beast when they sense their nests are threatened. I do not doubt that many readers have had encounters with aggressive Red-winged Blackbirds themselves. To those who have not had the experience I would not recommend it unless you happen to be wearing a catcher's mask or football helmet at the time. This is not a far-fetched suggestion. Ken Yasukawa offers this candid observation on the subject.

I have always been fascinated by the different "personalities" of individual redwings. Some are bold, some are calm, some are "nervous." But my favorites are the males who vigorously attack me when I check their nests and the females who scream bloody murder and incite the males to be more aggressive.

A few years ago we had a male who would fly into the back of my head as hard as possible, then circle up and whack me on the top of my head with his feet. Then he perched briefly on my research assistant's head (she was shorter than I) before starting the whole thing over again. He'd keep that up until we left the nest. It wasn't a big problem when we were just checking the contents of his nest, but the day that we banded his young was "interesting."

When I was a grad student working on a population at Yellowwood Lake in Brown County, Indiana, Cindy Patterson and I shared the study area. Cindy named one of the males the "terrible terror" because he was so aggressive when she searched his territory for nests. She got tired getting knocked in the back of the head, so she carried an umbrella when she went on to his territory. By the end of the season, the umbrella was full of holes. I used a hard hat when searching territories of aggressive males, but they quickly figured out not to hit the helmet, but to hit my back instead. One suggestion that I never tried was to put fake eyes on a hat and wear it backwards (eyes in the back of the head). Redwings only attack from behind, so it is supposed to prevent an attack.

Every breeding season I get "emergency" calls from people who say they were attacked by a redwing. I tell them that they probably got too close to an active nest and that the male was just defending his young. That usually satisfies them. I don't bother to point out that a male redwing weighs less than 3 ounces and can't really do anything to them.[11]

I should address an apparent discrepancy about the weight of a typical Red-winged Blackbird. I estimated George weighs about two ounces based on my reading of field guides. But the local subjects Ken Yasukawa studies he told me, tend to be larger.

Adult male redwings in this area weigh about 71 grams, on average. There are 28.3 grams in an ounce, therefore the mean weight in ounces is 2.5 oz., but in some populations the males are a bit larger, thus my "less than 3 ounces" statement.[12]

The sole targets of George's aggression this day were not ornithologists wearing hard hats or carrying umbrellas but the two male Red-winged Blackbird interlopers. As fierce as it appeared, their combat usually did not produce casualties but there was one confrontation where claws and beaks were used in midair so ferociously that I worried if any of the birds had been seriously hurt. When George visited the dock afterward I saw the unfortunate results. One of the feathers on his back was broken and protruding at a ninety-degree angle away from his torso. More alarming was that one of his wings was drooping. The right wing was noticeably lower than the left wing. Of course, this condition might have existed earlier but I had never noticed it before. Ironically it was George's droopy wing that became a visual marker to tell him apart from other male Red-winged Blackbirds at the pond.

Ken Yasukawa pointed out to me that it is the territory owner that begins singing and displaying his epaulets as soon as he ar-

[11]Ken Yasukawa, e-mail message, November 15, 2004.
[12]Ken Yasukawa, e-mail message, January 5, 2005.

rives on his territory. Knowing that gives more credence to the notion that the most aggressive of the three males involved in this and other skirmishes was George because that bird was also the one who sang "konk-la-ree" and showed his epaulets. If the more demonstrative male was George then he actually returned at least three weeks earlier than I had thought. That means he came back between early April and the middle of March. Unfortunately I did not make a note of the date I first saw the three males at the pond. If I had done so I would have a more accurate date of when to expect George's return next year. I am going to use March 15 as an educated guess for the date to begin searching for George at the start of the following breeding season. Believing he has already been back a month I must accept it that I have lost precious time observing him this year but I will not waste any more.

The majority of the Red-winged Blackbird behaviors I have described so far are not George's alone. But, I believe some of his behaviors may indeed be unique. For example, George deliberately perches where people congregate when most but not all other Red-winged Blackbirds would not remain in the proximity of humans for very long if at all. George not only comes close to people but he uses his perch at the dock as a stage from which to command their attention. His calls, songs and displays certainly have commanded mine. Curiously, George seems to communicate with people by adapting his "natural" Red-winged Blackbird behaviors into a kind of language that humans understand. I think there is more than a bit of irony in the fact that George tenaciously recruits people to provide him with a meal with his "konk-la-ree" song, "chek" calls and displays that scientists tell us are instinctive behaviors designed to attract females and challenge competitors. My theory, scientifically unproven and totally subjective, is that George accidentally learned that these actions induced people to feed him. I believe his discovery was serendipitous and not premeditated. I think on one or several occasions he attempted to scare off a human that came too close using the same behaviors he employs to chase a rival but found his efforts produced a treat instead of a retreat. The cause and effect evidently made a lasting impression on his bird brain.

When I first told Ken Yasukawa about the way in which George directs behaviors toward humans he offered these explanations as to how this wild Red-winged Blackbird might have found this un-expected means of expression.

> The interaction you describe is both interesting and unique, as far as I know. Song is probably associated primarily with an ag-gressive motivation, so perhaps the proximate explanation is that George is very excited by the possibility of acquiring food and this excitement "spills over" into singing behavior. This is an old concept in the biological study of animal behavior, which posited several "drive" systems (e.g., aggression, fear, hunger, mating, etc.). Sometimes, according to this idea, if a particular form of behavior is not expressed for a long time, the motivation to do it builds up to such an extent that the behavior occurs when it is inappropriate. Or it can "spill over" into an-other behavior, which would then be performed in otherwise unexpected contexts.[13]

It figures that George would use one of his aggressive modes of ex-pression because one only has to observe him for a short time to see that he possesses a forceful "personality."

During the hour and one-half I watched him, George came to the dock several times. He made six landings on my hand to take his pick of a mixture of dry-roasted unsalted peanuts and sun-flower seeds I carry precisely for these occasions. He selects the dry-roasted unsalted peanuts nearly every time. Occasionally, he flew some distance to eat his food. Just as often he hopped back onto the top of the fence to eat it while other Club George charter members and I watched. Make no mistake about it: these Club George members have not trained George to do their bidding, but George has trained Club George members to do his. Come to think of it someone might have taught George to do these things but I do not know who it was or how they could have done it. It is

[13]Ken Yasukawa, e-mail message, March 20, 2004.

widely recognized that birds can learn by imitating other birds' behavior. Is it possible George learned it by watching another bird like a Tufted Titmouse, for example, whose species is well-known to take food from people's hands? They also sometimes pull a hair out of animals, which they then use to line their nests. The hair on top of humans' heads is not immune from this activity. Presumably the Tufted Titmice have mastered these behaviors without human tutelage so why not George?[14] Of course, I am thankful that George has not taken to pulling hairs out of people's heads and hope he does not watch the titmice too closely lest he pick up that habit as well.

At this point you may have some thoughts about the safety issues these kinds of interactions raise. That is logical considering how much contact George makes with people. While George is careful to protect himself, admirers do not have to protect themselves from this diminutive fellow. What risk is there for him? A malevolent person could take advantage and do him harm but from his carefully selected position on the top of the eight-foot tall fence he does a fair job of controlling each encounter. People, perhaps excluding professional basketball players, would find it impossible to touch or, perish the thought, grab him. Then too, George has a greater degree of trust for people he recognizes. I believe he visually identifies certain people and possibly certain voices though the jury is still out on that issue. It is a fact that he interacts more with those with whom he is most familiar. I am struggling not to attribute too much intelligence to this Red-winged Blackbird, but there is no denying that George communicates, interacts and minimizes his risks with skill and panache.

After all this discussion about George's cross-species' relations and the breeding season with its associated behaviors it is ironic, is it not, that I have not yet seen female Red-winged Blackbirds at the pond. The males arrive before the females in order to claim and secure the breeding territory. The females not only arrive later but when they show up they tend to be reclusive or at least harder to

[14]Fred J. Alsop III, *Birds of North America: Eastern Region*, p. 518.

find. Perhaps the females are already at the pond. They may be waiting to see the outcome of the boys' territorial struggles. Or they are simply hard to see. Red-winged Blackbirds are sexually dimorphic: the females look different from the males. They are smaller, have mottled chocolate brown coloring with heavy dark streaking, a pinkish-peachy patch under their chins and prominent buff eyebrows. Their plumage provides them with camouflage so it's no wonder both sexes look like the females through their first year or a bit longer. Mature birds of both sexes have the same shape, though females tend to be slightly smaller. Males and females both have wing patches. However the adult female's wing patches vary widely in the amount of red and they do not attain the brilliant scarlet of the males' epaulets. Ken Yasukawa explained the variation in the female's epaulets is a "function of age, but it's also a function of conditions. Older females in good condition have large, relatively brighter epaulets."[15] The epaulets of the females then give the birder a rough indication of their age and health.

With their brown and buff streaked plumage the female Red-winged Blackbirds are often mistaken for sparrows. When I first began looking for them it took me weeks to be able to pick out the female Red-winged Blackbirds among the House Sparrows that habitually gather at the dock. After I learned how to recognize them I got more than a little satisfaction being able to point them out to more seasoned birders who could not find them. For myself and other beginners the ability to identify an adult female Red-winged Blackbird is a milestone in the development of one's bird-watching skills. You don't believe me? Wait until you inexperienced birds try to pick one out of a mixed flock then you will understand.

One reason why the sexes look different is that they do not have difficulty identifying one another. Surely George does not. I have watched him making deliberately slow display flights with his red epaulets fully exposed in an effort to impress a female or two. Some avian researchers theorize that the size and color of the epaulets indicate the health and stamina of the male and deter-

[15]Ken Yasukawa, e-mail message, November 30, 2004.

mine how strongly a male can both attract a female and send an aggressive visual message to rivals. However, experimental evidence suggests that while scarlet epaulets are positively crucial for defending territories against other males, they are less important for attracting a mate. Researchers blackened Red-winged Blackbirds' epaulets with dye and found that it did not make courtship more or less successful. That is important information, but I was concerned about the fate of the birds in the study. Did the researchers wash the dye off those Red-winged Blackbird wings when the experiment was finished?[16] I would hate to think they released those birds back into the wild without a proper suit of feathers but Ken Yasukawa assures me the effect was not permanent. During the next molt those dyed feathers would fall out naturally and be replaced by normally colored plumage.

[16]David Allen Sibley, *The Sibley Guide to Bird Life & Behavior,* p. 68.

Chapter 3 · April 24

Groovy Ruby

The big news today was that the ladies are back. I saw George flirt with a female Red-winged Blackbird. Truly, "pursue" is a more accurate word than flirt because for twenty minutes or more I watched him chase her. Whenever he got close she bolted several yards away. She would not let him perch within six feet of her. A few times George flew slowly and conspicuously across the pond making sure she would see him while he deliberately, and one might say audaciously, showed off. The object of his ardor remained unimpressed with his performance. Personally, I thought it was terrific. I began to wonder why the female did not seem impressed and how long George would persist in the face of continuous rejection. Although the female kept moving away from her

This is Ruby where she stood moments before she sang to George.

suitor she never completely left the area. She always remained within the invisible boundary outlining George's territory. If this lady really wanted to escape from George she could have flown outside his territory where she would be harder to find, but she did not leave. Therefore, I reasoned it was possible that she did not want to discourage him at all but was really playing hard to get. In fact I believed she was egging him on to pursue her. From the relentless effort George was making I would say that the lady's plan was working. It occurred to me too that George's showy behavior might have had a dual purpose. George was also sending a message to his two rivals. His body language and vocalizations were telling each of them, "This is my territory and my lady (or ladies) so hit the road Jack (or Jacks)."

At one point George chased the female in my direction. They both landed on the dock's wooden planking a few feet away from where Mack, another Club George charter member, and I stood. The female briskly walked away from us with George following directly behind. When she hopped off the north side of the dock and into the tall grasses at the water's edge George hopped after her.

Watching the Red-winged Blackbirds hopping, walking and at times running reminded me that it is abilities like these that make this species more intriguing for me than others. Some birds can only walk on the ground while others can only hop. Red-winged Blackbirds can walk, though they do waddle a bit, hop both forward and backward and run, albeit slowly. These skills are three of their talents that have helped make their species successful. They have been successful for a very long time. There are fossil records of Red-winged Blackbirds found in North America that are nearly 400,000 years old. I am not implying that they are world-class survivors because they can walk and hop forward and in reverse but because they are able to adapt to many situations and conditions. Here's another example. Most often they nest in freshwater marshes. That seems to be their preferred breeding ground but they are successful using other habitats such as saltwater marshes, hay fields, rice paddies, suburban landscapes and, just in case I forgot to remind you recently, urban parks. I have already discussed how they can change their diet to take best advantage of the available food supply (i.e., switching to grains vs. bugs and vice versa) but I did not mention a special ability related to their food gathering techniques. Red-winged Blackbirds are able to enlarge crevices or pry open objects by first inserting and then opening their beaks. Powerful muscles enable them to use their beaks to forcibly extract food "hiding in the sheathing of leaf bases of aquatic plants, under sticks, reeds or other objects on the ground or on floating vegetation, and under stones in streams" that other species could not reach.[1] They share this ability with other icterid or blackbird family members. Many experts consider gaping one of the reasons why they have been so successful and how they remain one of the most abundant birds in North American.[2] Of course they can pick up food with their beaks in the conventional tweezer-like fashion too. Red-winged Blackbirds have even more talents and I was about to witness how their musical ones are involved in their efforts to reproduce.

George and the female had moved to the lush vegetation growing in the shallow water. Mack and I rushed to the dock railing to see what the birds were going to do next. We expected, as circumstances suggested, that it would be something amorous. Luckily we could see both birds from a few feet away. Tellingly, the female had stopped fleeing George. We had a feeling that something special was about to happen. It did but it was not what we anticipated. The female stood facing away from George as he serenaded her with a subdued song and, theatrical fellow that he is, continued showing off his scarlet epaulets. When George stopped singing the female turned to face him. They were perfectly still, beak to beak. With his wings still held up and away from his torso, George moved closer to her. Then I heard a bird singing a soft high-pitched melody. Strangely I could not tell where the sound was coming from. It seemed to come from every direction at once. I asked Mack, "Where is that singing coming from?" Mack perceived what I had

[1] Ken Yasukawa and William A. Searcy, *Red-winged Blackbird*, p. 5.
[2] David Allen Sibley, *The Sibley Guide to Bird Life & Behavior*, p. 545.

not. "It's coming from her," he said pointing to the female Red-winged Blackbird. He was right. She was singing a song to George. We strained to hear her melody, but she sang too quietly for either of us to get more than a hint of it. When she finished she flew up and away, disappearing from view as she passed over the birch trees on George's Island heading toward the base of the cliff. George hastily followed her and he too passed out of sight.

I paused to reflect on what we had witnessed. We had been privy to an intimate moment in the Red-winged Blackbirds' lives. We had watched George's courtship behaviors and had heard both sexes sing their courtship songs. While doing so we had an exceptionally close look at what some perceive as the relatively reclusive female Red-winged Blackbird. The characteristic peachy-pinkish patch on her throat had been fairly easy to see even at a distance but the pattern of her mottled coloring and her prominent buff eyebrow was much finer and more intricate when viewed so near. Prior to this romantic interlude I had barely noticed that this female had muted red patches on her wings similar to George's but far lighter in color. As I learned from Ken Yasukawa it indicated that she was likely a mature female. I judged that the hue of her epaulets was more pronounced than those of other females I had seen either in the outdoors or in books. Since they were distinctive her epaulets could serve nicely as an identifying mark. To my mind it seemed quite appropriate therefore to name her Ruby, which I did.

Goose on the Loose

While touring other parts of the park before visiting George today the birds I saw were mainly the usual suspects, but in the Ramble I encountered three migrating birds for the first time. With the help of a field guide I recognized a Yellow-rumped Warbler, Louisiana Waterthrush, and two Hermit Thrushes. To the knowledgeable bird-watcher they are predictable visitors to the park in both the spring and fall migration but they were new to me. In the process of attempting to obtain their photos it did not take this inexperienced bird photographer long to learn that small birds like these move exceedingly fast and often. An important component of their survival strategy is the concept that a moving

I think the male has a whiter breast than the female so I am reasonably sure that this is Papa. Maybe.

target is harder to hit than one standing still. I can testify that it makes it hard for them to be shot, at least with a camera.

When I visited George he was preoccupied chasing the two Red-winged Blackbird males. He came to his perch on the dock only briefly and solely to use it as a lookout post. Hobnobbing with humans was not high on his agenda today. He appeared to be nervous and jerky as he relentlessly scanned his domain. His head spun to face the direction of each ambient sound. As soon as George got a visual fix on the other males he went into attack mode. His assault technique consisted mostly of high speed chasing, piercing choruses of the "konk-la-ree" song and an avalanche of "chek" and "seer" calls, but very little real physical contact among the birds occurred. On two occasions George did engage in brief violent bodily contact with his adversaries. I saw wings beating against wings, claws flashing and beaks pecking while they faced each other in midair, and heard what sounded like the combination of a dull roar and the hiss of a snake coming out of George. As alarming as it appeared none of the birds seemed to be damaged in these confrontations.

What I have witnessed since his arrival makes me think about how difficult his reproduction mission is and how much time George will have to accomplish it before he leaves his breeding territory. On last year's calendar I noted that my last sighting of him was on July 22. I was unable to look for him on July 23 but on July 24 I wrote "no George" on my calendar. I looked for him again on July 25 and again on July 28. I did not see him on these dates. That is how I have determined that George left the pond between July 22 and 24 of last year. I expect he will leave very close to those dates this year. Birds characteristically follow a repetitive time schedule for major events like the beginning and ending of breeding seasons or migration periods. Weather conditions may hasten or delay comings and goings a day or two or more if they are very severe, but the bird's timing will vary little.

Based on the departure dates from last year I believe George should remain on of his breeding ground for a total of four or five months if he arrived in early April or March as I assume he did. I will use the remaining three months to study him closely. I feel that because George volunteers to make himself so accessible he presents me with a unique opportunity to learn firsthand about a songbird's breeding cycle. I cannot be sure when such an opportunity might come again. I sense that I have been handed a privilege that I would be foolish to waste. I mean, how many people are there who can say that a wild creature literally sang and danced its way into their life and then provided them with a way to observe each step in its reproductive process? Not too many I would say.

Such close observations will take a considerable amount of time and dedication but it will not be a chore, it will be pure fun. Watching George will be my main objective but I anticipate there will be periods when he is out of sight and the wider world of birds tempts me. I sometimes feel disloyal to George when I am distracted by other species but when I do I recognize it as a sign that I am getting too obsessive and I snap out of it. Looking at other birds is not a distraction from the main attraction (i.e., George) as much as an additional privilege. Today, for example, I noticed one of George's bulkier, more gregarious and conspicuous neighbors. A Canada Goose was standing in the tall straw colored dormant grass on George's Island. Canada Geese come in what Sibley describes as six "races" that I have simplified as extra-small, small, medium, large, extra-large and really big. *The Birds of North America No. 682, 2002* lists even more. They say there are as many as eleven subspecies of Canada Geese. I would guess the goose on the island was somewhere between the large and really big varieties. He was about thirty-five inches long with a wingspan of forty inches or so. It would be hard not to notice his presence on any occasion, but it was especially true on this one because, as it turns out, he was not alone. After a while I perceived he was standing over a second goose that was lying low in the reeds. This other goose appeared to be deliberately hiding. In a flash of ornithological déjà vu the scene was familiar to me. I recalled that years ago in an industrial park parking lot, near the entrance to an office building in Mahwah, New Jersey, I saw two Canada Geese positioned in a similar manner in a clump of tall straw colored dormant grass. The hiding goose at that time proved to be a female sitting on her nest. The standing goose beside her was her mate. He was guarding his wife while she was incubating her eggs. In linking the two scenes I realized that the Canada Geese before me now were nesting on George's Island. According to several bird-watchers I queried, this pair of Canada Geese might be the first to raise a family in Central Park or at least in this section of the park. Whether this claim of a Central Park "first" is or is not correct did not matter much to me. What excited me was the thought that I would enjoy the added pleasure of watching the progress of these nesting Canada Geese on each successive visit to see George.

It seemed that only a few visitors to the dock noticed the male goose standing on the island and even fewer saw the female hiding in the grass. I, on the other hand, had become aware of them in a relatively short time. I do not mean to brag though I did give myself a pat on the back. Instead, I give credit for my quick detection of them to my Club George charter membership which has increased my sensitivity to my surroundings. I also freely admit luck played a big part in it too.

Later in the evening I followed up on my discovery by reading up on Canada Goose nesting practices. Only the female will incubate the eggs. It will take twenty-five to thirty days until they hatch. The chicks will be born covered with chartreuse colored down that will insulate them while they remain in the nest. It will also serve as a protective coat during their early launch into the world outside the nest. Remarkably, they will be able to leave the nest in one to two days after hatching. It will take between fifty and sixty days until they can fly. The smaller varieties of Canada Geese take less time to fledge than the larger. I do not know how significant this is but when I got a good look at Mama I thought she was noticeably smaller than Papa. The reference books I have do not mention a size difference in the sexes so I am left to wonder if this may be a marriage between the medium and large to really big varieties.

I could not resolve that issue but I do have knowledge, some of which I gathered firsthand, of what to expect in the future from these nesting Canada Geese. The adults have a strong bond that may last a lifetime and they are dedicated and highly organized parents. Both will ferociously defend the chicks and each other. When I say "ferociously" I am not kidding. In the Mahwah, New Jersey, parking lot where I first observed nesting Canada Geese, many employees entering and exiting the building had to pass by the nest. This proved to be a stressful experience for humans and Canada Geese alike. The male goose attacked anyone he thought came too close to the nest. Those who provoked his defensive instinct would get a warning of what was coming when the male lowered his outstretched neck until it was parallel to the ground. Then if they had not already made a run for the door they would hear him emit a series of loud honks followed by quieter but decidedly sinister hisses. Merely unlucky employees might be honked, hissed and chased by the charging male until they were forced to retreat to a distance the angry goose felt was acceptable. Intensely unlucky employees would have the dubious thrill of watching him fly through the air straight toward their head. No one stood still long enough for the Canada Goose to slam into his or her head, so I cannot say if the goose was bluffing or would have ultimately collided with them. Under the circumstances a near miss was unquestionably the best end result for both the target and the missile.

Sometimes the female would also honk, hiss and chase people, but I never saw or heard that she flew at anyone's head. In that respect this observer concluded that she was a tad less aggressive. I am happy to say that neither of the geese physically injured anyone but without a doubt many were intimidated if not temporarily terrified by them.

I can speak of this with some authority because the male Canada Goose in Mahwah, New Jersey, charged me on occasion but my experience differed significantly from the others'. The very first time he rushed toward me honking and hissing, I began talking calmly and steadily to him for no reason I could adequately explain then or now. It just seemed the right thing to do at that instant. Prior to this occurrence I had decided to call the male Murray and the female Mary because "Murray and Mary" seemed an easy, although admittedly droll, combination of names to remember. At the moment the male first threatened me I spontaneously said out loud, "Hello there Murray, how are you today, pal? You sure are looking good this morning." Murray stopped honking, hissing and, most importantly, he stopped charging. After staring at me for a few seconds he turned around and waddled back to his guard post near the nest. I do not know why my action had a soothing effect, but it was indisputably effective. I repeated it during the next encounter and found it had the same positive result. I felt I had an obligation to share my discovery. I spread the word around the office that I had found a foolproof field-tested defensive countermeasure against Canada Goose attacks. Those employees who adopted my method found it was 100% effective. Those who did not continued to run the risk of attack.

I doubt that the Canada Geese on George's Pond will have the opportunity or cause to attack anyone not because they are in New York and not in New Jersey but because these geese are unlikely to be in a position where they can easily come close to people. The island location of the nest is an ideal refuge that protects the geese from predators and people. The pond itself is nearly surrounded by a metal wire mesh fence with one area opening on a small patch of marsh, another onto a large rock and one more where a shear rock cliff blocks all access. The Canada Geese need not have any confrontation with the public unless either species deliberately moves beyond these barriers. In the remote possibility that there are reports of conflicts I am ready to share my knowledge of defensive Canada Goose countermeasures with anyone who desires to learn them.

Chapter 5 · April 30

Here's Looking at You Kid

The rewards derived from finding the nesting Canada Geese convinced me it was time to make a stronger effort to seek out more birds in other areas of the park. As I have explained my attachment to George made me reluctant to do so. There have been days when I started out with the intention of exploring a new bit of territory but have instead unconsciously gravitated toward George's Pond as if on autopilot. Now that I decided that I truly want to expand my range I have come up with a simple plan to do it. I will discipline myself with a predetermined daily route. I have worked out a fixed path allowing myself side trips only when compelling reasons arise. My course roughly encompasses a fifty-acre

There are other areas of the park I want to explore, but I unconsciously continue to gravitate toward George's Pond.

circle within which there are varying habitats. These include meadows, hills, ravines, cliffs, low and high shrubs, plots of weeds and herbaceous plants, thinly and thickly forested expanses, two ponds, one lake, one stream, two waterfalls, and one swamp. I will enter the park at 79th Street and Fifth Avenue, not far from the nest site of the New York City celebrity Red-tailed Hawks Pale Male and Lola, head west over Cedar Hill (also known as Dog Hill to generations of dog walkers), southwest through the Maintenance Meadow and the Ramble, after which I will push west to the Lake, turn north at Bow Bridge, move along the Lake's eastern shore until I reach its farthest point called the north lobe or, as I prefer to call to it, Bank Rock Bridge. Only from this point shall I end my session with a visit to George's Pond. I will keep George for last as I might a favorite dessert at the end of a scrumptious meal if I were not on a perpetual diet.

Keeping my mind on birds other than George should be a bit easier now because it is the end of April and the park, especially the Ramble, is frequented by spring migrant birds. The most common migrants I hope to see are numerous warblers, some thrushes and a few vireos. Most vary from four to eight inches in length. Their size, speed and mobility make them hard to find. I found binoculars are essential to view enough detail to recognize, name and study these small creatures. When I have tried finding them without binoculars I have more often caught fleeting glimpses of rapidly moving unidentified dark bird-like objects than birds I could categorize. It has also been my experience that the brilliant colors that should aid in the identification of birds like the American Redstart, Common Yellowthroat or Black-throated Blue Warbler are only apparent over unexpectedly short distances. Though you might think it improbable, a bright yellow patch the size of a nickel on a five and one-half inch long bird like a Yellow-rumped Warbler, for example, may not be evident at twenty-five feet without the assistance of a portable light gathering and image magnifying apparatus. Similarly, more subtly plumaged birds like the Hermit Thrush, Red-eyed Vireo and

Ovenbird may easily escape your attention because they blend in with their surroundings or are mistaken for one of the usual suspects, such as the House Sparrow, unless you see them through binoculars.

When I purchased my first pair of binoculars I did not have the benefit of field experience or the advice of experts to know what types are best for bird-watching or, for that matter, how to properly use them. Please do not make the same mistakes that I did. To avoid them here are my suggestions about how to select binoculars that will be right for you. Those of you who already are familiar with this information or are satisfied with the binoculars you now own may be less than thrilled by what follows. On the other hand, you beginners would be wise to slog on through it. This material will save you time, money and aggravation.

To begin with you need to ask yourself one essential question: "Do I have to spend a lot of money on binoculars?" The answer is a resoundingly unequivocal yes and no. This is not a cop-out. I shall explain.

You can get started with a modest expenditure of one hundred dollars or thereabouts for binoculars that will be adequate on a bright sunny day when and where there are no deep shadows to impair your viewing. Even low cost binoculars will make it much easier to recognize different species simply because they provide the benefit of magnification. The drawback with inexpensive binoculars is that they may distort the image, alter the color and are unlikely to be useful in the low light situations you may encounter in a shady forest, during an overcast day, early morning or early evening light.

Many new birders and even a few experienced ones make the mistake of thinking that higher magnification always results in better bird-watching. This is simply not so. Many experts recommend seven to eight and one-half power models. Higher power lenses narrow the field of vision and often lower brightness. For bird-watching this is less than desirable.[1] I warn you that you are likely to be seduced by nine or ten power models. You will think you will

[1]David Allen Sibley, *Sibley's Birding Basics,* p. 9.

be able to compensate for the trade-offs you must accept to obtain higher magnification. Do not do it. Unless you are a very experienced bird-watcher and are thoroughly familiar with the benefits (i.e., magnification) and limitations (i.e., less light, narrower field of view) of higher power you will not be happy with your choice. This is perhaps the most important of a few concepts that need to be understood before you can purchase the binoculars that will be right for your bird-watching needs and your budget.

Next you have to evaluate four specifications of each of the binoculars under consideration. They are power of magnification (usually referred to as simply "power"), size of the objective lens (the lens farthest away from your eye), angle of view (also referred to as field of view) and size of the exit pupil (the disk of light that comes into your pupil through the lens closest to your eye known as the ocular lens). Consider, as an example, binoculars with these specifications: 8×42, 6.5 degrees, and 5.25 mm exit pupil. Most binoculars will have similar values printed on them. Often the last number is not printed for reasons I do not comprehend. The major importance of that number will be revealed but the reason for its usual absence mystifies me.

The first number "8" in our example is the power of magnification. This number indicates an image will be enlarged eight times the size it appears to the naked eye. Therefore the object looks eight times closer. Most people find eight or even seven "power" to be more practical for reasons already discussed and the additional reason that higher power models make it harder to keep the visual image steady. If your hand shakes even a little bit higher power models may not be practical for you unless you use a tripod. If you just became paranoid at the suggestion that your hand might have the "shakes" remember that most people experience hand-shake to a small degree and a small degree is all that is necessary to ruin your viewing pleasure. Test them first. If the higher power works for you go for it.

The second number "42" refers to the size of the objective lens. Generally speaking the bigger the objective lens the more light that will be directed to your eye. This is a good thing. In low light situations the larger objective size will yield a brighter image, but therein lies a trade-off. As the size of the lens increases so do the weight and the cost. An objective lens value of forty serves as a reasonable benchmark. Binoculars with a smaller objective lens size, say twenty or twenty-five, could be less expensive but also less effective in low light. Many birders use 8×40 or 8.5×42 or similar specifications. But hey, an 8×20-ish pair will function well in broad daylight, may be small enough to fit in a jacket pocket and can usually be had for a lower price. If you are on a budget and a compact size is important the 8×20 may be the right choice for you.

The "6.5" degrees in our example refers to the angle of view or, in other words, how large an area the diameter of the image will be. Typically the numbers range from 5 to 8 degrees. The critical values here are 5 degrees or more. The higher the number the larger the diameter of the image and, you knew it all along, probably the higher the cost.

The size of the exit pupil determines how much light will enter your eye. This is the specification number in our example that is often inexplicably not printed on the binoculars or even in the accompanying literature. I do not know why that is the case but you need to know this number because the larger the exit pupil the better your vision will be in low light. But not to worry. It is easy to compute the size of the exit pupil: divide the diameter of the objective lens by the power of the binoculars. In our example, 42 (diameter of objective lens) divided by 8 (power) equals 5.25. That was the good news. The not so good news is that larger lenses are made with more glass than smaller lenses and more glass means more weight and, almost always, more cost. The exit pupil can range from 2 to 8 mm. A value of 5 mm or more is best for low light conditions. This is because in daylight the human pupil is 4 to 4.5 mm in diameter but in low light the pupil dilates from 7 to 7.5 mm.[2] So, a wider exit pupil can provide a larger disk of light to fill your eye's expanded pupil. Got it?

If you were able to maintain your concentration through the previous paragraphs you may now want to pause for a mild stimu-

---

[2]Swift Instruments, *How to Care for Your Binoculars by Swift* (Japan Swift Instruments, 2001).

lant (nothing illegal, mind you) like a cup of tea or coffee because we are poised to launch into a discussion about the two basic forms of binocular construction.

(PAUSE)

Hello, and welcome back. Now that you are refreshed we can continue.

In the traditional "porro" prism format the ocular and the objective lenses are not assembled in a straight line. This design translates into binoculars that are bulkier and heavier. They are often relatively less expensive because the manufacturing process is simpler not because they are inferior. The "roof" prism format is typically smaller and somewhat lighter. The ocular and objective lenses are assembled in a straight line forming the characteristic "H" shape for this type. Roof prism models are generally more expensive because they are more complicated in design and therefore more difficult to manufacture. Remember that neither design is inherently better than the other, so base your choice on price, the four specifications, ease of operation, weight and above all the quality of the visual image.[3]

Before you make a purchase, try out the binoculars in the store if it is at all possible. Having a hands-on test is so important that I would not recommend you buy binoculars through a catalog or over the Internet unless you are absolutely certain of the model you want. If you develop a severe case of "sticker shock" when you begin comparing prices you might consider buying a pair of used, or as it is phrased in automobile advertisements, "preowned" binoculars. It's one way to get a technologically superior model for a reduced price.

When you test-drive the binoculars answer these basic questions before you make a commitment.

1. Does the focus wheel adjust easily and precisely?
2. Do you see a clear completely circular image through each ocular lens when it is in focus? (Close one eye at a time to test

---

[3]"The Long View," *Consumer Reports*, May 2002, pp. 28–32.

this concept.) When you look through both ocular lenses at the same time do you see one clear round image? (Do I need to tell you to open both eyes to test this concept?)

3. Can you use the binoculars when you wear your glasses (i.e., are the rubber eyecups adjustable?) and is a "diopter" adjustment provided, typically at the tip of the right ocular lens, so you don't have to wear your glasses if you don't want to?

4. How close can you be to an object and still be in focus? Ten feet may be fine but twenty feet may not be practical.

5. Are the binoculars water resistant or waterproof?

6. Are they "armored" or do they have a shock resistant rubber coating?

7. Is a neck strap supplied or do you need to purchase one separately?

8. Is a case supplied and if not is there one available for purchase if you think you need one?

9. Are covers for the ocular lenses included so they will not get wet if they are splashed when you imprudently decide to walk with the binoculars around your neck in the rain?

10. Is there a warranty and what are its terms?

11. Are the binoculars a reasonable weight? The weight of the binoculars is too often overrated in importance. Sometimes lighter weight is achieved by sacrificing image quality. Be sure the binoculars you select provide an acceptable combination of image quality and weight. You may need to compromise between the two but I would not let weight be the deciding factor.

12. After you buy them do you solemnly swear to remember to keep the packaging, warranty, instructions and receipt just in case you decide to return them?

Here are some more words of wisdom that experts may not tell you because they assume you already know them. Using binoculars for bird-watching is not the same as using them to watch a sporting event, theatrical performance, ritual, concert or the odd unfeathered unidentified flying object. After all, unlike birds, athletes, actors, musicians and miscellaneous facilitators are normally not deliberately hiding from you unless they are fully conscious that they are putting in a dreadful performance. From what I have heard and seen on cable television a UFO may in fact be hiding from you but I do not profess any firsthand expertise on that subject.

First, listen for birds singing or calling and the rustling of leaves and other forms of vegetation. It may seem counterintuitive but it is a good bet that you may find a bird more often by listening than by looking. You need to respond to each movement and sound if you want to see a lot of birds. I was amused but not surprised when a friend told me that in his native British Isles bird-watchers are aptly called "twitchers" for their jerky physical responses to sounds and sights in the field.

Do not go stomping through the bushes and trees rustling the leaves and snapping twigs underfoot while singing a tune or talking on your cell phone. Remember that you have to be quiet or you will scare the birds away. Duh.

Alas, scanning for movement and sound may not be as effective on a windy, rainy or snowy day, but then you most likely will not be out there in the field will you? If you are, keep scanning and listening anyway. I do.

Quickly look over an area with your naked eye. Yes, I mean without those binoculars you agonizingly researched, test-drove and purchased at great expense. Look for any movement then zero in on it with your binoculars. You will find an eyes-only-scan of your surroundings will be more productive than scanning with your binoculars especially when you are a beginner.

When you pick a spot you want to search quickly raise your binoculars to your eyes and focus them without losing your target. Your focusing technique should be swift but smooth. Here is one major reason why you should have tried out the binoculars in the store before you bought them. You want to be sure you will be able to focus them quickly and accurately.

A good place to look for birds is at the "edges" where trees or bushes border on an open area. When many birds venture out into the open they do not go far from protective vegetative cover. It is likely you will catch sight of more birds here rather than in dense foliage or in an open field.

The shore is another excellent place to start bird-watching. Here however you may want to use a spotting scope and a tripod (i.e., a telescope specifically designed for birding) rather than binoculars. With my personal experience limited to urban birding I cannot offer you detailed suggestions about spotting scopes but reference books and the Internet abound with information.

These techniques must become automatic so that you do not have to think about them. You want them to come naturally so you do not waste time considering what to do next lest you miss a once in a lifetime chance to identify that rare giant Orange-vested Pixilated Condor that will make you a bird-watching legend and the envy of your family, friends and coworkers. Like any skill, you have to practice to become proficient.

Carrying a compact bird field guide with you can be very helpful, but I recommend that you use the book after you first have had a good look at the bird in question. For some, like myself, it is more valuable to search through reference books when you return home but only if you have a good visual memory. Make notes or sketches if you think you will need them later, but remember there is no substitute for looking at the actual real live bird in its real live environment.

Today, using these very instructions I was able to identify a number of migrant birds that were resting and refueling before resuming their journey northward. Some of these species were new to me and a few were familiar. I saw, in the order of their appearance, a Ruby-crowned Kinglet, Hermit Thrush, Wood Thrush, Yellow-rumped Warbler, Northern Waterthrush, Hooded Warbler, Savannah Sparrow, Black-and-white Warbler, Brown Thrasher, Rose-breasted Grosbeak, Barn Swallow, Northern Rough-winged Swallow and the uncommonly-seen-in-these-parts Red-headed Woodpecker. Except for the Red-headed Woodpecker these birds are all fairly small. Unless they had been only a few yards away the use of binoculars was necessary in order to identify them.

If, by the way, you are thinking I made up a name like "Yellow-rumped Warbler," as I obviously did the rare giant Orange-vested Pixilated Condor (you did realize I made that name up, right?), all I can say is, "Look it up for yourself, pal." After you have been a bird-watcher for a while you may begin to think it is too bad birds could not have had legal representation when some of their monikers were hung on them. I mean who would name their kid Yellow-rumped Sal, Northern Rough-winged Harry or Orange-vested Pixilated Thelma for that matter? Mr. Sibley offers an explanation for the inconsistent and sometimes seemingly capricious names inflicted upon our feathered friends.

Some species are named for people (Audubon's Oriole). Some are named for geographic locations (California Quail, which is common in that state; and Connecticut Warbler, which is rarely seen in Connecticut). Some are named for habitats (Marsh Wren, which is found in marshes; and Palm Warbler, which is usually not found in palm trees). Some are named for their songs or calls (Whip-poor-will, which says its name; and screech-owls, which do not screech). Some are named for a superficial similarity to other, unrelated, birds (water thrushes, which are not thrushes; and nighthawks, which are not hawks). Since the names were developed a century or longer ago, when bird study involved a shotgun and examination of museum specimens, we have birds named Yellow-bellied Sapsucker, Ring-necked Duck and Sharp-shinned Hawk. These names describe characteristics that might be evident if you are holding the bird in your hand but that are difficult or impossible to appreciate in the field.[4]

I have found that the names of several of the park's usual suspects do not bare close scrutiny and could easily be added to Mr. Sibley's list. After all the Green Heron does not look particularly green, except in just the right light. The Great Blue Heron is overwhelm-

[4]David Allen Sibley, *Sibley's Birding Basics,* pp. 55–56.

ingly more gray than blue, don't you think? Need I draw you a picture to explain that the Tufted Titmouse is not a mouse? The American Black Duck is only sort of black here and there. The American Robin is actually a thrush mistakenly named for its superficial similarity to the European Robin that is not a thrush. The Muted Swan is not mute; often quiet yes, but mute no. And who can look me in the eye and say that they know for a fact that the Hairy Woodpecker is truly hairy? For a broader discussion on the topic I recommend Diana Wells' *100 Birds and How They Got Their Names*. It's a real hoot, so to speak.

Chapter 6 • May 1

A Peek at Two Beaks

George was noticeably agitated. His trips to the dock were short and erratic. When he did perch at the dock he stood at the extreme edge closest to the water. His posture indicated he was ready to launch into the air at any moment. He called "chek" loudly. He sang "konk-la-ree" emphatically. He flashed his crimson epaulets ostentatiously. He bolted sporadically after one or the other of his rivals. After successfully chasing an interloper away George darted from one lookout perch to another making a complete circuit of his territory's perimeter until he returned to the dock where he repeated the process.

During one lull in his ongoing police action, George pre-

This broken beak unquestionably identifies its owner as Daffy, the Mallard, whom I will hereafter describe with no small measure of admiration, as a world-class survivor.

dictably came to the top of the fence at the dock but instead of standing on the end to reconnoiter he walked toward me. He stopped directly over my head and began to softly and slowly call "chek" a few times. I took this to mean that he was looking for a peanut but his laidback style was not in keeping with his normally extroverted communication techniques. I am probably reading too much into this but the gentleness of his vocalizations and calm demeanor were rather endearing. It seemed as if he was not going to put on a show to get my attention because he did not have to or maybe he was just tired. Well, I cannot know what he was thinking but George had undeniably fallen into a mellow mood that he did not often show.

I nearly always bring George peanuts, which he relishes, but I have been wondering if he might benefit from some variety. On this occasion I brought along a slice of whole-wheat pita bread in a "doggy-bag" left over from my lunch. I tore off a small piece and raised it up to George but he refused to take it. Once again George was exhibiting behavior I had never seen from him before. Since when did George start passing up a free meal? He sat perfectly still and stared at me. When I moved the bread closer to him, he literally turned his beak up at it. I offered him the bread three more times and three times he turned up his beak. On my next attempt, accompanied by pleading and baby talk (i.e., "Come on Georgie boy, eat the nice whole-wheat pita bread. Be a good birdie.") George took the bread, but still would not eat. Instead he examined it by gently turning it over and over in his beak for two or three seconds. His actions reminded me of a wine tasting where participants discreetly run their tongue inside their mouth to sample the liquid before spitting it out. And spit it out is exactly what George did. With an economy of motion and absence of emotion, he turned his head away from me and unceremoniously dropped the morsel into the water below. I made two more offerings. George dropped two additional pieces of pita bread into the water. Finally, as the bread began to sink under the water the thought sunk into my head that, no matter what, he was not going to eat it. To determine "A" if he was holding out for a peanut, or "B" he was not hungry, I simultaneously offered him a peanut and another piece of bread. George unhesitatingly snatched the peanut from my palm and ate it. Thus I came to the inescapable conclusion that "A" was the correct answer. George had unambiguously communicated his preference for peanuts. I might also add "C" as a corollary to the results of this impromptu taste test. George's actions could also be looked upon as a training session. If you accept that notion then you must also accept that I was the one being trained.

This event motivated me to investigate Red-winged Blackbird food preferences. You may be surprised that someone would endeavor to investigate Red-winged Blackbird food preferences but ornithologists are a thorough group. I have read the results of such a study. One of the findings supports what George had demonstrated for me. Researchers reported that the Red-winged Blackbird "in food choice tests shows preferences for seeds with high fat content."[1] As peanuts contain, I trust, more fat than pita bread the reason for George's choice becomes more understandable. Red-winged Blackbirds apparently favor fatty foods that are loaded with calories presumably because they reduce the effort needed to obtain daily calorie requirements. That seems logical but what remains mysterious to me is how George was able to make a choice by turning the food in his beak since taste and smell are supposedly not highly developed senses in songbirds. Just how could George figure out which foods have more fat? If he did not taste or smell did he "feel" the fat in the peanut and not in the bread? I suppose I could dig deeper for an answer but for now I am satisfied just knowing George's likes and dislikes.

Later, George launched another combat mission but this time he pursued his rival beyond his territorial border and kept on going. I spent the interval waiting for him to return by doing my own survey of his territory. Twenty or so Mallards, which had been attracted by the pieces of whole-wheat pita bread George had dropped into the water, were paddling around at the end of the dock looking for more of it. As the Mallards closed in I spied a fa-

---

[1]Ken Yasukawa and William A. Searcy, *Red-winged Blackbird*, p. 5.

miliar face, or to be precise, a familiar beak. One duck's beak had an unusual jagged edge, I thought, just like that of the gone-but-not-forgotten Mallard, Daffy. A still closer peek at his beak through binoculars left no doubt. To my delight I had found Daffy, the duck with the broken beak that I had last seen during the winter. It was a relief to know that, despite his injury, this Mallard had survived one of the cruelest winters the park had experienced in decades.

Not till I was home and writing notes on my calendar did I notice that this happened to be my first May Day visit to the Ramble as a novice bird-watcher. My newly educated eyes were delighted to have spotted a number of migrant birds: Ruby-crowned Kinglet, Hermit Thrush, Yellow Warbler, Yellow-rumped Warbler, Common Yellowthroat, Black-and-white Warbler, Northern Waterthrush, Hooded Warbler, Song Sparrow and White-throated Sparrow. At the time I spotted them I was not sure of the name of each species. I admit I had to use a field guide to confirm the identity of seven out of ten. At first feeling chagrined I reminded myself that no birder should ever feel inadequate when having to use a reference book to put a name to a bird. One of the most compelling aspects of bird-watching is to discover a "new" bird one has never seen before, but "newness" is not the only satisfaction. Another is enjoying and benefiting from the frequent accessibility of the usual suspects. Habitually seeing them provides an opportunity to gain familiarity with their behaviors. It can occasionally result in obtaining a bit of their trust. When they linger rather than flee it is easier to observe them in greater detail is it not? Some encounters provide the excitement of a first meeting and others the excitement of learning how they live their lives. Some birders prefer one type of experience to the other but I feel appreciating both makes my bird-watching sessions doubly enjoyable. This is a matter of choice or perhaps an expression of the viewer's personality. I would suggest all beginning birders give both approaches a try before becoming set in their bird-watching ways.

Chapter 7 · May 2

Bluish-Green Heron

The small swamp surrounding Bank Rock Bridge has served as a Green Heron nursery for several years. I have been told that last year two pairs of Green Herons raised four clutches of chicks in this locale. It was Ned who first told me that one pair had returned this season to build a nest in virtually the same spot as before. It is on a sturdy limb of an Oak Tree that protrudes two yards over the water from a height of about twenty feet. I did not have the good fortune to watch the birds building it, but through the grapevine I know others did. Both sexes contribute to its construction. Clearly this one is not yet finished but there is enough done for me to see

I have good reason to suspect that this is one of the nesting herons stalking prey on a log jutting out from George's Island. It is only a short flight to the Green Heron nursery at the northern end of the Lake at Bank Rock Bridge.

it is a roughly fashioned platform made of sticks and twigs with many small gaps showing between them. The loose weave is deceptively strong and the openings will permit precipitation and other undesirable material to exit freely. From my viewing angle it seems to be shallow too but it is at least two or more feet long. I expect a Green Heron nest would have to be commodious to accommodate both adults that are each between eighteen and twenty-two inches long with a wingspan of up to twenty-six inches and up to seven offspring. Of course individual nestlings are small and they average only four per nest but the structure has to be ready to accommodate the maximum number of chicks and adults just in case. Since they lay two to seven eggs things could get crowded. After the eggs are deposited both Mom and Dad will take turns incubating them for nineteen to twenty-five days.[1]

When the chicks hatch they will mature rapidly. The spacious nest will get progressively cozier over the next sixteen to seventeen days until they grow large enough to step outside to explore their environment. Before they can exit the chicks will have to eliminate their wastes inside the nest. Nature has evolved a way to deal with this sanitation issue. Nestlings' wastes are sealed in a mucous membrane wrapping known as a fecal sac that the parents can pick up for easy removal or, I would be remiss to dismiss, occasional ingestion. Think I am kidding? Here is Sibley's authoritative description.

> Parents must also clean the nest by picking up the chick's feces, which are wrapped in a mucous membrane called a fecal sac. Some adults eat the fecal sacs, while others carry them far from the nest and drop them.[2]

When chicks are strong and confident enough they will spend longer and longer intervals wandering farther and farther along adjacent branches of their nest tree first and then nearby trees. These short-range excursions give them a chance to exercise, gain

[1]Fred J. Alsop III, *Birds of North America Eastern Region*, p. 93.
[2]David Allen Sibley, *The Sibley Guide to Bird Life & Behavior*, p. 78.

coordination and begin to learn how to forage for themselves. The Green Heron adults will reuse the nest for a second brood so it is good sanitation strategy for the maturing chicks, who have ceased producing fecal sacs, to spend lengthy periods out of the nest where they can perform their excretory procedures outside their abode. This will help keep it that much cleaner for when they will huddle together inside for safety and warmth during the night and for the next brood should it come to be born.

In *Red-Tails in Love* Marie Winn described Green Heron nests in the same locale as early as 1998. When the birth of five Green Heron chicks in this spot was first publicized through the birder grapevine it spread to ultimately become a news item on the front page the *New York Times*.[3] I doubt the newborns I saw will achieve that amount of notoriety, but assuredly many bird-watchers will be stopping by to observe and pay their respects.

I have been thinking about last year's word-of-mouth history and what it might suggest about this year's yield of Green Heron nestlings. So far just one breeding pair is here but maybe another will turn up soon.

[3]Marie Winn, *Red-Tails in Love,* pp. 125–28.

Chapter 8 · May 4

A Mixture in the Picture

Visitors to Morton's Pond may occasionally wonder about the mysterious presence of beige stuff plastered on the trunks of one or two Cork Oak Trees. It really is no mystery. There is no doubt Harry, a bird-watcher and bird feeder of distinction, has put it there. Harry lovingly spreads his homemade mixture of bread, eggs, water and affection on the tree trunks. Many birds find it irresistible and so do I but for different reasons. They get to eat it and I get to watch them. Today I saw up to six House Sparrows at a time grab onto the tree bark and heartily feast on the mixture. Inevitably a Rock Pigeon or two interrupted their meal, but not for long. The much heavier pigeons at about thirteen ounces do not

Red-bellied Woodpeckers, ardent aficionados of his homemade mixture, are adept at extricating it from crevices in the tree bark where Harry placed it.

have the specialized legs and claws needed to maintain the gravity
defying position necessary to remain perpendicularly attached to
the tree. They quickly tired of trying to hold on and departed. A
Common Grackle of four and one half ounces and two European
Starlings of three ounces tried to chow down on Harry's mixture
too. I must report that they achieved poor to mediocre results. The
featherweight House Sparrows, at about one ounce, had no trouble remaining there for minutes at a time.

Red-bellied Woodpeckers and Downy Woodpeckers are also ardent aficionados of Harry's culinary creation. They are admirably
equipped to perch at seemingly impossible angles for extended periods. By the way beginning bird-watchers take note that female
and male Downy Woodpeckers are easy to distinguish. The male
has a red patch on the back of his head while the female has none.
You can easily tell the sexes of Red-bellied Woodpeckers too. The
male has red on the top of his head and nape of his neck while the
female has red only on her neck. Since both species are monogamous it is reasonable to conclude that these are male and female
pairs foraging here. Both species are territorial and would not permit other adults to be here especially during the breeding season.
It is exciting to think that the appearance of a fledgling woodpecker is possible and I have hopes to see one here but I think it is
too early for that.

Two Gray Squirrels were sporadically competing with the other
birds' collecting of Harry's mixture. I have personal knowledge of
just how aggressive the squirrels in this area can be. Last winter one
jumped onto my thigh on three separate occasions. I am sure these
were attempts to snatch seeds I held in my hand and not meant as
an expression of hostility. The squirrels did not hurt me. Harm, no.
Frighten, yes.

Gray Squirrels would eat a songbird if they could catch one but
so far in my observations they have not come close enough to do so
though I once saw one try. While I periodically check on the
whereabouts of these potentially pesky rodents the birds do a far
better job of squirrel detection than I ever could. When the squirrels make a move to get to Harry's mixture, for example, the birds

react to the clicking and scraping of their claws on the tree bark and head for safety in a heartbeat. Not only do birds know when a squirrel is closing in, but long before I learned it the hard way, they understood that where food is involved you cannot turn your back or your beak on a Central Park squirrel.

Around the perimeter of Morton's Pond the usual suspects were foraging together on the ground. In a crowd of dozens of House Sparrows, several Mourning Doves, Rock Pigeons, Common Grackles, precisely two Blue Jays and two or three Northern Cardinals depending on how many darted in and out at any particular moment were two male Red-winged Blackbirds, neither one of which was George. How do I know for sure neither was George? First, because this is breeding season and George is busy defending territory at "his" pond not this one. It is unlikely that he would leave it unguarded for long to venture so far away since food and water are plentiful within and just beyond his borders. Second, George's uniquely bold behavior with its song and dance routine that he directs at people would quickly identify him. Third, neither of these birds has a droopy wing like George. Fourth, George would not tolerate the presence of another male as these two do. Therefore I can conclude with a high degree of confidence that George is not one of them. In the past few days I have seen these two males together often and not in the company of females. I assume therefore that they do not have their own territories. If they had they would be fighting each other over the land and the ladies. No, I think these two are immature males. They are the kind of young floaters giving George a hard time at the pond. When they mature they will have a chance to establish their own breeding territories. Better luck next year boys.

I had heard other birders say that there were at least two other male Red-winged Blackbirds in the park that are known to take food from one's hand. One of these birds had been seen at the pond on the extreme south end where I do not often go, the other at the Bow Bridge where I do. None had been said to be at Morton's Pond. I was about to learn otherwise.

Standing against the low wire mesh fence surrounding the

pond I held out my open palm filled with a few peanuts and sun-flower seeds which I was about to toss to the aforementioned usual suspects. To my amazement one of the two male Red-winged Black-birds flew toward me, planted both feet in my palm, picked out the largest bit of peanut and raced off with it to a spot between two azalea plants a few feet away. Shielded from the eyes of the other birds and squirrels the Red-winged Blackbird ate his purloined prize. Before I got over the novelty of it a second Red-winged Blackbird also dashed toward me but his maneuvers had more complexity and bravado. This bird remained standing on my palm watching me intently until he had broken up his food and swallowed each crumb. Only when his meal was done did he fly a few feet away but even from a distance he kept looking at me closely and so did his friend. I soon knew why. Over the next five minutes both Red-winged Blackbirds repeated their trips to my hand each in his own personal style. As unpredictably as they had first taken food from my hand they raced off through the trees to the west and disappeared.

What promoted these birds to behave this way? It could be a case of "birdie-see-birdie-do" though precisely which birds they watched "seeing and doing," I cannot say. Might these two males be George's competitors and were they imitating his behavior? Are there itinerant Red-winged Blackbird trainers practicing their art inside Central Park or is it common for Red-winged Blackbirds to behave this way without training? If it is common how come I have not found a mention of it in the various field guides and texts? Could it be a trait of the Central Park Red-winged Blackbird population? I asked Ken Yasukawa these questions leaving out the one about itinerant Red-winged Blackbird trainers because you knew that was just a joke right? Ken thought it unusual to find Red-winged Blackbirds behaving this way.

> I'm not surprised that you can't find information about this phenomenon. It's not something that a biologist would write about in general. I would say that because the vast majority of redwings are not intimately involved with humans, this behav-

ior would be very rare, but only because the birds lack exposure to humans in this context. Redwings are able to make associations of all kinds (e.g., they can associate specific songs with individual neighboring males), perhaps especially those that will get them food.[1]

While ruminating on these questions it occurred to me that if I saw these two Red-winged Blackbirds again, as I believed I would, it would be helpful to have names to distinguish them. Naming one Red-winged Blackbird Squeaky was a logical consequence of the squeaky sound of his call. Naming the other bird Charlie was a whim for which I have no explanation.

Later my visit with George sharply contrasted with my visit with Squeaky and Charlie. George was preoccupied chasing his rivals and his two mates but he stopped intermittently to take nourishment from Gordon who is one of his favorite Club George members. It was not extraordinary for George to be busy but it was for him to take food from only one person and that one person was someone other than me. I could not comprehend why comparative strangers Squeaky and Charlie had interacted with me while George would not. What caused George to avoid me? I could not think what it might be but the more I considered it the more I realized I would be wise to put the brakes on my anthropomorphizing about George. I dropped the notion that George's behavior implied a personal rejection and considered another theory.

Could it be possible that George was aware of my visit with the other Red-winged Blackbirds, Charlie and Squeaky, and that he interpreted this as consorting with the enemy? I went as far to wonder if George could smell the scent of those other Red-winged Blackbirds on me. That is hardly likely. In fact my theorizing seemed to be getting so weird that I took it as a signal it was time to go home, replenish my blood sugar and rest. That is what I did and I soon regained my equilibrium. I reviewed the day's events rationally and calmly. I applied my powers of reason and accumulated

[1]Ken Yasukawa, e-mail message, January 11, 2005.

knowledge to comprehend and intelligently interpret what I had experienced during my walk especially what I witnessed at George's Pond. I concluded that George could not have known I had been with other Red-winged Blackbirds nor would it have mattered if he did. Do I sound convinced?

Chapter 9 · May 5

Mutual Trust

This was a perfect spring day. The air was comfortably warm and a gentle breeze was blowing. There was ample bright sunlight. As I walked through the Ramble it fell in thick shafts through openings between the leaves. The birds I saw did not require theatrical lighting to be attractive but when such a shaft illuminated one the added drama was not lost on me. Under these conditions I caught sight of several migrants that included the Yellow-rumped Warbler, Common Yellowthroat, Black-and-white Warbler, Prairie Warbler, Northern Flicker, Black-crowned Night Heron, Green Heron, Common Grackle, Savannah Sparrow, Pine Warbler, and Great Egret. There were more than a few of the usual suspects too:

George seemed to be in a contemplative mood too, if such a mental state exists in birds.

Red-bellied Woodpecker, Northern Cardinal, Mallard, American Robin, House Sparrow, Mourning Dove, Downy Woodpecker, Blue Jay, Tufted Titmouse and Rock Pigeon.

Most of those migrant birds were hard for me to identify. I frequently thought they were one of the usual suspects when I first saw them with my naked eye. By using my own, in this case, good advice as laid out in an earlier chapter I was able to systematically distinguish the migrants from the usual suspects. Whaddyah know, it really does work.

Maybe it was because of the balmy weather and the streaming sunlight through the trees but I was in a sensitive mood today. I felt extraordinarily peaceful and calm as I made my way along my route. I found myself focusing with greater clarity on both the details of each bird's appearance and their behaviors, or so it seemed. I thought a lot about how I have come to apply the same curiosity and attention to all the birds that I first directed solely toward George. Then memory of the uncomfortable feelings I had the last time I saw George flooded back. I knew it was silly but I was afraid that he might no longer trust me. The more I thought about it the faster I moved in the direction of George's Pond.

When I arrived there I expected the dock to be filled with people on such a glorious day but I found myself the only person there. I did not have to wait for George to arrive. He floated onto his favorite perch at the dock as I was arriving. When he makes his entrance at the same time as I do, as he often does, it is hard not to believe that he came at that moment because he had recognized me from a distance. His demeanor was different from his manic persona of yesterday. I supposed I was projecting my own mood onto George, but he too seemed to be in a contemplative mood, if such a mental state exists in birds. He was less animated and far less vocal than he has been of late. I know what you are thinking. Certainly I am anthropomorphizing George again, but be patient with me for a while as I describe George's behavior and why I felt the way I did about it.

George spent a long period on his perch at the dock quietly surveying his territory and making a soft "chek" call now and then. I stood watching as the breeze blew a few of his breast and nape feathers back and forth over and over again. Yesterday he shunned me but today he barely left my side during the hour and one half I was at the dock. He did leave to briefly forage on his island but mostly he stood perched just above my head. At times he walked a few steps closer to me, leaned over and made a slow series of muted "chek" calls that I took to mean he wanted a snack. I was correct in my interpretation. I also had the feeling that the calm quiet nature of George's calls meant that he was comfortable being with me. This is not an erroneous assumption on my part. Ken Yasukawa explained that the vocalizations and behavior I observed support the idea that George was indeed at ease.

> The behavior you describe when you are within a few feet of George indicates that he was not agitated at all by your proximity. The soft "check" calls you describe are part of an alert system. When all is well, the male gives a call every now then like the watchtower guard's "all is well." If George had been agitated by your proximity he would have switched to a different call and increased the rate of calling.[1]

He made no attempts to flash his epaulets, no slow display flights across the water or boisterous choruses of "konk-la-ree" to impress female or rival. No strangers or even a Club George charter member came along to break the mood. It seemed as if George and I were joined in quiet contemplation of the pond and its surroundings. The only sounds came from a few other birds I now cannot remember. I felt I suppose much like someone does about his or her pet. There was the sense of a shared mutual trust between this wild Red-winged Blackbird and myself. The gentleness of his demeanor and his comfort in my presence for that hour and one-half made me feel that for the duration George was not wild at all. Of course that was a daydream but it felt really good to indulge in it at the time.

[1]Ken Yasukawa, e-mail message, March 19, 2004.

Chapter 10 · May 6

An Uncommon Common Grackle

The usual suspects were foraging at Morton's Pond. There were two dozen House Sparrows, eight Common Grackles, and six Mourning Doves grazing together in the weeds and grass under the shrubs and between the trees. Now and then a Northern Cardinal was in and out of sight having stayed just long enough for me to remember it had been there. I was concentrating on how different species, like these four, can coexist, at least superficially, so peacefully. They were all in competition for many of the same resources but yet tolerated each other with only an occasional squawk or peck. Members of the same species seemed to have more disagreements with each other than with members of different breeds.

The Common Grackle can assume an uncommonly sinister expression, can it not?

Two male Red-winged Blackbirds joined them and I assumed they were the same two males I saw here two days ago. When the boldest of the pair came within a few feet of me several times I guessed it was Charlie. I held out my palm with a few nuts and seeds and he flew toward me, landed, grabbed a scrap of food and returned to the ground to eat. I had no doubt this was Charlie. It was the House Sparrows that took this as an opportune moment to break the interspecies truce by trying to take away Charlie's prize. Rather than fight he retreated to a more secluded spot to dine in peace. He made two more successful visits in this manner and then vanished leaving his companion Squeaky behind. This Red-winged Blackbird was content to keep his distance and continue foraging in the mixed flock by the waterside to which calm had returned.

It was my second close encounter with Charlie and Squeaky but I already could perceive obvious and subtle differences between them. Charlie was larger and more aggressive with humans and all other birds. Squeaky was smaller and shyer with people and birds of species other than his own.

Counting the addition of Squeaky there were five species represented in the mixed flock. They continued to feed spiritedly but he was noticeably losing enthusiasm. Squeaky pecked at the ground intermittently and with a lackluster effort. Something was distracting him. A female Red-winged Blackbird had slipped into the group having escaped my notice but not Squeaky's. He soon ceased foraging altogether and approached the female directly. He walked to her left and then to her right with his wings raised and his scarlet epaulets showed off to the maximum. He empathically sang out his Red-winged Blackbird song "konk-la-ree" several times. This was unmistakably a courtship ritual. Squeaky's feelings were transparent but I could not read the female's. She stood still, listening and watching but otherwise showing no response. Was she playing hard to get as George's mate had on the dock? My observations were cut short before I could make a judgment about that hypothesis.

While watching Squeaky and the female I stood extending my open palm unconsciously. I could not have known that an unlikely species was about to land on it. Without warning a mature Common Grackle made an uncommon two-point landing in the middle of my palm. Consider, if you will, that a male Red-winged Blackbird averages about eight and three-quarter inches in length and weighs around two ounces. In comparison, though the Common Grackle is closely related biologically to the Red-winged Blackbird, both belonging to the *Icteridae* family, the adult male is typically eleven to thirteen and one-half inches long and weighs up to four and one-half ounces. Both species are somewhat aggressive but the Common Grackle is more so. It not only eats insects, seeds, and fruit like its Red-winged Blackbird cousin, but also small fish and rodents and the occasional egg or chick of other birds. With a long sharply pointed stout bill and hooked talons on each foot these birds not only give the appearance of being formidable but they are in reality truly tough customers.[1]

Initially I was delighted but my elation rapidly degenerated into, shall we say, concern. Looking at this grackle I focused intensely on three of its physical characteristics. First, its large and sharp claws dominated my thoughts. To my relief they did not cut or scrape me, but I was highly aware of them pressing against my skin. Second, the long, stout, pointy and powerful beak worried me as it periodically dipped to pick up seeds but truthfully I barely felt its touch. Third, the bird's yellow eyes were positively eerie when seen close up. Those orbs would be put to good effect in a movie designed to scare your pants off. My pants were never in danger of falling off but I might not have noticed if they had because I was so focused on this wild creature standing on my hand. My concern deepened when it became clear this bird was not one to eat and run. No, this Common Grackle stayed put until my palm was picked clean. Only after every crumb had been taken did the bird push off to join seven thankfully more reserved grackles. I am sure

---

[1]Author's note: This is a good time to debunk a popular misconception among beginning birders. Many assume that a superficial resemblance between crows and grackles suggests they are related. They are not. In North America crows belong to the family *Corvidae* along with ravens, magpies and various jays including, surprising to some including me because of its coloration, the Blue Jay.

I will always remember the shock of this experience with a laugh and a bit of wonder. While I stress that the bird did not hurt me I would be irresponsible to recommend that any reader duplicate this feat. If either you or the bird should become startled one or both could be injured. In my case a temporary paralyzing fear kept me perfectly still thus forestalling a possible accident. Besides without realizing it I had been well prepared by having had practice with George and other birds. I knew what to expect so I did not flinch at the critical moment of contact. An inexperienced birder might jerk his or her hand away or worse they might take an involuntary defensive swipe at the bird. My advice plain and simple is do not put yourself in such a position. Try to keep common or uncommon grackles out of your hands at all times, okay?

David Allen Sibley tells a short but effective cautionary story about a particular Common Grackle. It better illustrates my claim that Common Grackles can be "tough customers" and supplies a good reason why you should maintain respect for them.

> One common Grackle in downtown Toronto would use buildings to its advantage to corner small passerines [perching birds] and then dispatch them with its large beak.[2]

There was one more unexpected bit of bird behavior in store for me directly after my encounter with the Common Grackle. Four Gray Squirrels, a rat[3] and six Rock Pigeons by then had joined the foraging flock. There were now six bird and two mammal species together for those who are counting. As I tossed a peanut toward the birds, a Red-bellied Woodpecker appeared from who knows where and snatched it in his beak while it sailed through the air. This is how I discovered that male and female Red-bellied Woodpeckers would play catch as long as they get to eat the ball. Of

---

[2]David Allen Sibley, *The Sibley Guide to Bird Life & Behavior*, p. 546.
[3]Author's note: Sorry but I cannot identify what type of rodent this was. My experience and exposure to them have been limited. Though my interest has increased it is not sufficient to have learned how to identify different species. I apologize to all rodent loving readers.

course, they also have to be familiar with you so they feel confident about your intentions. I am sure that this particular woodpecker had been watching me for quite some time, probably weeks, unseen on a perch above the pond. I have since learned that Red-bellied Woodpeckers "hawk" insects by hovering momentarily in the air in order to grab them. Peanut catching I suspect is an adaptation of their well-practiced instinctual bug catching behavior.

I had heard Red-bellied Woodpeckers calling out or tapping on a tree and had caught brief glimpses of them from a distance. Thanks to a tossed peanut I was now getting a detailed look at one. After having such an opportunity to study this creature I want to point out that the source for the name "Red-bellied" is not immediately apparent even in a close-up view. I can report that I found an extremely faint red wash, almost like a thin layer of watercolor paint, on the lower breast, abdomen and between its legs. The better field guides will warn you it is normally difficult to observe its red belly in the field. Save yourself aggravation and do not think your powers of observation are inadequate if you fail to see the Red-bellied Woodpecker's red belly yourself. Be confident you will see it in time.

Chapter 11 • May 7

Scene of Graphic Violence

WARNING: This chapter contains a scene of graphic violence. There may be more detail than you would have preferred to read or see. It is not my fault. This event would have happened with me or without me. I am only relating what occurred. If you decide to proceed be advised that parental guidance is suggested. If your parents are not available you are on your own. So what else is new? By the end of the chapter please do not say I did not warn you, okay?

———————————

I continue to follow my predetermined route through the park that passes through different types of habitat. My hope that I would find birds that specialize in each of those habitats has paid off handsomely. In the Ramble where the trees are relatively thick and much of the ground is covered with shrubs, grasses, herbaceous plants, weeds and wildflowers I consistently find woodpeckers, sparrows, thrushes, hawks, jays, cardinals, vireos, redstarts, grosbeaks, buntings and other species less likely to be seen in more open areas. Morton's Pond and the Gill, a winding stream, provide places where a variety of species congregate to feed, bathe and drink. It is a particularly attractive area for the annual migrants like waterthrushes, warblers and vireos. Willow Rock, with its crescent shaped cove provides a shoreline for sparrows, herons, egrets and a tree line where various migrants are interspersed with the usual suspects and perhaps a lurking raccoon. The landscape along the eastern shore of the Lake provides a transitional space where the trees line ends and the view opens onto twenty-two acres of water. Here I may find more herons, and egrets but also swans, geese, gulls, ducks, coots, swallows and other waterfowl. Of course lots of other birds come to the shore to drink and bathe too. Some, like the Red-winged Blackbirds, breed in the cattails and phragmites. At the northernmost end of the Lake there is the tiny swamp I have described where the Green Herons breed among other species that include American Robins, Gray Catbirds, Red-winged Black-birds and more. In the water, completely covered with a layer of green duckweed by summer, are not only minnows and bass but a host of other creatures including bullfrogs and turtles some of which are of the snapping variety. Farther to the east is a hill that affords some of the best views of the park. For some reason the vicinity attracts more woodpeckers and titmice than other spots I visit. Where the land slopes down toward the Delacorte Theater and George's Pond there is also the Shakespeare Garden where numerous species may even include hummingbirds during migration periods. On my way to visit George I pass through meadows sprinkled with trees and shrubs where robins, starlings and sparrows are common and when there are ripe berries to be had I may find a small flock of waxwings as well. Over those same meadows a towering spiral or two of gulls are not an unusual sight nor is the flight of a gliding hawk and the less common sight of one darting across the sky in full attack mode. Disciplining myself by keeping to this basic route has proven to be very satisfying. I recommend that the beginning birder do the same if possible. Of course if you do not have a variation of habitats available or do not have sufficient time to take advantage of them then a different strategy will be required. You can derive enjoyment studying a single habitat even if it is your own backyard, schoolyard, empty lot or, and I can testify to the productivity of this habitat, the parking lot in an industrial park. Wherever birds appear on a daily basis that is where your curiosity can and will be satisfied.

When I completed my route today and came to the dock I found George in a nervous state. He stood on the end of his perch on the fence jerking his head this way and that way: listening; looking; calling out. Every so often he sped off to pursue a rival or two or zeroed in on a particular edible creature or vegetative substance. He was nearly constantly in motion only perching long enough to select a new target to investigate or attack. While George was preoccupied with these activities I too had plenty to keep me busy. There were American Robins, Common Grackles and House Sparrows galore in the trees and shrubs beside the dock entrance. In the water three dozen Mallards were noisily engaging in three parts foraging and one part fighting each other, while the nesting Canada Geese went about their business with discretion so as not to attract attention.

I waited two hours but George disappeared without paying me a proper visit. That was disappointing but I remained on the dock well after dark anyway. I remember when I used to exit the park as soon as the sun was about to conclude its descent. This was for personal safety reasons. That was and still is a sensible strategy: there is inherent risk in remaining in an urban park when it is dark and I am not alluding to potential threats from wild animals but to those from the supposedly civilized kind. However I have allowed other priorities to undermine my more cautious judgment. The initial reason I began to linger was my hope to see the Black-crowned Night Herons that usually come out of hiding in the early evening to stalk prey among the plants and rocks in the shallow water. I have counted as many as seven Black-crowned Night Herons at one time around George's Pond's perimeter. Though they are mostly nocturnal the Black-crowned Night Herons are sometimes active in daylight. On occasion I have seen them partially concealed on a leafy branch or in the tall grass waiting for the light to fade so their inverted workday can begin. I have also seen a Black-crowned Night Heron stand in the open for an hour or more without making an attempt to hide from foe, friend or future food. That was on long summer evenings where the exposed Black-crowned Night Heron was standing on George's Island. I imagine it must have felt an added measure of security by being completely surrounded by water and that is why it did not try to conceal itself as it typically does.

George has behaviors too that he sometimes alters but he seldom alters his roosting habits. He prudently retires an hour or two before sundown. He does not risk running into a predator or other things that go bump in the night. Not George. Well not normally. On this particular evening well after sundown he returned to his favorite perch on the dock and began calling out. Even more uncharacteristically he flew across the width of the dock to a portion of the railing that is only about four feet high where he rarely perches. If George chose this less secure perch, I reasoned, it was likely he thought there were no strangers or predators about. I was wrong.

When I followed George to the opposite side of the dock I found myself positioned so that I could not help but notice a Black-crowned Night Heron standing in the shallow water below us. If George had not rested on this specific spot I doubt I would have seen it. George remained only long enough to nibble a bedtime snack and utter a few soft "chek" calls. Then he rushed off to retire to his island roost leaving me alone with the bird of prey standing statue-like beneath me about six feet away. A mature Black-crowned Night Heron like this one is twenty-five to twenty-eight inches long with a wingspan of forty-four to forty-five inches. Despite its considerable size it can be difficult to detect because it remains motionless and surrounded by vegetation for long periods. This particular heron gave no indication that it knew or cared that I was there. It was still and silent. Directly behind it was a shrub that largely obscured a boulder beneath which I knew there to be a rat's burrow. It became apparent the heron was aware of this as well. Hurriedly, but gracefully, the bird leaned over its left flank and made a short sharp lunge toward the base of the boulder. When the Black-crowned Night Heron turned back toward me I was stunned to see a rat hanging by its tail from its beak.

If I have alienated you at this juncture in my tale you may wish to move immediately to the next chapter.

———————

PLEASE TAKE A MOMENT TO DECIDE HOW YOU WILL PROCEED FROM HERE.

———————

All right, assuming you have made a decision, those of you who have elected to finish this chapter will now read and to some extent see the gory details.

The Black-crowned Night Heron still grasping the rat by its tail began to dunk the rat's head into the water over and over again like you or I might dunk a tea bag in a cup. It struck me as decidedly sadistic, but the heron continued in an almost machinelike fashion without any display of emotion. In sharp contrast the rat, as you would be correct in assuming, was an emotional wreck. In the brief interludes it emerged from the water the rat emitted high-pitched screams. As I watched I felt the hairs on the back of my neck stand up. I did not want to watch the action to its foregone conclusion but I could not look away. The scene was simultaneously ghastly and fascinating. I confess I have never been a rat enthusiast but in this situation I felt really sorry for the unfortunate creature. I was soon to feel even sorrier.

After several more dips in the water, the heron held the rat aloft then dropped it a short distance, catching it only to release and catch it again. The heron repeated this to reposition its grip farther along the animal's body. Starting from its tail, the Heron's beak advanced to the rump, torso, and shoulders until it held the rat by its throat. There the beak clamped shut. The rat gave a shriek that was to be its final comment on this situation or anything else. Simultaneously all four of its legs stretched out stiffly from its body. The rat went silent. Its limbs sank limply to its sides. In one smooth motion the heron swung the rat in a short arc into the air, let go of its tail and as it fell from the arc's zenith, swallowed it whole.

Sheesh.

THIS IS POSITIVELY YOUR LAST CHANCE TO AVOID A PHOTOGRAPH CONTAINING A SCENE OF GRAPHIC VIOLENCE. NO KIDDING.

I wanted to say or do something but I could not think of what that might be. The Black-crowned Night Heron showed no indecision whatsoever. Noiselessly the bird turned and walked slowly into the thick shore plants and disappeared from sight. I assumed it was on a mission to reprise its previous performance if it could.

You cannot say I did not warn you that this chapter contained a scene of graphic violence. Remember too that I am only reporting what I have witnessed: the good, bad, ugly and the birdie. With that in mind I must caution you once more. If you did not enjoy this story you are really going to despise this picture.

The Black-crowned Night Heron stands about two feet tall. It is not a small bird but it is not a huge one either. I thought the unfortunate rodent would be too large to be swallowed in one gulp but I learned firsthand what an easy maneuver that is for this adept predator.

Chapter 12 · May 8

Crested Breast Rodent?

At Morton's Pond the two male Red-winged Blackbirds, Charlie and Squeaky, were again feeding in a mixed group that included Common Grackles, Rock Pigeons, Mourning Doves and House Sparrows. One female Red-winged Blackbird that might or might not have been the same one I saw Squeaky courting a couple of days ago came and went briefly a couple of times. There was a frequent visitor that has joined my growing multitude of favorites. The Tufted Titmouse averages six and one-half inches long with a ten and three-quarter-inch wingspan. They weigh about eight-tenths of an ounce. I admire their energy, means of locomotion and their vocalizations. They are agile flyers and can hover with great skill. At will they can hang upside down from branches on which they hop

Crested Breast Rodent? No way.

as they seem to be in too much of a hurry to merely walk. They have a high-pitched raspy call that I especially am grateful for because it is readily identifiable as long as their close cousins the Black-capped Chickadees are not around to confuse me. Of course sometimes I wish the chickadees were here because I seldom see them at all. According to the birder's grapevine sightings of Black-capped Chickadees in the areas of the park I frequent have been rare for a couple of years. I have heard no reasonable explanation why that is so and they are reported to be in good numbers elsewhere in the region.

As cute as Tufted Titmice are their name is uncute. In fact, the name Tufted Titmouse, I confess, irks me. It is true they have a tuft on their heads, or a crest as it is more commonly called, but it does not require an ornithologist to determine that these birds neither resemble a "tit" nor a "mouse." I rely on Diana Wells' explanation of how the Tufted Titmouse got its name to make any sense of it. She says it is derived from the Old Icelandic "titr" meaning small and from the Anglo-Saxon "mase" meaning a small bird. I think "small, small bird," though redundant, makes sense but it does not mitigate the awkward image this moniker unavoidably conjures when I think of the contemporary meaning of each component of its name; tufted is a crest, tit is a breast and mouse is a rodent. Do you think "Crested Breast Rodent" is an appropriate appellation for this bird? I suggest an alternative. Since the Tufted Titmouse is so closely related to the chickadees I would prefer to call them "Tufted Chickadees" and let it go at that. Where did the name chickadee come from? Diana Wells says it is derived from its call. The Cherokee Indians called it the tsikilili derived from how they described its call, "tsik-i-li-li-li."[1] That seems pretty close to Alsop's description of its call as "chick-a-dee-dee-dee."

The Tufted Titmouse song is approximated in print by various field guides as "peter, peter, peter," "peto, peto, peto" or even "here, here, here" which are all in their way on the money, but other attempts to describe Tufted Titmouse vocalizations can produce curious results. That is because birdcalls and birdsongs, like

[1]Diana Wells, *100 Birds and How They Got Their Names,* p. 253.

human music, are so complex and nuanced. Efforts to describe these particular vocalizations serve as a good example of how difficult it can be to satisfactorily describe any sound using words. Please consider a sampling of some scholarly descriptions arranged in ascending levels of complexity. After you have read these I am confident you will begin to understand why there is no adequate substitute for hearing calls and songs straight from the bird's beak or a really, really, really good recording.

Fred Alsop:

Calls vary from high-pitched, thin squeaky notes to low, harsh, fussy scolding notes.[2]

Roger Tory Peterson:

Note similar to those of the chickadees, but more drawling, nasal, wheezy, and complaining.[3]

Kenn Kaufman:

Call notes: quite varied, include whining scold, "see-nyahh" and "sesee-jjeeer."[4]

Donald and Lillian Stokes:

Calls include a scolding "jweejweejwee" and "tseejwee."[5]

Then there is David Allen Sibley's attempt that is more musical to my ear though you might have to hear these calls a few times first to make sense of it.

[2]Fred J. Alsop III, *Birds of North America: Eastern Region*, p. 518.
[3]Roger Tory Peterson and Virginia Marie Peterson, *A Field Guide to the Birds of Eastern and Central North America*, p. 236.
[4]Kenn Kaufman, *Birds of North America*, p. 276.
[5]Donald and Lillian Stokes, *Stokes Field Guide to Birds, Eastern Region* p. 314.

Call a series of angry, nasal, rising notes often preceded by very
high, thin notes: "ti ti ti sii sii zhree zhree zhree."[6]

T. C. Grubb and V. V. Pravosudov make an even more ambitious
effort to reproduce the sound in print:

Several variations: a terse, scratchy "tschk-day"; a scratchy "tsee-
day-day-day," with a high-pitched first note; "see-sa-day-day,"
similar to the call just described; "see-tee-tee-tee," high-pitched
and thin and given with open bill; "see-tee" and "see-tee-tee-eh."

Grubb and Pravosudov go on to describe nine more vocaliza-
tions for those of you who are determined to dig deeper into
Tufted Titmouse lingo.[7] Also I strongly recommend Donald
Kroodsma's *The Singing Life of Birds* (New York: Houghton Mifflin
Company 2005), where the author, a bird vocalization specialist,
presents his provocative field research on the subject.

Compilations of recorded birdcalls and songs available on CD,
tape and Web sites are useful. By all means give these a try but remember that recordings should be used as a supplement to real
live bird vocalizations for at least one powerful reason. It is an
amazing though incontrovertible fact that birds can have local di-
alects. Yes, birds in different geographical regions have "accents"
so it is possible that a recording might sound "off" to you. I have
had that experience myself, but do not let it discourage you from
availing yourself of this useful tool. Hey, nothing's perfect.

Though I only saw one of them today at Morton's Pond there
are two Tufted Titmice that frequent the area. I believe they are
mates but the sexes look alike and I cannot tell them apart but one
of them is noticeably more aggressive than the other. It was this aggressive individual that unbidden flew toward me and hovered one
or two inches from my fingertips. The bird repeated this three
times. On the fourth approach the tiny creature landed, picked out

[6]David Allen Sibley, *The Sibley Field Guide to Birds of Eastern North America*, p. 299.
[7]T. C. Grubb and V. V. Pravosudov, *Tufted Titmouse*, p. 5.

a piece of peanut rejecting the sunflower seeds they are widely believed to crave, paused to stare at me for two seconds, then flew with its meal into a nearby tree. There the titmouse wedged the food in the crevice of the bark and pounded it to bits. When the meal was over the bird repeated the procedure and then hurried to another venue.

My visit to George revealed him to be in a very aggressive mode. He was feverishly chasing his two rival male Red-winged Blackbirds and was successful in expelling them. They were equally successful in sneaking back to the pond's perimeter but when they crossed over it was not for very long. George would not permit it, period. I marveled at the amount of energy George and his adversaries exerted in this ongoing war of wills. Eventually they quit but not because they were running out of steam. The sun was setting and it was time for them to go to their respective roosts. I made a reluctant and uncharacteristic early departure because it was I that had run out of steam and the sunset had nothing to do with it. Once I was sure George had roosted for the night I traveled toward my own roost.

Chapter 13 · May 9

A Bird in a Bag

In rapid succession I had three encounters with species for the first time in the Ramble. I saw, with certainty, an Eastern Towhee, Swamp Sparrow, and Magnolia Warbler. I qualified this statement with "certainty" because there was a previous instance when I learned after the fact that I had mistaken an Eastern Towhee for an American Robin hiding deep inside a bush, and was told on another occasion that a Swamp Sparrow stood within a group of White-throated Sparrows at my feet but I could not pick it out. Today I had no doubts at all about the identity of these three birds and felt a sense of "beginner's" satisfaction knowing I had gotten it

Here is George diving into the bag of peanuts. Moments later I moved in to hold the bag down, as he was about to shove it off the ledge on to the dock or into the water.

right. Later I followed the sound of loud drumming I assumed to be made by a Red-bellied or Downy Woodpecker but found the source to be the not-so-often-seen-in-these-parts-lately Hairy Woodpecker. That was not a first time sighting but it qualified as a-nice-surprise-contrary-to-my-expectations event.

Many of the usual suspects were out and about, especially around Morton's Pond where I saw male and female Downy Woodpeckers, Blue Jays, a Tufted Titmouse, Northern Cardinals, Common Grackles, House Sparrows, Mallards and the pair of peanut catching Red-bellied Woodpeckers.

When I arrived at the dock George was in the midst of coaxing some human newcomers to feed him. I never tire of watching strangers' reactions to George's routine. Almost everyone comprehends what George wants from him or her but there are a few who do not. These few would have a hard time accepting Club George charter membership because it is not likely that they would notice it had been offered. Three strangers, all receptive to George's message, lined up along the fence with their arms stretched up over their heads and their open palms filled with one kind of edible or another. Each hoped George would choose their offering. Over the course of ten minutes George visited each one to their great pleasure judging by the big smiles, giggles and exclamations.

When George finished with the newcomers he flew off across the pond. I prepared for his expected return by taking a plastic bag filled with peanuts out of my pocket. I put some in my hand and carelessly placed the bag on top of the railing at the end of the dock. I have rarely left the bag there for more than a moment because the breeze could blow it into the water, but I placed it there and forgot about it. When George came back to his perch on the dock I moved toward him as he excitedly called out. Instead of hopping down to get the food on my palm, as I thought he would, George flew inches over my head to literally dive into the open bag of peanuts lying on top of the railing at my back.

My first reaction was to laugh. I was terrifically amused that he had recognized the bag to be the source of the food and he had outsmarted me in heading for it when I assumed he was going to make a landing on my hand. His motivation was clear. Why should he settle for a few morsels when he could stuff his beak with a veritable mountain of food and not have to trust a human participant to get at it? His digging inside the bag was so vigorous however that I feared he might push it off the railing onto the deck or into the water below. I acted to stabilize the situation. I took a few cautious steps forward taking care not to startle him but by the time I reached for the bag he had sensed my approach and was backing out of it. However, he was not alarmed by my proximity. He patiently remained a few inches away alternately staring at the food and at me while I used both hands to roll up the plastic bag, widening the opening to better accommodate his entrances and exits. When I was done I backed away as far as I could without relinquishing my hold on the bag. With my outstretched arms I held the bag securely in place and waited to see what George would do.

George was indecisive. He continued turning his gaze from the bag to me over and over. Searching for a way to reassure him I spoke to him in a gentle tone. "Come on Georgie boy. Get your peanuts. Come on handsome. Come on boy," I said hoping that if anyone overheard me it would be a charter member of Club George who would understand my behavior. Arguably George did not require a dose of baby talk for motivation, the peanuts were motivation enough, but I suppose my soothing talk had a reassuring effect on him. George acted decisively. He ran to the bag and stuck his head inside while I continued to hold it in place for him. I was tickled to think that the fruits of bird and human teamwork could be so rewarding to each in his own way. George got food for the body and I got food for the soul.

He gorged on but it must have gotten stuffy inside the bag because, after a while, he altered his technique. George began taking a single piece of food out of the bag which he ate in the open air before reaching back inside to extract more. George kept on until he had emptied the bag. Once he had exhausted the supply he took off in search of another meal.

Chapter 14 · May 13

Morton and Mary

Over the last three days I had three first time sightings of migrant birds that included a Northern Parula, Black-throated Green Warbler and not one but two male Scarlet Tanagers at the same time. There were other migrants as well. Among those were the American Redstart, Common Nighthawk and several Common Yellowthroats. I emphasize that I saw "several" Common Yellowthroats because there appears to be a bumper crop of them this season. Other birders agree that they cannot remember seeing so many of them in the park at this time of year.

I also experienced another close-encounter-of-the-bird-kind on my walk that I would not have anticipated. While being entertained by the pair of peanut catching Red-bellied Woodpeckers

There really is no way to see if the feathers on Mary's back are downy, is there?

two Downy Woodpeckers came on the scene. I have mentioned that I often find these two individuals foraging together and they, especially the female, are enthusiastic fans of Harry's homemade mixture. The female, as usual, kept at least a dozen feet from me, but her mate, as is his custom, came closer. He became very conspicuous as he started circling around me making brief stops on successive branches to look me over before continuing on until he had made at least two full circuits. I reckoned his surveillance maneuvers were at an end when he perched directly opposite me on a truncated limb that is a favorite perch utilized by various species. Without having a hint of what he was contemplating the woodpecker leapt off his perch and flew at me. The tiny bird fluttered in the air an inch away from my fingertips where he was obviously considering a landing but aborted his mission to regain his perch and consider his next move. He cut short his ruminations and launched toward me again. This time the bold bird landed in my palm. For a second, he turned his head to one side focusing one eye into mine. He stood statue-like just staring. Then he rapidly bent forward, picked up a piece of food and streaked back to his perch. Still holding it in his beak he gingerly placed the morsel in a small indentation in the tree bark and then commenced to pound it into smithereens. When he was satisfied that the smithereens were of a suitable size he ate them after which he rested and preened for a short time. A little later, again without warning, he launched himself toward me once more. On this excursion he landed with both feet gripping my fingertips and hung upside down. Peering up from under my fingers he scrutinized me. I evidently passed the test because, still hanging from my fingertips, he swung himself up into my palm, grabbed a peanut, raced back to his perch to put the tidbit in the same indentation he had before and pounded it to smithereens that he greedily ate at once.

I had learned from *Red-tails in Love* that a Downy Woodpecker might behave this way but I was quite unprepared to experience it myself. It so impressed me that I thought such an audacious bird deserved special recognition. I decided to give him a name. The

name Morton came to mind at once. Since he is a Downy Woodpecker his full name would be Morton Downy. There is a well-
known media personality with the name Morton Downy whom I
hope would feel honored to know his moniker had been put to
such good use. I named Morton's bride too. Mary seemed appropriate. "Morton and Mary Downy" has a pleasing sound to it, don't
you agree?

I enjoyed coming up with these names so much that I got a little
carried away. As a further tribute I resolved to rename the pond in
Morton's honor. I have used the name Morton's Pond earlier in
this text and apologize if you tried but could not find it on a map of
Central Park. Since this pond is such a popular foraging place for
so many species of birds I had decided to deliberately obscure its
location as a way to discourage an increase in human visitors to the
site. After giving the woodpecker the name Morton it seemed convenient and logical to lend it to one of his favorite feeding spots.
You should know I did the same thing when I named George's
Pond. You will not find either name on a Central Park map.

As I have described Morton and Mary they are delicate diminutive creatures. Downy Woodpeckers are North America's smallest
Woodpeckers. They are also the most widespread. At between six
and three-quarter to seven inches, for comparison, they are just a
tad bigger than a House Sparrow. They have at least one claim to
fame. Their courtship display is said to be wonderfully theatrical.
Known as the Butterfly Flight, it is described as a kind of aerial bal-
let in *The Birds of North America.*

> The Butterfly Flight, one of the most spectacular displays of the
> Downy Woodpecker, is typically performed on sunny, warm
> spring days prior to nesting. Male and female follow (or chase)
> one another in a flight characterized by holding the wings high
> and flapping them slowly and weakly like a butterfly, moving
> dancelike through open spaces between trees, sometimes on a
> level course and at times in long, deep loops.[1]

[1]Jerome Jackson and Henri R. Ouellet, *Downy Woodpecker,* p. 12.

To my chagrin I have yet to observe it myself.

Downy Woodpecker mates share responsibilities in their division of their labors. Both sexes excavate the nest cavity and take turns incubating and brooding the chicks during the day but it is the male's sole responsibility during the night.[2] They are monogamous at least for each breeding season. It is not clear if they do or do not mate for life. In winter the female may leave the territory if food is not in sufficient supply for two but the pair will usually reunite later when the food supply improves.

Looking in my field guides at all the woodpecker species in North America it struck me as curious that the color scheme of white, black and red is the basic look for them all with the exception of Lewis's Woodpecker, which swaps gray for bright white and pinkish red for brilliant red. I suppose there was a similarly plumed ancestral woodpecker from which these birds decended but after millennia why do these species sport these particular colors? It is no accident that black is a dominant color of their tails. The black coloration is a consequence of a high concentration of melanin that structurally strengthens and diminishes the wear and tear of all birds' feathers. Morton and Mary, like the others of their kind, use their melanin reinforced black tails to brace themselves when they are climbing a tree trunk or branch. The tail and their two feet comprise a sturdy three-cornered platform that helps them hold on to vertical surfaces. The white color is prominent on Downy Woodpecker breasts, researchers theorize, because it reflects light onto whatever the bird is examining.[3] Why red is the color that differentiates the sexes in the Downy and other woodpeckers is not so easy to explain except that it makes it easier for them to identify each other out in a forest environment where shades of browns, greens and grays dominate. Male and female Downy Woodpeckers may look similar to beginning birders but like most woodpeckers they are sexually dimorphic. In this breed the most obvious difference is the place-

[2]Ibid., p. 14–16.
[3]Ibid., p. 22.

ment or absence of a red dot. Morton has a red spot on the back of his head and Mary has none. This identification system does not work for juvenile female and male Downy Woodpeckers. Both sexes have a red patch located on their foreheads and not the back of their heads.

What do Morton and Mary eat? The Downy Woodpecker diet consists of insects, spiders, larvae, snails, seeds, nuts, and berries. The couple forages together but they have different preferences about where they look for food. These differences reduce how much they compete with one another for limited resources. In general the females favor larger branches and thicker tree trunks while the males go for skinnier branches and stems of grasses but the sexes switch these preferences in different parts of their North American territory. What remains consistent with this species, it seems to me, is how the female and male try not to compete but instead cooperate to make the best use of their food supply.

I have no aesthetic qualms about its name but I have questioned why this woodpecker was officially named "Downy" by Carolus Linnaeus. Some say the name can be attributed to the overall softness of its feathers. One source suggests it was derived from the small bristles on its face that keep sawdust and wood-chips out of its nostrils when pecking away at a tree. "Not so," say Jerome Jackson and Henri R. Ouellet from *The Birds of North America* No.613, 2002.

> Linnaeus, however, . . . never saw a Downy Woodpecker, instead basing his description (Linnaeus 1776) on the work of the American colonial naturalist Paul Catesby. It was Catesby who gave the bird its common name, with "Downy" a reference to the soft white feathers of the white stripe on the lower back, in contrast to the similar, but more hairlike feathers there on the Hairy Woodpecker. . . . [4]

[4]Ibid., p. 2.

Incorporating this particular field mark in its name does not help a birder make proper identification. Since one cannot see from a distance that the white feathers in the stripe on its back are in fact "downy," or soft, the only way to know this to be true would be to hold the bird in one's hand. Even Morton would not hold still for that.

Chapter 15 • May 14

Yellow Cake and Black Skimmer

I had to cut my ornithological visiting time to 45 minutes because I had plans to meet my sister-in-law and my brother, her husband, and my nephew, accompanied by his increasingly significant other, at the Blue Smoke Grill where the only birds are on the menu. With this time constraint in mind I decided to pare down my birding mission to bare essentials. I would climb to the heights above George's Pond and try to find the Red-winged Blackbird nests Ned had recently told me about and then visit George. That was all I would have time for.

From the top of the cliff I concentrated my gaze on places where there were stands of cattails, phragmites, sedges or thick

I later found the cliff climbing Canada Geese foraging where I would normally expect them to be: on the ground. Two goslings and one adult escaped my camera lens just in time to miss this photo opportunity.

shrubs close to water. These were the places most likely to harbor Red-winged Blackbird nests but, to my disappointment, I could not find any.

Down at the dock, on his favorite perch, I thought George was acting oddly. He stood nearly motionless facing a small group of strangers chatting beneath him. George did not give me a sign of recognition as he usually does. Even an offering of peanuts could not get his attention. His gaze drilled past the food and me. I wondered whether I was mistaking a different Red-winged Blackbird for George but that droopy wing indicated that this was the real McCoy and besides this bird did not flinch when I came near. It had to be George.

As I studied him more closely I realized George was focused on a particular man with an infant strapped to his breast in one of those reverse papoose contraptions. The man was engaged in a flurry of baby talk and oblivious to the blackbird watching him. I never had cause to believe George would find baby talk so compelling, certainly not mine, but there was undeniably something about this fellow that commanded George's concentration. The man patted the baby's back with one hand and held a slice of yellow pound cake wrapped in clear plastic film in the other. At once I recognized the source of the attraction. Neither the man nor the baby had beguiled George. No, I was positive it was the yellow pound cake that caught and held his eye. When the man moved a few inches to the left or right George did likewise. Freeing both hands the man went about unfolding the clear plastic wrapping on the cake. Just as he raised it to his lips George jumped from the fence and, digging both feet into the yellow cake to steady himself, sank his beak into it and in one continuous motion pushed off into the air with a quarter's size chunk of cake firmly in his grasp. He sped to his island where he devoured it. The man was absolutely flabbergasted. He yelled to no one in particular, "Did you see what that bird did to me? Did you see that?" Yes, I saw it and at first I did not believe it either, but there could be no mistake that George had risen, or sunk depending on your point of view, to a level of boldness I had not imagined possible. Personally, I enjoyed it im-

mensely, but then it was not my cake he stole. After his initial shock
wore off the fellow was heartily laughing about the episode. He
told and retold it to one stranger after another. He had, I think at
the very least, recognized its value as a great icebreaker for the next
family or business gathering. Whether he had become a charter
member of Club George I do not know.

Still chuckling to myself about George's confectionary theft my
eyes gravitated to the scene directly behind him. What was interesting was what was not there. I searched for the female Canada
Goose sitting on her nest and realized she was missing. So was her
protective mate who has been dutifully patrolling the surrounding
waters for days. Where had they gone?

On a rocky ledge midway up the cliff I spied two adult Canada
Geese. It seemed incongruous for them to be in such an inaccessi-
ble spot. Walking up the jagged rock would be difficult for birds of
this size. Flying and landing on that narrow ledge would be a delicate and tricky maneuver or so it seemed to me. I even doubted if
these two birds were the missing nesting adults until I looked
through binoculars and spied six balls of greenish yellow fluff
stumbling around in a tiny patch of grass. These were the missing
adults and their newly hatched goslings. The family had chosen
this remote spot because it provided food and protection from
predators. But how had they gotten up there?

I watched and waited to see how the family would come safely
down the rocks and, conversely, that would tell me how they went
up. Walking was the only logical means since the goslings cannot
fly having just left the nest. After a while I watched Papa lead an orderly and meticulous descent of a single file line of goslings anchored by Mama following in the rear. The family carefully made
their way over the sharp rocks, past shrubs, through weeds and
reeds until, still in a single file, one by one they slipped into the water. They accomplished this with such aplomb that they looked like
they had done it all their lives when I knew that this had to have
been one of the family's very first forays away from the nest.

Thinking about this event I remembered that a day or two ago I had seen the male standing next to the nest instead of gliding on the water doing guard duty. It occurred to me then that his presence there might have meant that the chicks had hatched but I had no evidence of that until now. It turns out that my hunch had been proven delightfully correct. I cannot help it. I love it when that happens.

On George's Island there were more birds to see none of which I thought likely to steal anyone's yellow pound cake. An Eastern Kingbird stood on a log jutting into the water. This was notable because I have only seen kingbirds at a substantial distance and always on the highest of branches where they search for their insect prey. Over the next half hour a Great Egret, Green Heron and a Black-crowned Night Heron came and went from the island. The Black-crowned Night Heron, more often seen at night as you know, made one of its not to be missed appearances in the late afternoon. Two Double-crested Cormorants were putting on a seemingly effortless diving exhibition. At the end of each dive lasting ten to thirty seconds they surfaced nearly every time with a fish wiggling in their long beaks. The cormorants manipulated the fish deftly, turning them so that the head faced their open throats where it would be more easily swallowed whole. This bird can stay submerged from five to twenty-five feet for thirty to seventy seconds according to Alsop. A dozen Mallards paddled offshore while four Northern Rough-winged Swallows and four Barn Swallows caught their flying dinner over them. On the banks flanking the dock there were six Common Grackles, numerous European Starlings and House Sparrows either foraging together or at times segregated by species. At the far eastern end of the pond I found two White-crowned Sparrows, not seen with regularity in the park, mixed in with a flock of House Sparrows. All these birds were wonderful, but the bonus bird of the day was a Solitary Sandpiper hunting in the shallow water that had flooded the north shore of George's Island during a recent heavy rain.

George returned to the dock after the man with the yellow pound cake had gone but I could not stay with him. The time had come for me to leave for my family dinner date. With mixed emotions I made my way out of the park and into the subway where I experienced a kind of culture shock from the contrast between the park and train experiences. The trip was short but long enough for me to adjust my mental landscape from bucolic to urban.

We had a wonderful time but our dinner was over at an early hour. As there were still a couple of hours of daylight left I seized the opportunity to hurry back to the dock in the park. George was winding up his activities and soon flew to his roost on the island to retire for the evening. The other visitors to the dock drifted away and I was alone as the light faded. It was then that I saw it flying less than a foot off the surface of the water. I could see its silhouette and the line its lower beak made as it sliced through the water, but when it passed through the shafts of light from the street lamps lining the surrounding footpaths I could clearly see its black-and-white coloring. I was watching a Black Skimmer hunt for fish for the first time this season. These elegant creatures are about eighteen to nineteen inches long which makes them roughly the size of the American Crow, but the Black Skimmer's wingspan can be as large as fifty inches compared to the Crow's forty.

Black Skimmers are dramatically plumed with jet-black backs and snowy white underparts. Much of the rear edge of their long pointy wing is white as well. Their beak is bright red with a black tip. The bottom bill, or mandible, is a third longer than the top and shaped like a knife blade to minimize drag as it cuts through the water. When the lower beak makes physical contact with a fish it snaps shut. While continuing to fly the Black Skimmer swallows its prey and then resumes hunting without having to reposition itself. They are normally found in coastal waters but may accidentally venture inland when a storm blows them off course. Perhaps that is how a few Black Skimmers first discovered Central Park. They have been seen feeding here I am told for at least the past two seasons. The very first time I saw this bird it was on the same spot but the circumstances where atypical. That evening the New York Philharmonic Orchestra performed an outdoor concert on the adjacent meadow. During intermission I first saw the Black Skimmer. This subsequent sighting, nearly a year later, dispelled any notion I might have harbored that the Black Skimmer would only make its first appearance on George's Pond when accompanied by the New York Philharmonic Orchestra.

Chapter 16 • May 15

Bird Hygiene

The temperature was about fifty degrees, the air was heavy with dampness and low thick clouds threatened rain at any moment but the birds ignored the signs of an impending shower and so did I.

At Morton's Pond, Mary Downy began to shadow my movements but she would not come any closer than four or five feet. She wove in and out of the crowd of usual suspects stopping to feed and give me an occasional glance. Around her were ten Common Grackles, two dozen House Sparrows, one male Northern Cardinal, one Tufted Titmouse, one Blue Jay and one Red-bellied Woodpecker. There were also two dozen visiting White-throated Sparrows

These ducklings became separated from their mother, as I have seen them do many times. In this instance, Mother and children were soon safely re-united. They are not always so fortunate.

accompanied by a single Song Sparrow. In my walk through the Ramble I had also spied migrating warblers. I remain undecided because I only caught a fleeting look at it but I think I may have sighted a Worm-eating Warbler. If I had seen a Worm-eating Warbler, which looks something like a waterthrush, it would have been for the first time. Repeat customers included six or more Common Yellowthroats, an Ovenbird and a Louisiana Waterthrush, which you know by now is not a thrush. I did find thrushes. All four of them were Veeries, well except for the American Robins, that you know are not really robins and only some of which are migrants. Got that?

I have I believe sufficiently mentioned that the identification of warblers takes a lot of practice because of their small size, quickness, agility and the fact that physical differences between species, especially among females, can be maddeningly slight. If identifying warblers in the spring is difficult for a novice then identifying them in the fall can be positively intimidating. That is because after many warbler species molt in the fall the new plumage patterns of females and males can be exasperatingly similar. In my view too many have the common attributes of a greenish yellowish breast and an oliveish tanish color over most of the remaining parts. To visualize what I mean study a picture of a fall female Common Yellowthroat in your field guide. Alas, too many fall warblers look too much like this bird. If you think that I am exaggerating how hard it can be to differentiate warblers in autumn consider Roger Tory Peterson's classic field guide. In it you will find a chapter in the table of contents aptly entitled "Confusing Fall Warblers."[1] *Birds of North America: A Guide to Field Identification* goes one step further in highlighting the difficulties in identifying warblers. It has a chapter headed "Confusing Wood-Warblers in Fall" and another one headed "Confusing Wood-Warblers in Spring."[2] David Allen Sibley sums up the situation clearly in his tastefully understated style.

[1]Roger Tory Peterson and Virginia Marie Peterson, *A Field Guide to the Birds of Eastern and Central North America*, p. 278.
[2]Chandler S. Robbins, Bertel Brunn, and Herbert S. Zim, *Birds of North America*, p. 5.

> Identification of wood-warblers can be daunting Aug–Mar [i.e., fall migration] when most species show drab non-breeding plumage.[3]

You are not kidding, Mr. Sibley. Still, I know that with practice and patience the beginning birder will begin to recognize one warbler from another even in the fall. I know I can, sometimes.

The issue of confusing warblers brings to mind again the more common confusion new bird-watchers can face when having to deal with bird names that do not help them identify a species and can be downright misleading. For example, consider the Ovenbird. It does not remotely resemble an oven but it is said that its nest does. I do not know how the beginning bird-watcher might come across an Ovenbird nest and finding it make proper identification of this species. Perhaps a more eloquent and useful name could have been employed instead of such a pedestrian one utilizing a kitchen appliance. I have also been curious to find the rationalization for laying the title "Worm-eating" on another warbler. I did not find convincing evidence to justify its name because field guides like Sibley's and Alsop's say this bird almost always searches for food in low to mid-level vegetation. How many worms could they find up there? This bird, it turns out, seldom forages on the ground where it could find worms so the implication in its name that it specializes in the capture and ingestion of them may lead the inexperienced birder to search for them in the wrong place.

Before I leave this topic and get back to George's Pond I also want to express my opinion about the use of the word "common" in many bird names. Calling a bird a "Common this or that" unnecessarily implies a negative connotation. I do not see anything common about the so-called Common Yellowthroat other than they have been more commonly seen in Central Park during this spring migration than the last few. Common Tern, Common Crane, Common Eider, Common Grackle, Common Blackhawk and Common Loon are more examples of this practice. In this

---

[3]David Allen Sibley, *The Guide to Birds*, p. 442.

group the Common Loon gets my sympathy for the double whammy its name bestows upon it. Let us leave my consternations and return to my observations in the park.

From the cliff above George's Pond I saw a lot that made me want to get down to the dock in a hurry. Over the water there were four Barn Swallows and five Northern Rough-winged Swallows catching flying insects. At the highest point on one of the tallest trees perched an Eastern Kingbird no doubt waiting for a bug to flutter by. On a log jutting out from George's Island into the water stood a Green Heron and nearby stepped a Solitary Sandpiper, searching for edibles in the still flooded portion of George's Island. From the perimeter a noisy contingent of usual suspects comprised of House Sparrows, Common Grackles, European Starlings, American Robins and one Northern Cardinal made their presence known. The Canada Goose family paddled in their typically unerringly straight line past the Solitary Sandpiper. In sharp contrast were the comparatively chaotic movements of the Mallard ducklings and parent. I say parent because the male Mallard normally deserts his wife soon after he mates with her. Mallard families are of the single parent variety and consequently it seems the ducklings are not as closely supervised as goslings. I have watched ducklings on the water following their mother in a perfectly straight line only to see the configuration break down easily, early and often. The Mallards do not have the organized system that the Canada Geese families have. It saddens me to think about it but I have seen Mallard broods of as many as thirteen dwindle to four by the end of the breeding season. Mallards compensate for such typical losses by laying five to fourteen eggs per clutch. In comparison Canada Geese clutches range from four to seven eggs because more offspring will generally survive.

Today I spent quality time with George. He was insatiably hungry. He stood in my hand chowing down at a furious pace spilling nuts and seeds in his unruly enthusiasm. George is often enthusiastic but I have not known him to be a sloppy eater before. He returned for more food three or four times within a few minutes and ate with the same gusto. Then he did something unprecedented.

George concluded his frenzied feeding by gently rubbing his beak against my right index finger to wipe off the crumbs that clung to it. Oh, be still my heart! I was thrilled, delighted and astonished by his action.

"What was so special about him cleaning his beak?" you may well ask. It is that I understood George's action signaled a higher level of trust now existed between us. As a rule George, like birds of many species, rubs his bill against a branch or tree trunk to clean it. Human fingers are not known to be widely used for this purpose. As if that were not remarkable enough after resting for a short while he ate some more and then performed another round of beak cleaning utilizing my finger. I felt a rush of satisfaction followed immediately by a sense of responsibility. Then came a wave of guilt as I realized how strongly I was anthropomorphizing George. I could not help it. I knew I was interpreting his actions as an expression of friendship. Surely there could not be a mutual emotional attachment, at least not on George's part. Friendship is an inappropriate description for it but trust does not do it justice either. One, come to think of it, might interpret George's actions as a result of his ornithological-izing me. That is to say George is practicing reverse anthropomorphism by regarding me as he might another bird.

After George retired for the day, I waited to see what creatures might arrive later in the evening. While the last rays of the sun flooded the pond with that intense golden light that never fails to warm me inside though not necessarily outside, the Canada Goose family swam with controlled determination back toward the dock. When they came close they wheeled in formation toward George's Island. I watched Papa lead them out of the water and along the shore. He climbed up on a large flat rock that serves as the family's nighttime roost. The brown and chartreuse goslings dutifully followed without breaking ranks while Mama stayed behind in the water making sure they all followed Papa. When she too climbed up and lay down in the center of the rock the goslings snuggled under her right wing and disappeared from sight. Their father stood at attention, vigilantly on guard keeping his family in view at all times, and with good reason. On the far side of the island a Black-crowned Night Heron predator landed. Soon the resident raccoons would also be on the prowl. Unprotected goslings make a tempting target. I was glad these babes were well hidden.

A second and then a third Black-crowned Night Heron landed in the shallow water. I noticed they were spaced several feet away from one another no doubt to avoid conflicts over hunting rights. They all vanished into the vegetation. When it was darker I heard two "barks" coming from the center of the pond. I assumed the calls came from the herons. My binoculars scanned the approximate spot. I was able to make out two low flying silhouettes I assumed were Black-crowned Night Herons. One silhouette flew to the east end and the other to the west end of the pond. The one that went west landed in the water close to the shore where I would expect to see a Black-crowned Night Heron but the bird heading east continued flying close to the water's surface and it kept on going. When the bird flew through a shaft of lamplight I got a brief but clear view of it. Its long red beak, white underside and black wing with a white edge were unmistakable features of a Black Skimmer. When it passed out of the light I was only able to see the telltale trail its lower beak sliced through the water. This Black Skimmer and one of the Black-crowned Night Herons were the birds I heard earlier. It was these two that had the dispute over the center of the pond. The barks, I expect, came from the heron since the only call I have heard from a Black Skimmer was higher pitched like the sound you get when you squeeze a toddler's squeaky toy.

The interaction between heron and skimmer was terrific but nothing compared to George's act of beak hygiene.

Chapter 17 · May 16

A Beak Full of Chips

To enhance your bird-watching experience it is helpful to spend at least some portion of your sessions with more experienced bird-watchers. Just make sure you pick one who has patience and will be glad to answer your questions. Reference books are absolutely essential, but the birds in the wild rarely look exactly the way they are illustrated in them. Few field guides pull all the information together that you may need in the field. If they did they would be too large to carry on your walk. Often a brief physical description and a picture are not enough to identify a species especially when they share some characteristics with other breeds. You may need information about behavior (e.g., feeds its mate), habitat

This Red-bellied Woodpecker is hard at work transforming a dead tree into a living room. And you thought your home needs a facelift.

(e.g., feeds on shoreline), physical movements (e.g., pumps its tail), or vocalizations (e.g., its song is louder than a similar song from a similar but different species) to identify a species. A seasoned birder, with any luck, will have internalized and distilled information from many sources and then filtered it through his or her own personal insights. When you go into the field with such an expert he or she may impart this hard won information to you freely. Remember that a learned bird-watcher does not a helpful birder make. A helpful birder does not hoard knowledge and will not make you feel like a dope when you ask questions. If your expert is not as helpful as he or she is informed then my novice bird-watching aficionados, you are perching on the wrong branch. Find someone who is more simpatico, amigos. Otherwise you may end up more fraught than taught.

It can be helpful to join a group of bird-watchers too. Groups pool information and resources. They provide additional eyes and ears that will help you find many more birds than you are likely to on your own. The group might be a club, an association, or an informal gathering of friends or acquaintances. If you cannot find a birding group check with your local chapter of the Audubon Society or go on-line to find one. Personally, I most often go it alone because I am a lingerer. I stop to gather material for my journal or take photographs after everyone else has moved on just as my story will right now.

On the northwestern segment of today's walk I was on a narrow winding hillside path overlooking the Lake when I heard a series of muffled taps. I wished I had the assistance of an experienced bird-watcher to identify it for me but I imagined a woodpecker of some sort was responsible. I followed the sound to its source that seemed to be behind a leafy shrub. I carefully parted a few branches to find they concealed a dead tree stump riddled with more than a half dozen tennis ball sized holes. At the top of the stump the edges of one hole were light colored indicating it had recently been excavated. A head popped out of the hole pointing a substantial beak at me. The beak was attached to a male Red-bellied Woodpecker. As quickly as it came out it slipped back inside. I waited quietly though impatiently for the beak to return and in a minute it did. This time it was filled with bits of wood. The beak opened and the wood chips fell on my head. Watching some hit the ground I noticed that the ground was littered with them. What was this all about? I had discovered a Red-bellied Woodpecker in the act of excavating a cavity, very likely for a nest. Wow.

They can create one in about two weeks. This Red-bellied Woodpecker must have been working here for some time for him to be so deep inside the stump and for so many chips to have accumulated on the ground. The male starts the cavity but usually both the male and female work together if it is to be used as a nest.[1] It appeared that he was working alone at least for now so I could not tell if this was going to be a nursery or only a roost. I have never witnessed this process before and made a mental note to come back to check on the woodpecker's progress.

Finding this industrious woodpecker inspired me to search for the uncommonly seen Red-headed Woodpecker that Sam, a Club George charter member, said was in the Locust Tree Grove. On my way there I met a fellow on Bank Rock Bridge with a video camera set on a tripod pointing at another dead tree. I went to see what he was taping. Two or three feet from the bridge railing, at eye level, a robin sat on its nest. The bird impassively stared straight at us. It was snuggled down so tightly inside that there seemed to be no room to spare, not even for eggs. This nest was out in an open unprotected place with a relatively high volume of pedestrian traffic where it was also not uncommon to see a few potential sources of mayhem, like Black-crowned Night Herons, raccoons and Gray Squirrels. At first I thought the bird's choice of a nesting site ill-advised mainly because so many people came by but as I watched the stream of passersby I saw that hardly any of them noticed it. This American Robin had successfully hidden itself in plain sight like the evidence was hidden in Edgar Allan Poe's "The Purloined Letter."

I pressed on to resume my search for the uncommonly seen

[1]David Allen Sibley, *The Sibley Guide to Bird Life & Behavior,* pp. 374, 380–81.

Red-headed Woodpecker. When I got to the Locust Grove I was encouraged to hear what I knew to be the call of some kind of woodpecker. I just was not sure what kind. It sounded like a Red-bellied Woodpecker and, somewhat disappointingly, that is what it turned out to be. There would not be a "redhead" for me this day.

Walking toward George's Pond I heard his "konk-la-ree" song getting louder and louder. I found George chasing the two rival male Red-winged Blackbirds. Though he had more pressing priorities, George made frequent pit stops at the dock where he demanded to be fed, gobbled a snack then rushed off after those males. Ned joined me on the dock and reminded me why George was chasing the males. Looking down from the cliff Ned had found two active and possibly one deserted Red-winged Blackbird nest. So far I had been unable to find them myself even though I knew where and what to look for. Sigh.

While I have spoken repeatedly of George's role as protector and progenitor I have said little about the female's role. A single female will have constructed one of the nests Ned described. Each was made by weaving thin vegetation around stalks of reeds or other plants to form a frame. Then a platform of wet grasses and leaves was added. The outside of this structure was reinforced with more wet leaves and possibly decayed wood. An inner cup made of mud was lined with fine grass or weeds. If available, and they are here, sedges and cattail leaves are the preferred building materials. The female will usually lay four eggs, but the number can range from three to five. The female will incubate them for eleven to twelve days. When they hatch the chicks will be helpless or, as it called, altricial. They will be born naked and not covered with down to insulate them as other species are. The females will brood the chicks, keeping them warm, fed and hidden from predators for another ten to fourteen days. Usually Red-winged Blackbirds have one brood, a second is possible, but says Ken Yasukawa, very unlikely though they will replace failed clutches if they have the time and resources. The reference books say that in certain geographic regions the female feeds the chicks more often than the males.[2]

---

[2]Fred J. Alsop III, *Birds of North America,* p. 690

Northeastern males have been observed feeding offspring. I am interested to see what kind of father George will be.

Hey, wait just a minute. How many active nests did Ned say he saw? He said two or possibly three? Does that mean George has two or three different mates? Each active nest represents the work of an individual female. An inactive nest, one not visited by an adult bird, has most likely been abandoned. One of Ned's sightings fits the description of an inactive nest. Whether it produced offspring or not I cannot say with absolute certainty, thought I doubt it did because I saw no evidence of nestlings or fledglings being fed by parents. I can say with confidence that the third nest was also created by one of George's two mates.

Chapter 18 • May 18

A Poetic Place to Nest

Today's highlight was the discovery of another American Robin's nest in a most curious if not provocative location. It seems to this observer that the park's American Robins are reproducing at a remarkable rate. Not only are there a lot of nests but also the placement of some, like the one beside Bank Rock Bridge, sometimes borders on the astonishing. Well, in all of my experience to date, there is one nest whose placement crosses that border and plunges into the astonishing without a pit stop.

I had just come from the northwestern end of the Lake and was going to George's Pond with Michael when Stan, an experienced birder and insect expert whom I have been known to refer to as the

Could there be a better symbol of love, regeneration and hope than this one: partly man-made and partly bird-made? I do not think so.

"bug guy," greeted us. He had an enormous smile on his face. Stan urged us to proceed without haste to the statues of Shakespeare's characters, Romeo and Juliet, outside the Delacorte Theater. A pair of American Robins, he said, was tending a nest built in between Juliet's breasts. Intrigued by Stan's description, Michael and I picked up our pace and hurried along. We found adult male and female American Robins standing on the rim of a nest advantageously placed between Shakespeare's famous lovers.

Chapter 19 · May 20

A Bird's Nest Can Be a Hassle

I have not seen many migrant birds in the last few days but today I spotted four Common Yellowthroats, two American Redstarts, several Common Grackles and one Magnolia Warbler. Many of the usual suspects were highly visible especially at Morton's Pond where I found two Blue Jays, numerous House Sparrows, a few House Pigeons, many European Starlings and four Northern Cardinals. I recognized the call of the Red-bellied Woodpeckers, having had the benefit of a fair amount of practice listening to this species recently, but I did not see them. Morton and Mary Downy were there too and I was particularly happy to see not two but three Tufted Titmice. On close inspection I found one titmouse to be

George literally crashed into the Black-crowned Night Heron's side three times until he achieved the desired effect.

slightly but significantly different in appearance. It took me a while to figure out why one of them had a gray forehead and not a black one like the other two but eventually it dawned on me. The gray forehead indicated it was a fledgling. I had just made my first acquaintance with a Tufted Titmouse family albeit the realization arrived belatedly.

With such a goodly amount of birds in view, and my introduction to the Tufted Titmouse tot, I lost track of time at Morton's Pond. I wanted to be sure to have plenty of time to be with George but when I glanced at my watch I found I had far less than I had planned. I skipped some routine stops and hurriedly walked the long straight stretch north along the Lake. The sight of fresh sawdust on the ground at the base of a locust tree beside my path was the only thing that was strong enough to arrest my forward motion. It could not be ignored. I knew the wood chips had been dropped by a woodpecker. I examined the tree and found a freshly carved cavity. I wondered if the excavator was inside but I did not wonder for long. A Northern Flicker emerged from the hole. I knew this was a male by the presence of a black "moustache" under its beak. Beginning bird-watchers, if you do not know what a Northern Flicker looks like you should put down this book and dive into your field guide to get a look. Northern Flickers are arguably one of North America's most beautiful birds. They are a light brown all over with black barring on the back and tail. The buff breast has large black spots and there is a black crescent on the throat and a bright red patch on a field of gray on the back of the head. Except for the moustache males and females look alike. The eastern birds, like this one, are called "yellow shafted" because the feathers under their wings are brilliant yellow. This is one of the region's most colorful and intricately patterned birds. Sorry, but this specimen was in deep shadow so I cannot show you a decent photo of it but I will keep trying to get one.

After the thrill of finding the Northern Flicker dulled a tad I resumed a quickened pace but paused at Bank Rock Bridge to see the nests there. The American Robin's nest alongside the bridge was devoid of adults. Mom and Dad must have been away collecting food.

Nearby I needed binoculars to find it but I got a look at the back and head of an adult Green Heron sitting on a nest. That was unremarkable. What was news was that this was a nest I had not seen before. A second pair of adult Green Herons has returned to breed here just as they did last year.

Farther to the northeast between Romeo and Juliet's breasts on the sculpture outside the Delacorte Theater both American Robin parents were actively transporting food to the chicks tucked inside.

At George's Pond two female Red-winged Blackbirds scoured the shoreline for food in tandem. They were acting in a way I had never noticed before. These two carefully worked their way along the bases of the phragmites and sedges closest to the water one reed at a time. It was clear to me that there was something specific they were after, but at the time I did not have a clue what it was. When they found whatever it was they flew to the far side of George's Island and disappeared behind the vegetation. I thought I heard at least one of them call out something that sounded like, "tee-tee-tee-tee-tee" as I lost track of them. What was that all about? The females have been keeping a low profile up till now but today they gave me a show and a lot to think about. I interpreted the females' high visibility, frequent trips to specific patches of thick vegetation and the unfamiliar call as signs to support Ned's story about finding nests. I guessed the ladies were gathering insects to feed nestlings hidden on the south side of the island.

When I did my reading later on I uncovered facts that supported my theory. Both females had been collecting insects as they emerged from their larval stage and crawled out of the water along the plant stems where they would dry their wings and bodies before dispersing. The period of their emergence is brief but not so uncoincidentally coincides with the Red-winged Blackbird breeding phase. Huge numbers of creatures come out of the water at different points in the season. For example, Beletsky recounts research

done in Washington State that found that insects emerged from
April through June but that gnats, midges and mosquitoes peaked
in May and dragonflies and damselflies peaked in June. Some
species tended to come out early in the day and others at midday.
This staggered schedule meant there was a steady supply of food
for the local Red-winged Blackbirds over a period of several hours
every day for months.[1] The Red-winged Blackbird females at
George's Pond obviously knew just where, when and how to am-
bush them. What about the call I heard? *The Birds of North America*[2]
describes the call the female makes coming and going from the
nest as a "chit" call. A "ti" call, which I think is what I described as a
"tee" call, is either an alarm or a vocalization made prior to mating.
The context in which I heard the "ti" seemed to be associated with
nesting. Perhaps the female was signaling George about a threat to
the nest that I could not see or maybe these females speak with a
New York accent.

There came a point later that afternoon when a Black-crowned
Night Heron came out of hiding and moved toward the south side
of the island. The bird's presence in that specific spot provoked
George. He charged the heron repeatedly screaming high-pitched
"cheer" calls as the books describe them, or "seer" calls as I hear
them, that got my attention more than they got the heron's. When
that had no tangible effect George intensified his assault. He literally crashed into the Black-crowned Night Heron's side twice, but
after the third hit the Black-crowned Night Heron lifted off to seek
relief in another section of the neighborhood. I recalled that
George was oblivious to the Black-crowned Night Herons earlier in
the season. The fact that George had stopped tolerating them
added to the growing body of evidence that there were or about to
be Red-winged Blackbird nestlings hidden in the vegetation on the
south side of the island.

---

[1]Les Beletsky, *The Red-winged Blackbird, The Biology of a Strongly Polygynous Songbird*, p. 56.
[2]Ken Yasukawa and William A. Searcy, *The Red-winged Blackbird*, Birds of North America, *No. 184,
1995*, pp. 6–7.

Chapter 20 · May 21

A Heaping Helping of Ducklings

It had rained earlier in the day and a continually threatening sky kept many people away from the park, especially from Morton's Pond. I confess I was pleased there were hardly any other people around because the birds are sometimes more active when they do not have an audience of more than one or two. There were some migrants in the Ramble like the Wood Thrush, Northern Waterthrush, American Redstart, and Canada Warbler and the usual suspects surrounding the pond included three Blue Jays, two male Northern Cardinals, only one of the Tufted Titmouse clan, Charlie the Red-winged Blackbird, Mary and Morton Downy.

I acted on a notion I have considered to try and get a look at the

Always be extra careful when you walk in the woods. You never know where you might step.

Green Heron nest from a new angle. I climbed down a short steep slope at the side of the path and headed to the Lake shoreline. I walked as quietly and deliberately as I could, not wanting to disturb the nesting herons. Passing behind a wide tree trunk I was stopped dead in my tracks by the scene before me. It was a very good thing I had advanced with great care because virtually lying at my feet were ten Mallard ducklings huddled together in a pile of leaves. Mother Mallard was standing over them but her eyes were glued on me. I expected to hear her yell "quack" a few dozen times and see the kids scurry for cover but the ducks surprised me. Mother Mallard remained calm, almost serene, and the ducklings did not so much as wiggle. Though it was accidental I had intruded and I wanted to extricate myself quickly but without provoking a reaction. As a small parting gesture I slowly reached down to the ground to leave a hefty handful of nuts and seeds for the ducks. Then I made my exit. If Mother Mallard had demonstrated a mild apprehension about my intrusion she demonstrated a tremendous enthusiasm for the food. She dived on it. One by one the snoozing ducklings lifted their head to see what Mother Mallard was excited about but the food did not sustain their interest. Several tiny heads slumped back down as the ducklings snuggled even more tightly together in that heap of feathers and down.

I backtracked to my more customary spot to watch the Green Heron nestlings from the paved path. I found an adult Green Heron on a branch about a foot over the water. As if the director had said, "Lights, camera, action," this heron flew up, onto and then into a nest. After a spell of waggling, the bird settled down, presumably to warm a clutch of eggs. Upon leaving I was struck by the juxtaposition of the newborn ducklings below and the soon to be born herons above.

Then it was off to George's Pond where George was pursuing rivals and mates. The two females were busier than ever collecting insects in the tall grasses at the edge of the shoreline. By now the weather had deteriorated and it was drizzling on and off. It did not affect the Red-winged Blackbirds as it did me. I stuffed my camera and binoculars inside my zippered jacket to keep them dry and opened my small folding umbrella. The rain prompted a quick exit of the few park-goers that were there but I was not George's only visitor. Two women I had not met previously approached me. They asked if I could tell them anything about "the Red-winged Blackbird" that they heard lived at the pond. Would you believe that at that moment George came in for a landing on the fence? Well, maybe you cannot but that is what he did. He ran along the top of the bird blind toward me, stopped, hopped into my hand and started to eat. "Yes," I said without missing a beat and acting as nonchalant as I could, "I know about the Red-winged Blackbird." The two women were stunned but they recovered quickly and all three of us had a good laugh about George's fortuitous timing.

As the drizzle increased the activity around the pond decreased but there was still plenty to see. The Canada Goose family took advantage of the solitude and commandeered an adjacent meadow where there were no picnickers to inhibit them. The goslings were nibbling grass and giving Mama and Papa a workout when they would individually stray from the group. This was a new behavior they practiced with increasing frequency. No doubt these small displays of independence hinted at a significant stage in the goslings' development. Meanwhile on the flat rock on the shore of George's Island a Green Heron was reconnoitering. A Great Egret and four Black-crowned Night Herons were all hunting up a meal in total disregard of the drizzling sky.

I had hoped to photograph George and his two mates but the rain put a damper on that. I did manage to catch one female peeking out at me through the reeds. I shot some film of George chasing his intruders but those pictures would likely be a blurry mess. The birds were too fast for my camera's abilities. When it began to rain harder I started for home but stopped at the east end of the pond to take my customary last look. When I walked along the rock toward the water a Black Skimmer swooped past and an instant later a Common Nighthawk flew overhead.

A gray rainy day had turned out to be a winner.

Chapter 21 · May 22

Kissing Cardinals

I saw a male and female Northern Cardinal in love today. At least that is how they looked to me. The two birds were on the ground facing each other. They moved closer until they touched beaks. It appeared as if they were kissing but it also seemed as if the male had placed something in her beak at the same time. In a little while the male again approached the female that had been waiting for him in exactly the same spot. After watching this process for the second time I understood what was happening. The male was feeding the female. She had accepted his second gift but rather than stay for a third she flew off with the male following close behind her. I am accustomed to seeing the more aggressive male cardinals

It may seem like peanuts to you, but this female Northern Cardinal eagerly accepted the gift her mate had given her.

shove the female out of the way when there is food to be had so this display of a kinder gentler behavior startled me. I assumed it must be part of the Northern Cardinal's courtship ritual. In my reference books at home, I had no trouble finding an explanation. It is standard operating procedure for Northern Cardinals not only through courtship, but also the entire period the female will spend incubating her eggs.[1] If it is so common why had I not noticed it before? I can only thank my Club George charter membership for giving me the awareness to see what had probably been staring me in the face on many other occasions. I just had not paid close enough attention.

The "kissing cardinals" were the first personal "first of the day." A second "first" occurred when I hand-fed a Blue Jay. There were three Blue Jays at Morton's Pond where I was distributing seeds to House Sparrows, Northern Cardinals, Common Grackles and European Starlings. I paused to rest my open palm on the top of the wire mesh fence. My peripheral vision alerted me to movement on my right flank. A Blue Jay had landed on the fence and was carefully making its way toward me one cautious step at a time. When the bird was about two inches away it leaned over, grabbed a peanut and took it to a branch above me where it summarily gulped it down without benefit of crushing or chomping. In a few moments one of the three Blue Jays, and I cannot be sure which of the three it was, unexpectedly rocketed toward me again from the right side, at high speed. Once more I picked up its approach through my peripheral vision. The jay snatched a peanut in its beak and pushed off my palm using both feet to make its ricochet retreat. The Blue Jay had not landed on my hand as much as strafed it scattering the remaining food on the ground.

Remember my story about the Common Grackle that landed in my hand? When the grackle stood on my palm I gained a new appreciation of its prodigious beak and claws. I similarly reassessed the physical attributes of this marauding Blue Jay. It appeared to be considerably more formidable than it looked when at a farther dis-

[1]Fred J. Alsop III, *Birds of North America: Eastern Region*, p. 678.

tance. A mature Blue Jay is about eleven inches long with a wingspan of sixteen inches. It weighs, however, a mere three ounces. For comparison consider that it is larger than an American Robin but smaller than a Rock Pigeon. Close-up-and-personal its physical features were not as menacing as the Common Grackle's, but the Blue Jay does have a long powerful beak and pointy claws. You would not, for example, want to hold any of your fingers in its mouth to see what might happen should the beak shut forcefully. While I would be acting irresponsibly to suggest that Blue Jays are a threat to birders I will point out that though the majority of its diet is plant material, insects, frogs, fish, small mammals and the occasional petite reptile are on its menu. It also will take the eggs and young of other birds. This is not a shy, gentle songbird like those kissing cardinals is it?

One Tufted Titmouse and Charlie the Red-winged Blackbird, perhaps inspired by the Blue Jays, also came to be hand-fed. Charlie was especially vocal about his intentions. He called loudly to give me warning that he was about to visit. Morton and Mary Downy, the woodpecker couple, were on the periphery all the while, but they did not come close. The Red-bellied Woodpecker male made a brief appearance without his mate. I thought he might want to play catch-the-peanut but he had other plans.

The local Gray Squirrels stepped up their aggressive behavior as they usually do when they see me feeding the birds. After the third time I had the misfortune to involuntarily find a squirrel clinging to my thigh I had resolved to keep my food supply hidden from sight. That may mean shoving it in my pants pocket or under my shirt when no other suitable storage space is available. I no longer feed Gray Squirrels, though I used to, because it excites and emboldens them to behave, well, like Gray Squirrels. At Morton's Pond they are so frisky and unpredictable that I instinctively check the area around my legs and feet periodically to see if any are closing in on me as they often do. I especially keep an eye on a particular Gray Squirrel with numerous scars and what I think is a bad case of mange. It is no wonder he has those prominent scars because this is one wild rodent. I have discouraged the squirrel's advances many times with a "Scat!" and stamp of my foot but these tactics have had only short-term results. This New York critter is not discouraged easily.

I visited the Northern Flicker nest on the lakeshore in my ongoing effort to get a good photo of this bird. I patiently waited to see if the Northern Flicker would show. I did not have to wait long. He popped his head out of his hole and I took my shot but the light just was not good enough and I did not want to frighten him at such close range with the flash.

I have made comments about the prominent reproductive activities of the American Robins. I have more evidence to offer. In addition to the American Robin nests at Bank Rock Bridge and between Juliet's breasts at the Delacorte Theater, I have found two more nests that are nearly as easy to spot and each is at eye level. One is in a shrub at the lakeshore not far from the Northern Flicker cavity. I had not noticed it as I stood surveying the water but when I turned to leave I found myself eye-to-eye with an an American Robin in a nest three feet away. I found the other nest about fifty feet farther along the same path. This one was at the top of a tree trunk where it had been broken in two. The robins had placed the nest inside the torn jagged edges of the two halves of the severed tree. Neither of these nests was the least bit camouflaged. After finding four nests placed so blatantly out in the open I begin to wonder if American Robins have little or no fear of predators though I am at a loss to know why or how such a strategy can be advantageous. Regardless of my questions about the logic of American Robin nest placement the bottom line is that they reproduce successfully year after year and continue to be present in significant numbers in Central Park and elsewhere. They are obviously doing something right even if they are not particularly subtle going about it.

On George's Pond babies are either on display, hidden or at some point along the line in the manufacturing process. This spot is becoming a veritable bird nursery. The formerly tiny Canada Geese goslings continue growing at an amazing rate. Mallard ducklings, also early on the scene, are more in evidence than before. There are now two Mallard families on the pond.

I hoped to find at least one Red-winged Blackbird nest but I failed again. George was in his hypervigilant mode chasing intruders on sight. He spent little time on the dock and when he did his visits were short. George's two mates were also busy bees. They continued making frequent trips to the reeds on the perimeter of the pond to gather food. Sometimes they came up on the dock to perch momentarily or to walk across the wooden deck looking for crumbs and seeds people had dropped but they did not linger.

In tracking George with my binoculars on one of his forays I found some surreptitious birds that had gone unnoticed. Hiding in the tall reeds were a Green Heron and two Black-crowned Night Herons. Impossible to miss with or without binoculars was a Great Egret. I also noticed what I did not notice. That is to say I did not see the Barn Swallows and Northern Rough-winged Swallows that have been prominent at the pond this spring.

A vocal group that I have been regularly visiting on my way home in the evenings is gone. In a thick bed of shrubs fifty or more White-throated Sparrows have been perching and serenading one another and me with their "Poor-Sam-Peabody-Peabody-Peabody" song for weeks. There are those who claim the White-throated Sparrows are really singing, "Pure-Sweet-Canada-Canada-Canada" but I do not wish to take sides on this issue and risk becoming embroiled in a potential international dispute.[2] Besides I am sure some of my material has raised an eyebrow or two already.

Still I really would like to know where the White-throated Sparrows went no matter what song they are singing.

[2]Fred J. Alsop III, *Birds of North America: Eastern Region*, p. 667.

Chapter 22 · May 25

Narrow Escapes

This is Memorial Day weekend. The temperature is an uncooperative 59 degrees and it drizzles lightly now and then. Normally on a holiday weekend there are measurably larger crowds in the park but this weather will likely discourage them.

What I thought to be unusual is, as I now know, quite usual among Northern Cardinals in breeding season. At Morton's Pond I again watched a male feed his mate. This time he gingerly placed an inanimate pale green object, formerly a grasshopper, into her beak.

I crept up surreptitiously as I could to check the status of the American Robin nest along the east shore of the Lake. Congratulating myself on having arrived at a respectable distance undetected I peered into the nest only to find two impassive eyes staring

Not all the attention George received today was in his best interests.

back into mine. The female must have seen me coming but did not react. The Northern Flicker in the nearby locust tree was way ahead of me too. In fact without binoculars I could see his head was poking out of his cavity inspecting me before I could inspect him. The robin nest across the path looked deserted. I suspect the nestlings have already fledged and are getting their first life lessons on the wing.

I had no luck finding the American Robins at their nest beside Bank Rock Bridge or the Green Herons in either of the two nests. I even tried climbing off the path onto a narrow dirt trail on the opposite shore hoping that would yield results. Rather than finding a better vantage point it took me five full minutes to relocate the nests. When I found them there still were no Green Herons to be seen. I felt discouraged but coming back onto the path I experienced some totally unexpected excitement. There I was confronted by a Red-winged Blackbird with whom I was not acquainted. This keyed up male loudly called "chek" repeatedly. He hopped from branch to branch, came down to the ground, went back up into the tree, then down and then up again. I was baffled by his behavior. He was acting aggressively but not as if he were defending his territory or nest. If that had been his intention he would have dived at the back of my head in typical Red-winged Blackbird fashion. His motivation must have been different, I reasoned, because he did not physically threaten me and remained a short but safe distance away. Having rejected the idea that this could be an attack I wondered if he might be asking for food. It was easy to test that hypothesis. I dropped a peanut on the ground near his feet. He stopped calling and picked up the food. He ate it a few feet farther away. A minute later he repeated the action but when he finished eating he flew off to chase another male Red-winged Blackbird that had snuck into his territory while he was busy shaking me down for a meal. He did not return for a third course. "How about these Red-winged Blackbirds?" I said to myself out loud. "Is it something in the Central Park air or water that makes them this way?" I was kidding (mostly) of course but I still would like to have a solid explanation for this behavior. This is the fourth male I have encountered this season that has asked to be fed and I have heard through the grapevine there is another male at Bow Bridge, known as Larry, that does the same thing.

There were three Club George members standing in a row on the dock hoping to get their favorite bird's attention when I arrived there. Two of them were strangers to me. The third was Gordon the Club George charter member. The Ramble had been fairly empty, I thought due to the weather, but there was no shortage of people here on the dock. Except for the three Club George charter members most of the crowd were only casually aware of George's presence except for a girl I judged to be ten years old. George unmistakably entranced her but her intentions proved to be sinister. When George left his favorite perch to make a landing on a lower ledge that is only four feet high the young girl lurched toward him. She attempted to grab him with both hands. Impulsively, I screamed, "Don't do that!" as I felt an adrenaline-rush race through my body. In that instant I imagine I felt like a parent whose child was in mortal danger. Luckily the child's mother leapt to her feet to pull her daughter away. George escaped her clutches, but the experience had frightened him. He fled to his island where he sat on his favorite island perch near the top of a birch tree. He spent nearly twenty minutes fluffing and preening his feathers over and over again. I believe he was doing this to calm down after his narrow escape. This served as a wake-up call for me as I hoped it did for George. I was graphically reminded that it could be dangerous for birds or any wild animals to interact with people. Besides the possibility of an accident there are individuals, whose reasons I cannot fathom, who will act in irresponsible, ignorant or violent ways that can be injurious or even deadly. I interact with birds in what I believe is a responsible, careful, respectful manner as I hope I have amply demonstrated. It is possible however that my interaction with the birds encourages others to emulate and interpret my behavior in ways I do not approve and cannot abide. For the future I will try to be less conspicuous about feeding birds when there are strangers watching. How that might affect my relationship with George is to be seen. Lately he not only comes to me on the dock but also sometimes seeks me out if I walk along the northern shore of the pond far from our usual meeting place. If I think for a moment that I might avoid him I am deluding myself. Could I really resist him? I think not.

I knew when George recovered his equilibrium: he stopped his compulsive preening. When he returned to the dock he spent much of his time with Gordon. George stood for nearly a full minute in Gordon's palm eating enthusiastically. That was an un-usually long time. I would have thought after his harrowing experi-ence George would have stayed clear of humans at least for the rest of the day, but he did the reverse. He lingered with the assembled Club George charter members and interacted with renewed gusto.

On the water there were two mother Mallards with their duck-lings and the Canada Geese couple with their goslings. They were all about to play a role in a drama that would remind me that peo-ple are not the only source of danger but that violence can erupt from the most idyllic scene at any time. When one duckling strayed from its mother to commingle with the goslings this observer thought it an innocent occurrence. "How adorable," I thought to myself. "Look at that cute duckling mixing in with the goslings." The male Canada Goose did not share my sentiments. Papa Goose rushed up to the duckling and grabbed it in his bill. Then he shoved the duckling beneath the water where he held it for what seemed a disastrously long time. The other goslings and ducklings scattered in panic. Water splashed in all directions. Ducklings and goslings screamed. Mother Mallard rushed to her baby's defense, but the male Canada Goose repulsed her with a honk, a hiss and a lunge. I assumed the victimized duckling was lost. Then, when the violence subsided, I saw a lone duckling paddling furiously toward its mother and siblings. The dunked duckling had survived, slipped out of the danger zone undetected and had reunited with its family. If you came to the pond at that moment you would have seen the Mallard and Canada Goose families peacefully foraging a few yards apart and you would not have a clue that a life-threatening situation had just come and gone. Why did the male Canada Goose attack the duckling? I do not believe the goose was looking for a duckling dinner. Instead I think Papa Goose saw the duckling as a potential threat to his goslings, as illogical as that might seem.

I gradually began to regain my composure after these acts of violence but no sooner had things calmed down than a new violent outbreak erupted on the perimeter of the pond. Two Great Egrets had a noisy disagreement about who was going to fish where. One Great Egret let loose a string of throaty honks and chased the other up into and through the air. The pursued bird sized up the state of affairs and decided to try its luck at another location. These brief but intense bursts of violence including George's near miss with a ten-year-old human communicated a clear but complex message. Even here on this postcard perfect peaceful pond in spring reality is more complicated and morally ambiguous than it seems on the surface.

Though the pond quickly regained its facade of tranquility I found it took me more time to regain mine. I had detected a new sources for potential violence lurking in the form of the Green Heron and the Black-crowned Night Heron that were strategically spaced in the reeds. Though at the moment appearing stoic and static they served as a reminder that violence is but a beak's length away. A calming effect again started to take hold during my observation of a migrant Brown Thrasher on the shore but then I recalled it was using its long curved beak to slaughter insects and small amphibians hiding under the leaves. There seemed to be no relief in any direction even if I looked up. In between bouts of drizzle, four Barn Swallows were gracefully and artfully dispatching flying bugs in midair. There were mayhem and carnage everywhere.

Was I getting carried away with this? Of course I was.

As the sun went down I began to mellow out once more if only because there were fewer potential sources of violence to see in the fading light. I saw not one, not two but three Common Nighthawks, which thrilled me, as they are not often seen here, but they too were slaughtering insects in the sky. Regardless of their activity watching them was a treat. Its flight can be erratic, almost mothlike, which is appropriate for a creature that eats moths don't you think? Common Nighthawks average about 2.2 ounces in weight, are about eight to ten inches long, and have boomerang shaped wings that span twenty-one to twenty-four inches with a distinctive white bar on each. The male has another white bar across its tail distinguishing it from the females. The Common Nighthawk presents to me another irksome example of a poorly named bird. Why? The Nighthawk is not a hawk at all. It is in the Nightjar family along with the widely known Whip-poor-will. What's a Nightjar? These include the Chuck-will's-widow and Whip-poor-will, for two examples. Named for their respective songs, they catch insects, often at night. Don Kroodsma poetically suggests the name Nightjar derives from their distinctive calls that "jar the night, endlessly, relentlessly, with a never-ending song performance."[1] After re-considering the violent acts I witnessed today I consoled myself with the idea that I also witnessed a number of exhilarating narrow escapes. I decided to focus on the half-full glass and not on the half-empty one.

[1] Don Kroodsma, *The Singing Life of Birds*, p. 288.

Chapter 23 · May 26

Love with a Many Splendored Wing

The skies have often been overcast for nearly two weeks. The bird-watcher in me has had to cope with frequent rain or drizzle and poor lighting conditions. The photographer in me has been even more frustrated with the situation. A hat and a folding umbrella have become fashion accessories that have salvaged many birding sessions but they cannot salvage photo opportunities lost to deep shadows or always provide enough precipitation protection for my camera gear. Today's Weather Channel forecast was again

Most nights the Canada Geese family climbs up on this flat rock on the shore of George's Island. After a prodigious amount of preening they will roost here for the night. Papa will stand guard. Mama will lie down and the goslings will snuggle up under her wing. To satisfy your curiosity I will explain that the material on the rock is a biological by-product I prefer not to discuss in any detail. Suffice it to say, I often refer to this spot as Poop Rock.

disheartening. It ranged from the uncertain to the miserable. The Doppler radar picture graphically confirmed the disappointing verbal prediction. On the map I saw heavy rain heading this way. In spite of this forewarning I chose to risk a walk albeit a short one. George's Pond would be my sole destination.

Early on even this modest plan seemed to be overly optimistic. The rain arrived while I was en route and for a time drove me to seek shelter under the Willow Oak Tree near the dock. When the wind blew the rain horizontally I hugged the tree trunk flattening myself against it in a desperate attempt to stay dry. It looked like the rain was going to defeat me and I would have to slosh home feeling cheated of my favorite pastime but the sky cleared quite suddenly. The birds that had no doubt done some tree hugging in their own way resumed their activities. The Common Grackles, House Sparrows, American Robins and European Starlings came noisily back to work. Six Northern Rough-winged Swallows, the tenants I had missed on my last visit four days ago, were soon flying low over the pond. Four Barn Swallows, also recently missing, joined them in a vigorous aerial bug hunt. The insects too had obviously also gone back to work. George came out of his island birch tree roost but he did not go back to work. He had something else on his bird mind. George began to pursue a female in his now familiar theatrically amorous style. The female acted in her characteristic manner too. She was playing hard to get, but not too hard.

The chase moved onto the rocks at the base of the cliff where I saw George showing off his epaulets for his girlfriend. She must have changed her mind about him because she had stopped running and turned to face him. Standing with his wings raised and his head lowered parallel to the ground George's scarlet epaulets were visible without binoculars one hundred feet away. He walked toward her, she turned away and then he mounted her. I remained watching without benefit of my binoculars but standing beside me Ned was looking through his state-of-the-art model, one greatly admired by those Central Park birders in the know. He saw what followed in all its romantic glory but alas I did not. This was my second opportunity to see Red-winged Blackbirds mate and why I did not recognize that it was about to happen and how come I did not get my binoculars in place quickly enough are a mystery even unto myself. Since I cannot give you a more complete eyewitness account, I will quote from *The Birds of North America* instead. I added a few explanatory notes in brackets to make some portions, shall we say, more explicit. You may suppose some words are missing from the quote but they are not. The text in *The Birds of North America* series often omits articles (e.g., the), conjunctions (e.g., and), and pronouns (e.g., it) presumably to save the reader time but these omissions have the opposite effect on me. I find this series indispensable but the style sometimes impedes my comprehension of the material as I reflexively try to supply the missing words. Oh one more thing. This quote may not be appropriate for minors. I defer to the reader's discretion and delicacy of sensibilities.

Copulation is difficult to observe in most habitats. It is most frequent just before and during egg-laying period (Gray 1994). Male pre-coition display is full-intensity Crouch with *ti-ti-ti* vocalization and rapid fluttering of wings. Epaulet feathers are erected and vibrated for maximum conspicuousness. In full expression, male walks or hops toward female while displaying (Nero 1956a, Orians and Christman 1968). Female pre-coition display is typical of passerines [i.e., perching songbirds]. Legs are flexed, body is horizontal or tipped forward, tail is closed and elevated, bill is raised, soft *ti-ti-ti* vocalization is given (Nero 1956a, Orians and Christman 1968). Copulation is also typical of passerines. Male mounts crouching female, flexes legs, and flutters wings while twisting tail beneath elevated tail of female to bring cloacal vents into brief (1–2s) [i.e., one to two seconds] contact. No specific postcopulatory display, but male frequently gives Song Spread [i.e., he sings his "konk-la-ree" song and displays his epaulets] immediately after copulation, and may be aggressive toward other males and females if they are nearby (Orians and Christman 1968).[1]

[1]Ken Yasukawa and William A. Searcy, *Red-winged Blackbird*, p. 10. Author's Note: Ornithologists vary in their spelling of bird vocalizations. I have used Alsop's spelling of "konk-la-ree" throughout *Club George*. Yasukawa and Searcy spell it "oak-a-lee." Beletsky, for another example, spells it "conc-a-ree." If George knows the preferred spelling, he, at least on this subject, is not talking.

After such a rousing and possibly arousing passage you might want
to take a moment to compose yourself before we continue with
more pedestrian topics. George, by the way, unambiguously indulged in a "victory lap" immediately after this event. He sang and
displayed then sailed slowly across the north-south axis of his realm
impressing all with his good looks and letting his rivals know who
was boss.

Meanwhile a female Mallard with two ducklings, the products
of an intimate encounter that I did not witness, had climbed
through a fence and on to the dock. Mother Mallard walked toward me with the ducklings following behind. She stopped two feet
away and began making soft peeping-murmuring sounds as she
turned her head slowly from side to side and looked at me. I could
not be sure if I had fed these particular birds before but I had no
doubt that Mother Mallard was asking for a handout. I threw down
some sunflower seeds intended for the whole family, but Mother
Mallard shoved her ducklings out of the way and ate the food herself. She thwarted every attempt by the little ones to get a share.
Talk about a strict upbringing. The situation became more complex when two adult male Mallards slipped through the same
opening in the fence. Now it was the boys that shoved Mother Mallard aside, dived into the remaining seeds and at times one another. Things got out of hand after Mother Mallard persisted in
her attempts to regain her share. The males turned on her and
chased Mother Mallard and her ducklings off the dock, onto a path
and around a tree where I could not see them but I could hear
them fighting. The Mallards got so carried away with their battle
they forgot about the free lunch and none came back to finish the
seeds. Perhaps it is behavior like this that has given a pejorative
connotation to the term "birdbrain" but this is how Mallards often
act. The Mallards did calm down and a few minutes later I was relieved to see the ducklings back on the water with their mother.
None appeared to have been damaged in the fracas.

I have been watching this particular female for days and have not
been impressed by her parenting skills. She often neglects to keep
track of her babies. Several times I have watched one of her panic-

stricken ducklings, having discovered Mother Mallard had left it behind, frantically racing around the pond until it could relocate and
rejoin its family. I reckoned that this adult female must have been inexperienced at raising a family or she was just an incompetent parent. Adult Mallards can be rough with each other but this female
treated her brood more harshly than any other I had encountered.
There were five ducklings in her care only a short while ago. Now
there were only two. In her defense the losses her brood suffered
are only moderately higher than those of the other Mallard family
on the pond. I counted eleven ducklings in that group and they are
now six. That is about a fifty-five percent survival rate compared to a
forty percent rate for Mother Mallard's brood.

I do not recommend watching Mallards mate to the faint of
heart. It often is a crude and rude affair. The males may brutally
take females seemingly against their will. It is not unusual to see
the male shove the female completely underwater and not release
her until he has had his way with her. In comparison the Red-
winged Blackbird mating is a genteel elegant affair. Ken Yasukawa
offered this technical explanation of how the male Mallards are
equipped to overpower the females and characterizes how they use
that ability.

> Male Mallards have an intromittent organ so they can force fe-
> males to copulate with them. Often, attempts at forced copula-
> tion are quite violent and can involve several males "ganging
> up" on one female.[2]

Ken was careful to remind me that as a scientist his intention was
not meant to be critical. Mallard mating behavior can be undeniably ruthless but as Ken pointed out nature is amoral and it is illogical to judge animal behavior as we would that of humans. I will
try to remember that and strive to be impartial the next time I see
Mallards roughing up one another, but it will take a conscious effort not to be judgmental.

[2]Ken Yasukawa, e-mail message, November 30, 2004.

While Mallard mania had dominated the dock, the five North-ern Rough-winged Swallows had perched side by side on a fence. They were taking a break. This was an uncommon opportunity to get a good look at them because they spend a high percentage of their time in the air. A sixth Northern Rough-winged Swallow was maintaining its reputation as a workaholic. This individual kept up its airborne pursuit of flying insects and showed no signs of resting like its companions.

By now the sun was close to setting. Over the cliff I heard the un-mistakable high-pitched chatter of Chimney Swifts. I counted eight of them high over the cliff. A Common Nighthawk entered the same airspace zigzagging through the sky at an almost comically rapid pace as it called out "beers," or something like it, repeatedly.

After the sun went down the Red-winged Blackbirds went silent. There was very little sound at all without their insistent vocaliza-tions. The Canada Goose family came across the water and pre-serving their orderly formation climbed on to the flat rock on the shore of George's Island. They immediately commenced their eve-ning preening. The surroundings were so quiet that I could hear the click of their beaks as the Canada Goose family worked over their feathers. When they finished grooming, Mom squatted down on the rock. She nudged the goslings with her beak until they all were under her right wing. They squirmed and pushed each other to get the best positions while Dad stood guard over them. He faced east and Mom faced west so that between them they could see any approaching danger. These parents are so diligent that I have wondered if they sleep at all. Studies involving Mallards, for example, have shown that they keep one eye open to watch for predators while the other eye is closed and the corresponding side of the brain sleeps. Throughout the night the bird alternates the sleeping and conscious sides of its brain. It may sound like science fiction but it is science fact that they can literally be half asleep and keep watch at the same time.[3]

When it was dark two Black-crowned Night Herons silently

[3]Nancy Drilling, Rodger Titman, and Frank McKinney, *Mallard*, p. 13.

drifted over the water and landed in the shallows by the shore. One barked. The other bird some twenty feet away did not reply. On the periphery there were more calls to disrupt the quiet. The American Robins were calling more loudly and frequently than they had in daylight. To my ear they sounded agitated as if they were fighting among themselves and I soon saw pairs of them were involved in numerous chases. They did not let up even when I assumed there was not enough light for them to see where they were flying.

I did not see a Black Skimmer this evening just the ghostly outlines of the two Black-crowned Night Herons standing in breaks among the reeds. On my last look at the pond the erratic flight of four bats got my attention. I imagine that this too was a family unit. They were looking for a meal and I went home to look for mine.

Chapter 24 · May 27

Feeding Frenzy

Not only does Harry spread his mixture on the Cork Oak Tree a few times a week but also Allen sits on in his favorite bench dispensing peanuts to all comers. The birds would undoubtedly come to Morton's Pond anyway but I am convinced that the supplemental food attracts them in greater numbers than would be the case otherwise. My own nutritional contributions have no doubt helped to alter their behavior. Many other folks not necessarily bird-watchers also find this spot conducive to providing handouts. The birds have come to expect it but knowing that did not prepare me for the feeding frenzy that I witnessed today.

About a dozen House Sparrows gathered on either side of me along the top of the wire mesh fence. Out of the corner of my eye I

Two turtles at George's Pond were catching some rays.

saw a blurry shape slowly inching his way toward my open palm. "Left foot, right foot, stop": it repeated this cautious pattern as it progressed. I held perfectly still to see if the bird would take food from my hand. I dared not turn my head for fear I would frighten away the creature but that meant I could not identify it as it approached. I assumed it was one of the sparrows but I was wrong. It was Morton Downy who had surreptitiously mixed in with them and bamboozled me. The Woodpecker leaned over, stretched out, grabbed a piece of food and flew off to smash it to smithereens, which he then ate in his customary fashion.

Morton's action apparently had a compelling effect on the surrounding usual suspects. There were three Blue Jays overhead in the trees that had been watching very closely. As soon as Morton departed one Blue Jay took his place on the fence. The remaining House Sparrows would not socialize with the Blue Jay as they had with a Downy Woodpecker and they joined their flock foraging in the grass. The Blue Jay, like Morton, inched its way along the top of the fence and paused beside my hand. The bird was statue-like until it lunged to snap up a peanut and sped back to its former position overhead to swallow whole its catch. About thirty seconds later the Blue Jay came back for seconds. This time the bird made a flying approach and pushed off with both feet as it got the target inside its beak. The first time I saw a Blue Jay this close I thought it looked a bit menacing, but not this time. It looked quite benign in fact. I guess, like the Blue Jay, I am getting used to this.

The House Sparrows had obviously been eyeing the Blue Jay and had determined that they would attempt it themselves. About a dozen male House Sparrows took turns hovering in midair at my fingertips, but not one had the gumption to take the food.

The Northern Cardinals too were inspired. Three males lined up on the fence. For several minutes they looked at me intensely. They came closer and looked some more, but finally decided not to trust me and they went back to gathering food from a less exotic source.

No sooner had the Northern Cardinals given up than Charlie

the Red-winged Blackbird came hurtling from out of the west. Streaking toward me he made a pinpoint landing on my palm then took his food ten or twelve feet away. He repeated this twice more and then, poof, he disappeared from whence he came.

If ever someone wanted evidence to show that birds imitate the behavior of others I imagine this feeding frenzy would serve that purpose well. This situation changed when Ned came along. He was not as familiar to the usual suspects. Not to imply anything negative about Ned but I think the presence of a stranger caused the bird to lose their bravado and resume conventional food gathering instead. It was just as well. I know Ned does not approve of hand-feeding birds and a continuation might have been a source of tension between us.

I decided to move on. I especially wanted to visit the Northern Flicker and Red-bellied Woodpecker cavities on the eastern shore of the Lake. Ned was glad to come along. As we walked Ned spotted and identified birds with such rapidity that I had to accept his word that I had actually seen an Eastern Wood-peewee, Canada Warbler and Swainson Thrush. My novice skills could not process the visual information as fast as Ned's accomplished skills could at what seemed to me a lightning pace. His skills however could not help us find the Northern Flicker or the Red-bellied Woodpecker at home. At the Green Heron breeding ground we could not locate the juveniles and I began to feel it is time to assume they have fledged and gone but we did see an adult incubating eggs on the new nest.

Ned, like myself, has gotten into the habit of winding up his bird-watching walk at George's Pond. His timing is tied more closely to the hope of spotting a Black Skimmer than it is to keeping up with George though he is not adverse to doing so. There were a few people on the dock primarily interested in the turtles swirling around in the water at the foot of the dock. A Black-crowned Night Heron was standing out in the open on George's Island. Mel, George's neighbor, seemed to be in especially good voice today not to imply that the rest of the Red-winged Blackbirds were not. From several directions came the sounds of American

Robins, Common Grackles and House Sparrows. The two Mallard families were shuttling in and out of the phragmites and cattails in the shallow water. Sadly the family with six ducklings has been reduced to five but the Canada Goose family has maintained its numbers. All six goslings dutifully kept in formation until they reached an area of vegetation where they could fan out and forage for themselves in relative safety without either of their parents standing directly over them but they were never far away.

George was busy chasing rivals and his lady friends. His trips to the dock were short and few. Julio had been at the dock for some time and I asked him to give me an update on George's activities. He told a frightening story. A young man and a woman had attempted to abduct George. Ironically they had tried to lure George with a piece of bread and then, working together, snare him in a butterfly net. George had been interested in the bread but wary of the couple's actions. Luckily George kept clear of the net long enough for Julio's admonishments to convince the errant couple to give up their selfish, cruel and I may add illegal activity.

I was shocked and very angry. It was fortuitous that I had not been present when this occurred. Certainly I would have lost my temper. I had not been aware of it before this episode but I learned from Ned that there is a market for "exotic" animals to be sold as pets and wild birds, even widespread species like Red-winged Blackbirds, are targeted. It is illegal to conduct activities that may endanger birds that migrate across international borders in North America and Red-winged Blackbirds fit that description but there is no easy way to stop poachers if they are determined and persistent.

The thought of anyone putting George in a cage strikes me as obscenely cruel and hopelessly ignorant. I cannot imagine how callous a person could have become to be capable of doing that. How much more beautiful and rewarding it is to watch wild birds live the life they were born to rather than see them diminished to the status of dust collecting household bric-a-brac. One only has to see birds in the their natural habitat to know what freedom means to them and to ourselves.

I do not remember much else that I saw after hearing this disturbing story except that it was comforting to watch the Canada Geese preparing to roost. The goslings have gotten to a size where they do not all fit economically under Mom's wing. We laughed watching one gosling pop out as one wiggled in. Eventually they all managed to hold on to a spot but it will not be long before all of them will not fit. Where will they sleep then? I hope to find out.

Chapter 25 · May 29

Goose vs. Goose

I t rained yesterday but I got in an hour of bird-watching before the weather forced me to return home. On and off, mostly on, I stood under my umbrella during my visit to George's Pond. There was little bird activity but one sighting was well worth enduring the rain. In the phragmites on the south shore stood an immature Black-crowned Night Heron and two adults I assumed to be its parents. The youngster was nearly the same size as the adults but had very different coloring. It was a mottled brown and streaked so heavily that I imagined it looked like a giant mutant sparrow. This juvenile is one more I can add to my list of species in the virtual nursery the pond has become but I very much doubt that the Black-crowned Night Heron fledgling was born here. They are colonial nesters. As

Canada Geese had always impressed me as being rather tolerant of one another. Until today.

stealthy as Black-crowned Night Herons can be they could not have hidden a breeding colony or even a single nest at George's Pond without a park birder discovering it and passing its location along the grapevine. I wanted to stay to watch this trio but the rain intensified and I retreated.

Today in the late afternoon I looked out the window to discover that the sun had come out. This was its first meaningful appearance in days. I rushed to take advantage of the light for birdwatching and picture taking. I found the Red-winged Blackbirds at George's Pond were taking advantage of the weather too. Ruby and her harem-mate were working through the reeds at the edge of the water. George was foraging for himself. If he was taking food to the hidden nests as I assumed his mates were I did not see him do it. I still could not locate a nest even though I watched the two female Red-winged Blackbirds' movements like, dare I say it, a hawk. (I dared.)

I could not know it of course but on this first sunny day in a succession of gray ones I was going to have a stirring lesson in Canada Goose behavior. In larger congregations of ten to fifty or so Canada Geese that I have observed on the Reservoir or the Lake I have never witnessed the kind of belligerent bickering that Mallards engage in. Canada Geese have impressed me as being rather tolerant of one another. So when I watched six additional adult Canada Geese arrive at George's Pond I expected them to be accepted by the family that was already here. I was mistaken.

As the six newcomers were splashing down on the water's surface the Canada Goose parents began herding their goslings to a point about thirty or more feet away from them. Then Mama and Papa Canada Goose lifted up into the air and traveling at great speed barely inches above the water flew toward the six new arrivals. With their outstretched necks in line with their bodies they plunged into their targets like living cruise missiles. They burst into the knot of visiting Canada Geese and sent them scurrying and squawking in all directions. I could hear Mama and Papa honking and hissing from where I stood on the opposite end of the pond. I tried to begin to understand what I had seen but before I could the attackers launched another strike. The parents repeated their attacks at least a half dozen times before stopping abruptly. Then regaining their composure in a heartbeat Mama and Papa resumed their typically peaceful foraging with the children as if no problems had ever existed in the world. The parents had not succeeded in driving the visiting birds away but they evidently were satisfied that the other geese had learned that it would be in their own best self-interest to keep away from their family. It must have worked because as far as I know the six newcomers did not come close to the goslings again.

Another surprise, this one doubly sweet, awaited me. A passing bird-watcher I had never met before led me from the dock to a single tree in which both Baltimore Orioles and Orchard Orioles had built nests. I will be adding oriole chicks to the list of babies in this growing bird nursery if all goes well.

This bird-watching session would yield still one more notable event that I must categorize as a cautionary tale. I had a late start because of the weather, as I have explained, and had intended only to visit George's Pond but I made a last minute decision to make a quick survey of the Ramble. As I entered the Ramble I noticed the sun was about to slip beneath the tree line. There would soon be too little light to see birds even if they had not already gone to roost. I admitted the folly of going forward and reversed course. I headed back to the dock knowing I had plenty of time to look for Black-crowned Night Herons, Common Nighthawks, bats and the possible arrival of a Black Skimmer. Walking down an empty path lined by trees and other thick vegetation I heard rustling in the underbrush. I initially assumed the noise came from a squirrel but I quickly reconsidered that explanation knowing they had retired for the night. Maybe it was a dog or a cat? I did not know but I was intrigued. The rustling escalated into swaying as I watched a moving line advance toward me through the plants. The sound of grunts and a low growl came from the edge of the path where the movement stopped. I was stumped. I was a nervous too. In hindsight I recognize this as the point when I should have left but did not. The plants parted and out stepped a furry four-legged animal:

a petite baby Common Raccoon. This creature could not have been more than ten inches long. It came forward waddling as if it were drunk. Grunting and grumbling the raccoon stood on the path three feet in front of me. Holding still for a few seconds it looked up at me. It was breathing heavily. With a loud snort it waddled on past me, off the path, back into the weeds and under the branches of the shrubs. I could still hear it grunting and grumbling and saw the plants rustling as it moved away and disappeared. I was not sure how to interpret any of this. At first I wondered if this raccoon had been separated from its mother and was searching for her. Could it have mistaken me for its mother? Had it mistaken me for its dinner? I have seen many a raccoon before but never at such a young age and none had moved or vocalized as this one did. Then it dawned on me that this baby could have been ill. It might even have been delirious with a fever. That would explain its grunts, grumbles, snorts and its wobbly gait. If that were the case then I had just had a narrow escape. Had it gotten closer to me I might have been introduced to some microbe I would prefer never to meet. Before I saw the raccoon I should have made a hasty exit. Beginning bird-watchers take heed and learn from my inaction and poor judgment. Be advised to steer clear of wobbling, grunting and grumbling wild animals of any size and any age.

Chapter 26 · May 30

Plan A or Plan B?

There was a violent thunderstorm today. Afterward the sky remained ominously dark through the late afternoon and early evening. I had felt trapped by monsoon-like rain and was anxious to get outside. At 7:00 PM I tuned to the Weather Channel to review the most recent Doppler radar image. It did not show evidence of precipitation in, around or close to the area. I made a calculated decision to launch a bird-watching excursion. To minimize the potential risk I carried my folding umbrella and planned to limit my walk to a visit with George.

I saw few people on my way into the park, but on the dock I found George standing in Gordon's palm gorging on birdseed.

In this region there are those that might sum up George's forceful personality with one word: chutzpah.

More people arrived. Three additional Club George charter members stood with outstretched palms filled with offerings for George but still he preferred Gordon's hand. The three supplicants looked like fanatical fans desperately seeking a celebrity's autograph. The intensity of feeling George inspired in these people, as he did in myself, did not escape my notice. Logic prevents me from assuming George might draw his own inspiration from the adulation of his fans but there is no doubt he reacts strongly to the attention he receives. If he were a human I might describe him as being a supremely self-confident fellow with a strong sense of self-entitlement and boundless energy. In a person these traits are not always attractive but in this little bird they become, well, for lack of a better word, charming. Watching him with his admirers boosted my admiration for him. George is a living example of how the combination of tenacity, courage, and boldness tempered by caution, discipline and experience can lead to success. In this region there are those that might sum up his forceful personality with one word: chutzpah. You do not have to be a New Yorker to know a little of that can go a long way.

At the end of the day the Canada Goose family continued the practice of climbing onto the flat rock on the northern edge of George's Island but there was a change in the gosling's routine. I have reported that they all had reached sufficient size to create difficulties when snuggling up under Mama's wing at the same time. This evening the six goslings switched to plan "B." They huddled together away from Mama in the center of the rock. They remained that way until the temperature dropped noticeably. That prompted the goslings to abandon plan "B" and revert to plan "A." Once again they pushed and shoved each other trying to get a spot under Mama's sheltering wing. They all fit underneath but it took a great effort.

There were two unusually vocal Green Herons here. At times I saw them briefly standing together. Their close proximity and conversation made me wonder if they were a male and female pair and very likely one that was nesting near Bank Rock Bridge. The Barn Swallows returned too but not the Chimney Swifts or the Common

Nighthawks that have been on view lately. Closer to sunset I saw two Northern Rough-winged Swallows and one Little Brown Bat out for a hunt.

I remained at the dock long after it was dark. The grapevine had spread word that the Black Skimmer had been sighted at George's Pond with regularity since May 14, the day I first saw it, and the number of evening bird-watchers willing to wait to see it has been slowly increasing. Tonight about a dozen gathered. They were enough to fill the width of the dock lined up two deep. At 8:30 PM we saw a shadow moving through the air toward the middle of the pond. We hoped it was the skimmer. When we heard a loud bark the consensus was it was more likely a Black-crowned Night Heron but then the shadow landed in a tree and not in the shallow water where we expected a Black-crowned Night Heron would at this hour. Training my binoculars on it I recognized it was neither a Black-crowned Night Heron nor the Black Skimmer. It was instead a Great Egret. For several minutes the bird searched out and tested different perches. We were not sure why. When the Great Egret finally settled on one we realized it was going to spend the night here. This gathering of bird-watchers agreed this was the first time any of us had watched a lone Great Egret come to roost at George's Pond. Personally after witnessing that I did not mind if the Black Skimmer did not show up.

Chapter 27 · June 1

Soggy Bread

hand-fed Morton Downy several times at the pond I have named for him. He typically spends less than a second on my hand but today Morton stood on my fingertips and stared into my eyes for about two or possibly three seconds before grabbing a bit of food and taking off with it. That may not seem like a long time to you but to me it seemed an extraordinary amount of time. It is a rare delight to get a close-up look at any wild creature and who knows, maybe Morton was looking at me and thinking the same thing.

Morton's action was the opening salvo in another feeding frenzy. A Tufted Titmouse relentlessly returned for meal after meal. House Sparrows followed my every step and at least one half

Morton is captured in the act of creating smithereens.

dozen of them took food from me. Charlie, the Red-Winged Black-bird, flew from a distance of thirty feet straight into my hand with such precision that an observer might suppose the two of us had rehearsed this but then, come to think of it, we have. Though Charlie's landings appeared effortless his attempts to hold onto his food did not go smoothly because the Common Grackles kept taking much of it away to his obvious consternation as his volleys of calls and one great hiss attested. Male and female Northern Cardinals lined up waiting for me to toss them something but there were no hand-feeders in this group.

I wondered what the relationship was between these four individual cardinals. I suspected that they formed a family unit. Since it is breeding season the territory owners would chase other adults and their lingering offspring, born the prior year, off their turf. I guessed that of the four, one male and one female were juveniles but I did not have the skill to positively identify them as youngsters. Often one, maybe the same male circled me. A few times he came within inches of my hand but no closer. I imagined this bold fellow might be "Papa." I found I was taking increasing delight in watching Northern Cardinals watching me. It was the way they looked at me that I found captivating. Their eyes are widely spaced on either side of their heads so they do not have highly developed stereovision. They often turn their heads from side to side using one eye at a time to give something or someone a close look. The extraordinary control they have of the crest on top of their heads fascinates me most. The various degrees to which they can move it up and down in the context of their different activities and reactions to situations suggest they use it to signal their disposition, intention and emotion. How crested birds can move the feathers on top of their heads is a neat trick of physiology. Each feather is attached to a specialized group of muscles that makes dexterous control possible. If you do not have a conveniently located Northern Cardinal to examine consider visiting a local pet shop instead. Take a look at the Cockatiels or other parrots. I think you will agree that they use their crests to communicate but remember not to attempt to feed pet shop birds for their safety and your own and remain at a reasonable distance from them or you may find you are being escorted to the door. Should you be inspired by the demonstration of this concept I do not recommend that you spend time standing in front of the mirror trying to get your hair to rise and fall in a similar manner because human hair follicles and associated muscles do not function in precisely the same way. If by some chance you discover you posses a comparable skill get yourself an agent and business manager. Handled correctly you could make a fortune.

A high priority today was to track down the rumors Julio and Michael have told me about bird-watchers claiming to have seen George in the company of a fledgling. These stories have become so commonplace that I now accept them as fact. I am frustrated that I have not found a nest much less seen one of George's chicks. I was determined to investigate these stories thoroughly.

When I stepped on to the dock a couple of Club George charter members, whose names I did not know, told me that they had seen not one but two Red-winged Blackbird chicks on and around George's Island. Two chicks? It was bad enough when I believed I was one chick short but to learn that I was two chicks short was just too much.

There were at least a half dozen of his fans alternately feeding, admiring and vying for George's attention. Few were disappointed because George returned every few minutes to take food from most of them: much more quickly and indiscriminately, or so I thought, than is his custom. Once he had the food he did not linger but rushed to the shrubs on his island where he disappeared for a couple of minutes before racing back to collect more and then repeat the cycle. There was no doubt in my mind that he was shuttling back and forth to nestlings—or was it fledglings?—hidden behind the leaves.

George exhibited another behavior for which I had no immediate explanation. He had suddenly changed his two top food preferences. Rather than choosing peanuts first and wild birdseed second his top preference has mysteriously become bread and the others have been demoted to a distant second and third. I watched him repeatedly turn up his beak at peanuts and seeds he normally would gobble up with gusto. I was puzzled. Why had his enthusiasm been redirected to an edible he regularly accepts as a food of last resort? I was so mystified that I decided this observation required scientific testing. I offered him different combinations of peanuts, birdseed and bread several times to see which he would select. He chose the bread nearly every time except in a few instances when he ate a smidgen of peanut before racing off with white bread in his beak. Michael performed the test himself to provide a control for my experiment. He thought the shape of the food might be a key factor so he offered George similarly sized and shaped bits of bread and peanut placed side by side. George unhesitatingly chose the bread. No, the determining factor was not shape or size.

Tellingly we did not see George actually eat the bread. Instead we noted that he took it to a spot covered by thick vegetation on the island. Closer examinations however revealed another layer to this deepening mystery. We watched George carry pieces of bread to a specific spot on the shore where he dipped them in the water, sometimes repeatedly, before taking them into the bushes. He did this three or four times in succession. Now, I admit it was not possible for us to see what George did with the wet bread once he was behind the leaves but I believe he fed it to his offspring.

Why feed them soggy bread? I theorized that the wet bread could be easier for him to deposit inside the beaks of baby birds and it might be easier for chicks to swallow than crushed seeds and peanuts. My idea simply put was that George was collecting and wetting bread to create a mush-like baby food. As this occurred to me the voice inside my head asked two questions, "Just how intelligent is George anyway?" and "Are you getting carried away again?" I will not make a stab at replying to either of those questions but I did try to find data about this provocative behavior.

I have not read that adult Red-winged Blackbirds soak food routinely either for themselves or their progeny. Ken Yasukawa could not offer me any information about it. There may be a naturally occurring foodstuff that George would normally process in this way if bread were not available but I do not know what that food could be. No one I asked remembers seeing George soak seeds, peanuts, bugs or any other of his usual foods.

In searching my collection of Red-winged Blackbird literature it was difficult to run down any references to bread. Not unexpectedly I could not find the topic listed in indexes or tables of contents. I did, however, come across a note in Robert Nero's *Redwings* that is applicable if not definitive.

> It is curious that Redwings respond so readily to the sight of white bread as food. I once dropped a piece of bread on the shoulder of a road beside a wet ditch where there were a few Redwings. Very shortly after I backed my car away, the resident male flew down to feed on the bread.[1]

What tantalizes me is the author's mention of the proximity to water. Nero does not say so but I would like to know if this Red-winged Blackbird dipped the white bread into the water. The author does state that the bird ate the bread but not that he took it with him to feed nestlings or fledglings. Nero also notes in *Redwings* that the majority of Red-winged Blackbirds in his study, unlike George, were consistently fond of white bread. In my experience, scientific though it may not be, not only do Central Park Red-winged Blackbirds prefer peanuts to any type of bread, so do many of the other seed eating species I have encountered. Perhaps this can be explained in terms of a regional food preference? For example, the majority of New Yorkers, it is commonly said, prefer to put mustard on a pastrami sandwich where those in another geographic location might prefer mayonnaise. Am I making any sense or am I grasping at straws here?

Does anybody want to buy a pound of straw?

[1]Robert W. Nero, *Redwings*, p. 40.

Chapter 28 · June 2

Hunting Techniques

Today's weather was my idea of what summer weather ought to be. There was a surplus of brilliant sunshine; the kind sentimental writers like to refer to as golden, and a seventy-degree temperature that suited my outdoor and indoor comfort zone to perfection.

The climatic excellence raised my spirits and the hope that this was the day I would see George's offspring myself. I rushed down to George's Pond, camera in hand, with a mental image of finding George industriously gathering food from the natural environs that he fed to his chicks. Curiously yesterday's hankering for bread was at an end. Not only had George reverted to his predilection for peanuts but he also ate them without conveying so much as a single

Roger Egret nabs a fish.

beak-full to his progeny. Maybe he was eating to compensate for a loss of calories yesterday. Meanwhile the two Mrs. Georges were briskly harvesting food that they obviously shuttled to offspring I still could not see.

In one magical fleeting instance I discerned the silhouettes of two Red-winged Blackbirds behind a screen of sedges on the island. From their postures I thought it reasonable to assume that I saw an obviously larger adult bending over to feed an obviously smaller chick. At last I had some tangible proof that at least one fledgling existed but because the scene was obscured I was not fully satisfied.

After seeing these silhouettes I began to imagine I saw Red-winged Blackbird chicks in other places. Once I thought a juvenile male Red-winged Blackbird was perched on one of the dock's supporting pillars. The bird's dull red epaulets led me to rashly conclude it was a young male but a closer look revealed my imagination was working overtime. It was not a juvenile. It was Ruby the mature female Red-winged Blackbird.

An agitated Great Egret distracted me from my ruminations about the elusive Red-winged Blackbird babies. Normally Great Egrets make few superfluous moves during a hunt. Every motion is calculated and considered before energy is expended. These birds raise the economy of motion to an art form. So why was this particular bird acting so uncharacteristically? This Great Egret was making repetitious and seemingly random strikes at one spot in the water. I supposed there must have been a school of fish around its feet providing a confusion of targets that inspired this hyperactivity but the bird's wild lunges succeeded only in splashing a great deal of water. When the egret paused to rest or perhaps to reevaluate its tactics it stretched its wings. That stretch revealed a gap in one wing where a flight feather was missing. The missing feather was a distinguishing mark I used to identify Roger Egret, a frequent pond visitor, from one and sometimes two other Great Egrets that feed here. This streak of errant beak strikes was so unlike Roger Egret's familiar style that I wondered if there were other variations in the bird's hunting techniques that I might not have noticed in the past. When Roger Egret reverted to a more cautious technique the bird's luck changed. It nabbed three fish in as many attempts. Along with a few other onlookers I found myself cheering out loud for the Great Egret. I also silently gave a sympathetic thought about the fate of those summarily dispatched fish.

The arrival of another Great Egret acted as a catalyst to launch Roger Egret into another flurry of activity, this one better characterized as a fit of aggression. Roger Egret sprang into the air heading straight for the newcomer that sprang into the air a fraction of a second later. Watching two creatures of such size (they are more or less forty inches long) oppose one another in midair would have been an eye-opener under any circumstances but these birds chose to rumble at a low altitude, at about fifteen to twenty feet over the water. At first Roger Egret, the territory owner, succeeded in routing his opponent but the situation changed when the newcomer twirled around. Now the two egrets sparred beak-to-beak in midair. As they swiped claws and beaks they emitted a torrent of harsh squawks. The two continued the battle with a series of loops over the center of the pond where they started to tumble and fall toward the water. To the awestruck crowd below on the dock this was like a state-of-the-art audiovisual spectacular disaster movie but the looming crash did not occur. Both birds gained altitude and the chase rerouted toward the dock. Directly, and I emphasize directly, over our heads the two birds again turned to face each other. They seemed to hang in the air as they flailed at one another with beaks and claws. They came so close to us that we feared we were going to be accidentally struck. Bruce, positive he was about to be knocked in the noggin, let out a loud "Wooooo!" and in a stooped posture reminiscent of Groucho Marx in a hurry dashed clear of the battling birds. The birds too dashed off. Neither Bruce nor anyone else was injured but we had all been dealt a fright. The shock of it dissipated quickly enough as we all erupted into laughter. The victorious Roger Egret returned in a moment to resume fishing. The bird's calm demeanor contrasted jarringly with its violent behavior we had witnessed only minutes before.

There were more hunting technique demonstrations awaiting

me. While they would not be quite as ardent they could not be described as dainty either. For the first time I watched a Green Heron catch a fish. On previous occasions I have seen motionless Green Herons stare into patches of water for extended periods without ever seeing one lunge or peck at a victim. Today from the tip of a log jutting off the island I watched a Green Heron catch a fish using a stalking and lunging technique reminiscent of the Great Egret. The method employed in the ingestion of the catch was quite different. The much smaller Green Heron did not swallow its catch whole as I have seen the Great Egret or the Black-crowned Night Heron do. Instead this heron deftly ripped the fish into three segments and swallowed each separately. That particular fish was far too large for it to swallow whole.

It was an unusual coincidence but soon after witnessing the Great Egret intraspecies hostilities I saw a related but less theatrical display from the Green Heron. This was the same Green Heron that I described cutting up its food. It attacked a second Green Heron seconds after it landed two yards away. A high-pitched bark came out of one of these birds but I could not tell from which. Their ensuing chase described a wide circle over the pond's perimeter. After a complete circuit the intruder chose to set down on the far eastern end of the pond. The attacking bird seemed content with this compromise and returned to the island on the western half of the pond. For the next half hour I watched two motionless Green Egrets staring into patches of water waiting for the right moment to grab an unsuspecting fish. I did not see either bird budge the whole time.

On the shore of George's Island close to one of those Green Herons a lone Spotted Sandpiper was hunting up a meal. Moving slowly but steadily along it stabbed at prey often and with good results. The Spotted Sandpiper is only about seven and a half inches long and feeds on insects and their larvae, other small invertebrates and tiny fish if it can get them. So it was no wonder that from a distance I could not see the food it was grabbing and swallowing with such frequency.

Five Northern Rough-winged Swallows and two Barn Swallows

hunted insects on the wing as they often do but I do not recall having watched them swoop down to the water to get a drink as often as they did today. As they dipped their beaks to scoop up the liquid they did not appear to slow their forward motion at all. I found that maneuver to be most impressive. Above this mixed group of swallows six Chimney Swifts were twittering away as they too hunted. Seeing all three species at the same time made me think back to last year when I saw each for the first time and was unable to distinguish them. Many beginners experience the same confusion. All three species share superficial similarities the most common being their size and methods of hunting their prey in flight but I have found ways to tell them apart easily. Swifts and swallows may look somewhat similar but they are not closely related. Swifts are physiologically nearer to hummingbirds than they are to swallows and swallows are more closely related to songbirds.

Roger Tory Peterson has described Chimney Swifts as resembling a "cigar with wings," which is an excellent aid to help you recognize them in the field. These dark gray birds have a stubby rounded tail that looks like the part of a cigar that an aficionado would place between his or her lips as opposed to the end they would ignite. They soar speedily, elegantly and sometimes erratically, often at a height where they are barely visible. Swifts are after flying insects and "ballooning" spiders (i.e., juvenile spiders using silk caught in the breeze as a means to disperse). Some describe their flying style as similar to that of a bat. These visual clues are helpful but I have learned to identify Chimney Swifts from their loud high-pitched twittering calls alone. Their unmistakable vocalizations carry over distances farther than one might expect from such a small bird. Chimney Swifts will not perch on horizontal surfaces where you might get a good look at them not because they are shy but because they have tiny feet and short legs best suited to grabbing onto vertical surfaces. They belong to the family *Apodidae* that literally means "without feet." Chimney Swifts are so named because they spend most of their workday flying. In fact Sibley says, "They not only capture their food in flight, but also, bathe, drink, and sometimes even copulate and spend the night in the air."[1] So it is safe to say that they do not perch often. They are also distinguished by their construction of nests inside chimneys and air shafts. They roost inside those structures in groups that can number in the hundreds depending on the size of their accommodations.

Swallows also hunt flying insects and perform similar kinds of aerial maneuvers. Generally I see them at lower altitudes than Chimney Swifts but that is not a rule. Swallows are members of the family *Hirundinidae*. You may get a chance to see them perch, mostly singly but sometimes in small groups. I have found that an examination of their tails is key in distinguishing the three most common species in Central Park. Northern Rough-winged are named for small barbs on the leading edge of their primary flight feathers but the purpose of these structures is speculative at best and few bird-watchers will ever get to see them. Why were they named for a physical attribute the birder may never see? Who knows, it's just one more unhelpful name we all have to deal with.

Northern Rough-winged Swallows are medium brown with gray-ish brown or tannish throats and light beige graduating to white underparts. Their brown tails tinged with black have a slightly angled edge that ends in a shallow, sometimes nearly imperceptible notch in the center. Tree Swallows have intense bluish green upperparts and white underparts and white throats. Their tails are also ever so slightly notched. The books say Barn Swallows have a grayish blue back but in the field I sometimes have difficulty distinguishing it from the bluish green of the Tree Swallow. More definitive markers are the reddish chestnut throat and deeply forked tail of the Barn Swallow. If you remember these hints you will be able to distinguish each species in far less time than it took me. Should there be more species of swifts and swallows in your region I am afraid you are on your own.

1. Chimney Swifts resemble a "flying cigar" because they have a cigar shaped tail end. Their flight can be erratic almost

[1]David Allen Sibley, *The Sibley Guide to Bird Life & Behavior*, p. 353.

bat-like and their loud frequent twittering calls can be heard from a substantial distance.

2. Northern Rough-winged Swallows have medium brown upperparts, grayish brown throats graduating to white underparts, and a lightly forked brown tail tinged with black.

3. Tree Swallows have iridescent bluish green upperparts, a white throat and underparts, and a slightly notched tail.

4. Barn Swallows have dark iridescent grayish blue upperparts, a reddish chestnut throat, and a deeply forked tail.

Chapter 29 • June 3

Babes in Pond Land

t drizzled most of the day. George's mates were gathering food for their offspring that I, to my chagrin, was having difficulty locating. After watching the adult females for a while I noticed something different about the appearance of one sitting in the sedges at the water's edge. This bird seemed a bit smaller than I remembered it should be. When I compared it to the other female Red-winged Blackbird I was certain it was not the same size. I had been mistaken about identifying one before but I thought to myself, "This has to be it. It's George's kid." I ran through the clues: smaller size, looks like female Red-winged Blackbird but does not have pinkish peachy throat, and it's hiding." Duh! There was no doubt about it.

Five of the six Canada Goose goslings are strutting their stuff on the rock at the east end of George's Pond. My how they have grown.

I had found one of George's offspring. I congratulated myself for having recognized a Red-winged Blackbird fledgling but I was a little humbled by the disproportionate effort I had to make to do it. As to the sex of the babe I did not have a clue but that was not necessarily a lack of skill on my part. At this stage of development experts would not readily tell females from males if they could at all.

This fledgling would have been motionless except that the reed it clung to swayed gently in the breeze. But when its mother arrived the young blackbird became animated and behaved in a manner consistent with the other bird babies around the pond. It called loudly and fluttered its wings rapidly. Ruby, the adult female, stilled her child by slipping her beak down its throat where she deposited the food she carried. This was just the right composition I wanted for my photograph, but the dim light, drizzle and distance were insurmountable obstacles. That was okay. It was a thrill for me just to see one of George's children.

If the stories are right about the existence of another fledgling, is Ruby also its mother or does George's other as yet unnamed mate also have one? That will be fun to figure out. Should I be able to catch each adult female simultaneously feeding their own fledgling I will know that they are both mothers.

It has been a while since I have mentioned it but George's neighbors Mary and Mel have been highly visible and audible. I am convinced that they too have a nest. It is located in the cattails and irises on the southern peninsula very close to the water. I cannot see the structure but I have watched both adults repeatedly enter and exit from precisely the same spot. When he is not foraging or fighting Mel perches above the location on one of two cattails that he favors. Clearly he is on sentinel duty. Without a doubt George's neighbors are also feeding nestlings.

The Canada Goose adults and goslings stopped at the foot of the dock where some people were feeding a congregation of turtles. The geese muscled their way in between the turtles and began taking a large share of the offerings. Meanwhile a very excited spaniel straining at its leash pulled its master down the length of the dock. The spaniel thrust its head through the bars of the fence where it was greeted by a series of loud hisses from Papa Goose in the water about four feet below. The hisses were a warning that Papa Goose was prepared to attack the spaniel but as the goose was down there and the dog was up here there was no immediate cause for alarm. Still the formerly frisky and now chastened spaniel pulled its head out from the bars and backed away a good two or three feet. From that safe distance, where neither potential combatant could see the other, the spaniel tried to make a good show of it by wagging its tail and uttering a couple of halfhearted muffled barks but the dog did not fool anyone. We all knew who came out best in the confrontation. Without further canine comments the Canada Geese family resumed consumption of the processed baked goods raining down on them.

The drizzle intensified and I decided to leave but I stopped long enough to check the status of the Baltimore Oriole and Orchard Oriole nests located in the same tree on the meadow north of the pond. The grapevine has reported the presence of nestlings in the Baltimore Oriole nest. I had not had the good luck to see them myself. What I saw were the long tail feathers of an adult female Baltimore Oriole sticking out of the nest. Was she incubating eggs or brooding chicks? I could not say. In the adjacent Orchard Oriole nest I saw no birds at all.

Orioles of either kind are not rare but few breed in Central Park. It heartens the bird-watching community to know that the park suits these birds. The fact that any migratory species would choose to nest here is interpreted as a good sign. It suggests that the park is becoming increasingly wild bird friendly. It is well deserved when bird-watchers praise the work of the Central Park Conservancy and the New York City Department of Parks and Recreation that has resurrected a critically ill park, nursed it back to health and continues to make improvements from year to year. The Central Park rehabilitation story is also an ecological success story but is not always recognized as such. Contemporary visitors admire the park's physical beauty but have little appreciation of the continual efforts it takes to keep the guiding spirit of its designers alive and steer a steady course through competing priorities and conflicting agendas for more than 150 years. Its champions have managed to preserve Central Park as an oasis for humans, animals and plants alike. This success is not merely a comforting thought but it is also proof that even in one of the most urbanized zones on this planet a balance can be struck between the needs of nature and civilization. Central Park is a symbol to all of what can be done if people have the will to make it happen or to paraphrase the popular song "if parks can make it here, parks can make it anywhere, and here's the proof, New York, New York."

Chapter 30 · June 6

A Cruel Eviction

The rain has been interrupted only by brief periods of drizzle since June third. On June fourth, I chose to remain indoors because the precipitation was too intense. By June fifth I found myself with a severe case of cabin fever, but mercifully the weather cleared sufficiently for me to make a short trip to George's Pond.

I watched George from the dock as usual. His two mates were going about their typical Red-winged Blackbird activities one

I took this photograph moments after the Red-bellied Woodpecker lost its tree cavity to the European Starling. The best thing I can say about this particular bird is that it did not drop sawdust on my head, as did the former tenant though I would gladly suffer the indignity again if it meant that the Red-bellied Woodpecker could recover its home. In Chapter 17: A Beak Full of Chips there is a photograph of the Red-bellied Woodpecker in the same pose, in the same spot taken at nearly the same angle.

would expect from new parents. They were engaged in food collection and delivery. It was clear that George too was ferrying food to at least one little one hidden in the shrubbery on his island headquarters. At one point George quit collecting and began pursuing one of his mates until they both landed on the path leading to the dock entrance. If the birds were vocalizing I could not hear it but the curious way they stood close facing each other on the ground was recognizable. I suspected something amorous was about to transpire. It did.

George broke into song, lifted his wings away from his body and walked briskly, and a bit wobbly, toward the female. When they were nearly beak-to-beak the female turned her back toward George. George lifted up just enough to mount the crouching female. Before I could say, "Wow, I do not believe this" the action was completed. This time I had a clear unobstructed view of the mating process but did I have the presence of mind to take a photograph or two? No I did not. Oh well, it may have been another missed photo opportunity but the experience was no less thrilling for me and presumably more so for George and his companion even though it lasted all of two seconds. I have read that field researchers do not have many opportunities to witness this particular act and it "is difficult to observe in most habitats."[1] Maybe researchers should come and do their work here? Mating is one more behavior George is inclined to put on display for the world to see. What an exhibitionist.

Since Red-winged Blackbirds usually mate prior to egg laying I would say I had just seen strong circumstantial evidence that another clutch of eggs is in the works. I tried to keep my eyes on the female to see what she would do next but after this romantic interlude she showed no provocative behaviors. She flew off to the island and dropped out of sight. I was frustrated too that I could not figure out which of the two females she was. George flew to his favorite perch on the top of the fence, pointed his beak skyward, blasted forth with a "konk-la-ree" song, ruffled his feathers, and then preened for a

[1] Ken Yasukawa and William A. Searcy, *Red-winged Blackbird*, p. 10.

minute before launching into what I believe was the second victory lap I have watched him make after an amorous episode.

This week I bought a monopod to steady my camera because too many of my photographs are going into the recycling bin as opposed to the photo album. The longer the camera lens the more critical it becomes to reduce "hand-shake." From the number of my wasted shots it is clear my 300-millimeter telephoto lens has shaken too many hands. I had used the monopod once before and thought I had worked out all the necessary logistics but somehow I managed to tangle the straps of the binoculars, camera and camera case into one large knot around my neck. In my haste to get the camera into position I became painfully aware that I was literally choking myself in an effort to take a picture. I got free of the mess and accepted that there was a larger learning curve I would have to master than I had anticipated. A little organization and practice at home before I took this show on the road again were definitely in order.

Today June sixth I spent some time looking for birds I have neglected. I could not find the American Robins in their nests near the Lake and there was no indication the Northern Flicker was in its tree cavity in the locust tree. I did not see the nesting Green Heron. These disappointments evaporated when I heard the call of a Red-bellied Woodpecker from behind the leaves covering the tree stump I had discovered when the cavity was under early construction. I quietly approached, parted the branches and was stunned by what I saw. The Red-bellied Woodpecker was there all right but not where I expected it to be. It was on the outside on the tree trunk not inside its tree cavity. Poking out of the opening was the head of a European Starling. I had read descriptions about what I was witnessing but its full impact did not really strike me until then. I had come along at the precise moment when a European Starling was evicting the Red-bellied Woodpecker from its home.

The word European in the name European Starling accurately identifies these birds as a transplanted species. They are not natives but were deliberately brought here with good intentions that produced unfortunate results. The European Starlings spread across the continent to quickly become one of our most numerous breeds and a tough competitor for several resident species. Various wood-peckers in particular are faced with a challenge ever since this star-ling arrived. European Starlings though smaller than Red-bellied Woodpeckers excel at forcibly taking their tree cavities away from them. Diana Wells explains how a well-meaning bird-watcher has been credited with almost single-handedly creating this trouble-some situation.

> The common starling, *Sturnus vulgaris*, was deliberately brought to New York in 1890, when the American Acclimatization Soci-ety, led by Eugene Schieffelin, let loose forty pairs in Central Park. It is said that Schieffelin, who was also president of the Brooklyn Bird Club, was planning to bring all of Shakespeare's birds and flowers to America (although Shakespeare men-tioned the starling only once, in *Henry IV*.) More likely Schieffe-lin's group was hoping the starlings would destroy insect pests. But the birds increased rapidly, eating more grain and fruit than insects and becoming pests themselves.[2]

The Red-bellied Woodpecker has other troublesome housing com-petitors that are natives. I kid you not, the Flying Squirrel, the House Sparrow when attacking in small flocks and another wood-pecker species, the Northern Flicker are known to evict them. In a few instances the Red-bellied Woodpecker does prevail but in the majority, especially those involving European Starlings, they be-come homeless. The Red-bellied Woodpecker can carve out an-other cavity in a tree but it takes about two weeks to do it. In a seeming contradiction to their relative passivity toward the Europe-an Starling and other opponents the Red-bellied Woodpecker is highly aggressive with two particular species. It not only fights off invading Red-cockaded Woodpeckers but also has been observed grabbing them by the bill and pulling them out of their tree cavities, sometimes injuring or killing them in the process. The Golden-fronted Woodpecker is also the object of the Red-bellied Wood-

[2]Diana Wells, *100 Birds and How They Got Their Names*, pp. 235–36.

pecker's selective wrath and may be the reason that bird does not expand its range in Texas.[3] Why is the average nine and one-quarter inch Red-bellied Woodpecker tougher with the eight and one-half inch Red-cockaded Woodpecker than with a European Starling of the same size? I cannot say for sure but I have noticed in the bird world bulk is not the sole determining factor in conflict. Often a determined attitude more than compensates for physical limitations. How else can you explain, for example, how small songbirds like George mob hawks, egrets, and herons yet typically escape unscathed? How can an itty-bitty Tufted Titmouse risk its life to pluck a hair out of a "raccoon, opossum, dog, fox squirrel, red squirrel, rabbit, horse, cow, cat, mouse, woodchuck and humans" and get away with it most of the time?[4] Perhaps for the same reason the European Starling successfully evicts the Red-bellied Woodpeckers: because they believe they can. Sounds familiar doesn't it?

Standing on the northern peninsula that is the DMZ between George and Mel's territories I found both birds in a classic pose astride their invisible boundary line. Separated by just a few feet the birds perched facing each other. Periodically one would tilt its beak up at about a forty-five degree angle. The other bird would reply with the same action. I recognized this as a signal of Red-winged Blackbird aggression. Depending on how much anger they need to express they will hold their beaks from a forty-five degree angle, like George and Mel, to nearly a ninety-degree angle. Ornithologists refer to this as "bill tilt" or "bill up." It is the equivalent, if you will forgive the analogy, to the human antagonistic gesture involving the display of a middle finger and often referred to, coincidentally or not, as "flipping the bird." While this behavior generally communicates a low level of antagonism in both species, Red-winged Blackbirds and humans have lots of more dramatic ways to show how annoyed they can be. I will illustrate one more

[3]Clifford E. Shackelford, Raymond E. Brown, and Richard N. Conner, *Red-bellied Woodpecker*, p. 12.
[4]T. C. Grubb and V. V. Pravosudov, *Tufted Titmouse*, p. 8.

from the Red-winged Blackbird repertoire. Discussing human aggression will be left for some other occasion when it presents itself as I am sure it will.

Just across the water from where George and Mel perched the Great Egret was stalking a meal along the edge of the reeds. When the Great Egret reached a certain point Mel launched into the air and dived at the bird's back. I understood Mel's concern. The Great Egret was closing in on the spot where Mel and Mary's nest was hidden. Mel's effort did not dissuade the Great Egret and it kept on course. Then with a loud "te-te-te-te" Mary shot out of the reeds to join Mel in the attack. The male and female Red-winged Blackbird team hovered within inches of the Great Egret now blasting out shrill "seer" calls. The Great Egret seemed to ignore their hostilities even when Mel literally bounced off the big bird's back. When the Great Egret eventually passed by the crucial spot without disturbing the nest the Red-winged Blackbirds quit their attack only to resume it after the Great Egret turned around and came stalking back from the opposite direction. The stoic egret calmly walked along as the two angry screaming birds fluttered and crashed into its back and rump until it again passed out of the contested zone. The Red-winged Blackbird nest was not harmed and the Great Egret continued on to find a meal elsewhere.

Chapter 31

Apparel That Will Wear Well

believe it reasonable to assume that if you have reached this point in the text you have already or are about to engage in outdoor birdwatching instead of the armchair variety. If either is the case then the following advice, hard-won through personal experience, comes at an opportune moment. Your bird-watching apparel will no doubt be influenced by your personal sense of style

The Northern Cardinal is a conspicuous member of the usual suspects that becomes even more conspicuous in winter. For those of you who might think otherwise this particular bird does not need to go on a diet. Many a new birder does not realize that birds can substantially alter their appearance by fluffing up their feathers in order to trap air, which absorbs body heat to keep it warm. That down jacket hanging in your closet works in the same way to keep you warm except that you do not have to fluff it up each time you put it on.

but there are practical matters the prudent bird-watcher should consider.

I will focus on the conditions in the temperate zone with which I am most familiar. Some discussion of environmental extremes I have encountered will hopefully be helpful to readers in a variety of climatic zones. Polar explorers, desert trekkers and rain forest ramblers however may want to look elsewhere for guidance.

Common sense dictates that you dress comfortably and appropriately to suit your environment. If you are birding on your lunch hour in an industrial park or an urban park your work clothes will serve you for short walks of a half hour or so. Beyond that you could find your "business casual" or more formal clothing restrictive. Bear in mind that tramping into a patch of brush or negotiating a soggy meadow may not be reasonable pursuits if you expect to remain presentable upon your return to the workplace. Also even a brief period of pedestrian activity may tire or strain feet that are squeezed into dress shoes. Wearing comfortable and supportive footgear is a critical aspect of any birding session of significant duration in any geographic location or clime. Athletic shoes will serve you well if they provide the support and traction you need but if your route includes wet or slippery surfaces waterproof hiking shoes are a better choice.

I speak with authority when I caution you not to wear open-toed sandals or shoes while bird-watching. This is so important that it bears repeating: do not wear open-toed sandals or shoes while bird-watching. Should you stray from a man-made path or manicured lawn you will inevitably encounter twigs, stones, thorns, insects and other obstacles with the potential to ruin your walk, day or worse. If for no other reason open-toed shoes should be shunned because birders spend a disproportionate amount of time looking up as compared to looking down. This exponentially increases the possibility for the birder to accidentally step where one would otherwise prefer not to step. Putting it simply you may stub your toe, suffer a scrape or come into contact with unwholesome materials up to and including biological waste products. When I found myself in the latter situation I was more than a little thankful that I had the foresight to wear protective footgear. The damage done was therefore limited but time-consumingly corrected with the judicious application of a sharp stick.

Loose fitting trousers or jeans are fine for birding but cargo-pants are a better selection for birders that feel compelled to lug along an assortment of accessories. Those extra pockets free your hands if you plan to take along a field guide, camera, snack, bottled water or a small folding umbrella like the one I occasionally carry. A backpack will work as well but if you take along a bag your hands will not be free to manipulate your binoculars or other gear.

As in any outdoor activity judicious layering of clothing will allow one to cope with changing weather conditions. In moderate weather a windbreaker or jacket tied around my waist comes in handy if the breeze picks up or the temperature dips. A sweater or sweatshirt will do the same, of course. If you are out in the noonday sun, when most birds have the good sense not to be, a hat and sunscreen are recommended. For those of you who are especially sensitive to the sun's rays they are a must.

When my bird walking sessions increased from intervals of minutes to hours I found that my socks were wearing out at an unprecedented rate. The solution, I was informed by Betsey, was to have on socks with reinforced heels and toes. Sporting goods and sports clothing stores are one place to find them if you do not know where else to look. They can be pricey but I have found that even the inexpensive kind is effective.

There are other related questions you must ask that are not about apparel but should be addressed at this juncture. For example, are there restroom facilities available along your route or might some improvisation be required? Is there a water fountain or vendor from whom you can purchase clean drinking water because you are not going to sip water from a source whose purity you cannot attest to, are you? In case of emergency, especially if you are alone, will there be a telephone within a reasonable distance or will you carry a cellular phone? You will avoid entering areas where large carnivorous predators are known to roam and you will not ramble around the woods during hunting season, right?

The color of your birding apparel is something to mull over too. Some advise birders not to wear bright colors because they may act as a deterrent or an alarm that will prompt birds to flee at the sight of you. Should you experience rejection when so attired please do not misinterpret it as clothing criticism. There is no scientific evidence that I know of suggesting that birds have fashion preferences but colors like bright red, orange or yellow are ofttimes discouraged by experienced birders. I have not tested this hypothesis in the field myself but from the time I began birding I avoided wearing bright colors. I still do not wear them, taking special care to avoid the color red that Red-winged Blackbirds, with whom I associate throughout the breeding season, use to signal rivals and mates. At some time I may conduct my own tests to see if bright colored clothing does or does not make a difference but until then I will play it safe and wear subdued colors.

For those who live in regions where hunting is a popular pastime my advice about which colors to wear is the complete opposite of what I have just told you. In those territories bright colors must be worn to avoid becoming an accidental target. My brother Walter lives in such a region. He places great faith in his collection of bright please-do-not-shoot-me-orange hats, vests, parkas and jackets. He keeps these handy for family and friends to put on should they venture beyond the safety of his garden during hunting season. Do yourself a favor and follow my brother's advice. None of our please-do-not-shoot-me-orange clad family members or friends has been shot. It has worked for us and it will work for you.

The previous generalized suggestions will serve you well in any situation but modifications are necessary where more extreme conditions exist. Summer in temperate zones or perennially hot climates present issues the birder must not ignore. A hat and bottled water are obvious helpful accessories but the judicious application of insect repellent is of equal importance. There are some people, like Michael for instance, who are especially attractive to biting insects while other people, such as myself, even while sharing the same arthropod infested environment may remain virtually unscathed. The insect attractors among us must be hypervigilant when it comes to preventing bug bites. Other commonsense cautions are not to overexert yourself, wear sunscreen, rest when you feel the need, keep hydrated and do what the birdies do: go out in the morning and late afternoon but shun the hottest part of the day.

In fall when the temperatures can be wildly variable, layering of apparel allows the birder to adapt to rapidly changing conditions. The first layer to consider is that of the undergarments. As it gets cooler a T-shirt beneath a long sleeved shirt will suffice. Achieving thermal regulation can be as easy as rolling up your sleeves and opening buttons, to a point that is socially acceptable in your community. If you are not warm enough a long sleeved T-shirt can furnish the right quantity of additional insulation. If it's cooler still that jacket or sweater you remembered to tie around your waist or put in a backpack or bag will come in handy too, won't it?

When you consider what type of jacket is best I suggest that you select one that is either water-resistant or waterproof especially during the season your region most often receives precipitation, experiences lower temperatures, or both. With the addition of a hood the garment will provide enhanced protection from inclement weather. If you are hoodless a hat is a good idea too.

Winter presents the birder with more complicated apparel challenges. When your long sleeved T-shirt or long sleeved shirt and a light jacket no longer suffice it is time to add a sweater or sweatshirt to your ensemble. The bulk these garments add will depend on each individual's thermal requirements. Your choice must also be adjusted for the amount of physical exertion involved in addition to climatic conditions. In other words even if it's cold outside you may want to wear lighter layers if you anticipate working up a sweat. On still colder days one of the simplest and effective options is to put on long underwear. There are different types designed to deal with various temperature ranges so read the product labels carefully before you make a purchase. You can wear jeans or other casual pants of varying thicknesses over your thermal undergarments but if it is brutally cold there are ways to cope with that too. Fleece lined warm-up clothing is excellent by itself but can be further enhanced with the addition of long johns. Ski or snow pants are good alternatives. If all this fails to provide enough insulation my advice it to give up and stay indoors to wait for more hospitable weather.

Betsey offered a cautionary note on this subject that may be of significance to the more socially active birder. What you decide to wear under your coat may also need to be appropriate for activities other than birding. If you run into a friend, for example, who asks you to join her or him for a cup of hot coffee or tea the multilayered cold weather birder must ask him or herself if their attire is suitable for public exposure. By failing to plan for the possibility of such an encounter you may find you have worn clothing that might best be hidden from the eyes of all but the most intimate of acquaintances. In plain English, if you meet a friend take a moment to recall what apparel lies beneath your coat before you inadvertently display your long johns in public.

Your coat should be warm but lightweight because unfettered movement is crucial. You do not want to be so protectively padded that you cannot lift your binoculars into position or you cannot bend over to tie a shoelace. Along with the coat a hood, or a hat, a scarf and gloves are vital, but the latter present a special challenge for bird-watchers. Arguably, the warmest option would be to wear mittens but they will not provide the necessary dexterity in your fingertips. Gloves make those things easier but not without significant trade-offs. There is no escaping the fact that there will come a time when every intrepid winter bird-watcher will remove one or both gloves to do what must be done thus exposing their hands to harsh conditions. I solve this problem by wearing a second pair of gloves. Under my thermal lined gloves I wear glove liners. The liners are made of fleece that permits a fair degree of maneuverability and warmth and reduces the number of times you may have to expose a bare hand to the elements. If you cannot find retail vendors that sell these gloves try this improvisation. Get a pair of fleece or wool gloves that fit snuggly and a pair of thermal gloves that are a size too large. If you can slip your fleece or wool clad hand inside the thermal gloves you may congratulate yourself on having successfully created your own personal appendage thermal regulating system. You may be asking why in the world I would be outside when it is so cold that I have to wear two pairs of gloves? Well, when the deciduous trees lose their leaves in winter some birds become much easier to find. Most notably I have had more sighting of raptors, including the Central Park Red-tailed Hawks Pale Male and Lola made famous in literature, television and film. The Northern Cardinals, a personal favorite, are easier to find and their brilliant red coloring is all the more dazzling when contrasted against white snow. In Central Park during the winter there is also the possibility of finding a visiting owl's roost and waiting until sunset to watch it fly out to go hunting. Make no mistake; it takes both a determined and appropriately dressed birder to stand around on a frigid January evening in New York City waiting for an owl to go to work.

Experienced birders know that as long as they continue walking their feet are likely to remain warm except in the bitterest cold but birders spend a considerable time immobilized staring at birds while their tootsies begin to freeze. This is why specialized footwear is a necessity. Thermal socks, with reinforced heels and toes naturally, are very helpful but make sure you read the product labels to get the right socks for the conditions you will face. There are socks designed for hikers, snowboarders, hunters and other outdoor enthusiasts. Any of these may serve but I prefer the kind that stretches over the calf. Alas, warm hosiery alone might not suffice. In that case insulated shoes or boots are in order. Thermo-this or thermo-that linings designed to retain body heat are similar to those in parkas or gloves. In their usage may lie the warmth you seek.

If you plan to purchase insulated waterproof boots be sure that you have a reasonable expectation as to their reliability. I once purchased a pair of boots with the label of a well-known sporting goods manufacturer not normally associated with shoes. During the fourth week of slogging through wet snow and standing in puddles I experienced a sudden numbing cold spreading from the heel of my right foot, along the sole and on to my toes. Later at home I discovered that a section of the synthetic sole had worn away from the heel exposing a hollow inner core where a solid one should have been. In less than a month the right heel had worn out allowing ice water to gush into my boot. The left heel had only a paper-thin layer of material remaining. It too would soon give way and allow the cold and moisture to enter. My next purchase of insulated waterproof boots was more closely considered, as should yours.

Finally, putting on all this gear, especially multiple layers in winter, can be daunting especially for a fast-paced urban birder or for impatient people of any locale. The willingness to be belabored layering on clothing with the knowledge that those layers will only have to be removed is directly proportional to the bird-watcher's desire to go birding.

The ultimate choice of apparel is yours. Choose wisely.

Chapter 32 · June 10

Would a Woodpecker Spy?

When I got to Morton's Pond the sun was very low in the sky and the light barely broke through the dense foliage above. There were still a few streaks of light filtering to the ground. After a short wait a few birds came into focus. The first I saw were a mother American Robin and a fledgling that were likely the same pair I have seen on previous days. In the open area adjacent to the pond a crowd of usual suspects and acquaintances gathered. Rock Pigeons, Common Grackles, European Starlings, House Sparrows, Gray Squirrels and one petite rat of a species I am unable to identify were among them. More birds arrived. A male Red-winged Blackbird mixed in with the others on the ground and a Tufted Titmouse flitted from tree to tree energetically. In a single mod-

Morton checked me out prior to launch.

estly sized shrub there appeared Morton Downy, the woodpecker, a Northern Cardinal and three House Sparrows all perching together for several minutes until they simultaneously went about their business elsewhere.

While I composed yet another picture of the adult robin and fledgling I heard a series of scraping sounds coming from the far side of the tree I stood beside. Not recognizing the noise I turned to see what was causing it. Poking around the tree trunk was the petite head of a male Downy Woodpecker. Since this was Morton Downy's territory I assumed it was he but I was not sure. A simple test would establish the veracity of my assumption. I put a few bits of peanuts into my palm and stretched my arm toward the woodpecker. The bird stared at me for a while. Then he moved up a couple of inches and then down until we were eyeball to eyeball. The woodpecker advanced in short hops from the back of the trunk to the front and stopped directly across from me. There he stretched and leaned forward as far as he could and still grip the tree bark. I knew what would happen next and it did. The bird popped from the tree and into my hand. Yes, there was no doubt that this particular specimen was Morton Downy. For the next twenty minutes, while I waited for the robins to wander into one or the other beam of bright sunlight to facilitate the taking of more photos of them, Morton periodically repeated his visits. On each he first checked me out from the safety of the far side of the tree trunk and, when satisfied with what he saw, cautiously worked his way around until he was in front of me. Then he made his move. Twice he paused in my hand with a peanut clasped firmly in his beak, and turning his head from side to side scrutinized me keenly before flying to the far side of the tree to eat his catch out of my sight.

When a Gray Squirrel began to move closer to the tree I knew the furry rodent's action did not bode well for continuation of Morton's forays into peanut-land. After the squirrel slipped behind the tree beneath Morton's assumed position I heard the clicking sound of claws and then the flutter of wings as Morton made a hasty retreat and vanished. An uneasy silence followed. It was broken not by a sound but by a sight. A tiny fuzzy ear materialized at the side of the tree. The ear stopped and then began to move again. Slowly the entire head of the Gray Squirrel came into view. The rodent peeked at me from the very spot Morton had launched his last visit only a short time before. The squirrel held still for a while, and then it did something I felt was as odd as it was ominous. Without ever taking its eyes off me the squirrel violently tore a strip of bark off the tree, chewed it a few of times and then mindlessly let it fall to the ground. I took this as a sign of aggressive intent. The message was clear: this squirrel wanted to get to my stash of peanuts in the worst way with an emphasis on the "worst." Luckily the squirrel grew dispirited when I backed away and it left to seek out easier fare elsewhere.

At George's Pond I found more evidence that the bird nursery there was growing. In addition to the goslings, ducklings, and grackles I found two more baby starlings and several infant sparrows. Most alluring was the sight of the mother and father Baltimore Orioles ferrying food to their nest. There can be no doubt that there are baby orioles inside but I still have not seen them. I did not see George's babes or his mates either come to think of it.

The Black Skimmer watch contingent at first consisted of Mark, Bruce, Michael and I but soon more people joined us. They were not necessarily skimmer lovers. More likely the newcomers were opera lovers, a few of the thousands gathering to listen to a live outdoor performance of Giacomo Puccini's *Turandot* by the Metropolitan Opera on the Great Lawn. The conditions for a skimmer or opera sighting were optimal: a warm clear evening with almost no breeze and an orchestra. At 9:00 PM, the same time as last night, one Black Skimmer noiselessly glided onto the scene. I have read some scholarly explanations as to how it is able to skim over the water with seeming ease but no description does justice to watching this bird in action. It can turn in a tiny radius in any direction in a New York heartbeat. I have tried to photograph it in action but how do you get a picture of a bird speeding through the dimming twilight over inky black water with the faint shafts of light filtered through random openings in the foliage slightly swaying in the breeze? This is a task for a photographer armed with a powerful (i.e., expensive) strobe light, a fast (i.e., expensive) telephoto lens and professional (i.e., expensive) camera mounted on a state-of-the-art (i.e., expensive) tripod. In my opinion the cost is worth it but after carefully considering its potential budgetary impact I have decided to content myself with watching as opposed to picturing it for now.

Chapter 33 · June 11

Berry in a Beak

It was seventy-five degrees today with a relative humidity of eighty-nine percent. This was not the kind of weather I enjoy but when I considered that there may be days in July and August when both the temperature and humidity surge into the nineties and the Big Apple seems more like the Big Baked Apple I readjusted my attitude and headed outside. No sooner had I entered the park than I began to sing the birder's lament, "Where Have All the Birdies Gone?"

The female Baltimore Oriole is grasping the side of her hanging nest under which numerous pedestrians walk unaware of the activity going on above them. I have not yet seen nestlings but the behavior of this female suggests that she is about to deliver food to newborn chicks deep inside the nest. I am not sure how this female managed to bend her tail in this position but I can assure you that she was able to straighten it afterward.

At Morton's Pond the majority of birds consisted of eight irritable Common Grackles. Like myself I thought the weather had put them in a funk. They seemed to be uncommonly antagonistic toward one another. In particular there were a few grackles that interrupted their food gathering to engage in some ostentatious bill-up displays signaling their mutual disdain. Perhaps seeing George and Mel do this the other day has sensitized me to it but I did not remember seeing grackles do it so much. Examining the grackles more closely I discovered that there were four pairs of males and females. Only the males were dissing or flipping the bird to one another.

House Sparrows and Rock Pigeons were fewer than in recent days but unlike the Common Grackles they were peaceful. I fleetingly glimpsed two male and one female Northern Cardinal and one female Downy Woodpecker, very likely Mary, Morton's mate, but they scampered away quickly. My only up-close-and-personal visitor was Charlie the Red-winged Blackbird. He whooshed in and out of my hand three times in rapid succession to snatch a peanut then exited with the same frenetic energy. The heat and humidity had not slowed Charlie down.

My photo mission once again targeted parents and babies but I saw few and they stubbornly clung to the shadows where my camera could not record their images. It was only proper that these birds were keeping the lowest profile possible so as not to call attention to themselves and their offspring. They were hiding from potential predators and not necessarily photographers. In addition to the local American Robin family there were two House Sparrow families. The juvenile robins are easy to distinguish. Besides being smaller than the adults they have spotted breasts. This is the only phase in their lives that American Robins will show this characteristic plumage common in the thrush family. The House Sparrow chicks however are only slightly smaller than the adults and both sexes resemble the female. These juveniles are harder to pick out in the crowd but their begging behavior gives them away.

Distinct from these familiar creatures and deep under the shrubs and ubiquitous Japanese Knotweed I saw a bird with an ex-

traordinary physical feature. Its plumage was unremarkable. The
bird's back was medium to dark brown, its breast was buff with dark
spots, which I recognized as characteristic young robinlike features
but what was I to make of its astonishing beak? It was spherical and
bright red. I was stumped. What bird in North America has such a
beak? None. I was excited because I thought no one might ever
have found a bird like this one before. I stared at the creature
thinking of how I was going to cause a commotion through the
birders' grapevine with the story of my amazing discovery and give
press interviews and sign autographs but as I kept my eyes riveted
on the bird the red spherical bill fell to the ground. What was going on here? The red sphere was a berry held none too firmly in
the beak of a fledgling American Robin. I laughed at myself. Coincidentally I had viewed the berry and beak straight on. From my
vantage point the berry and beak were in a perfectly straight line
and looked as if they constituted a discrete anatomical feature.
There is no denying this was a goofy misperception on my part but
the story does illustrate a situation birders may face at some point.

Sometimes field conditions can obscure a bird's identity. The
amount and character of natural lighting can easily distort their
appearance. Shadows can hide key anatomical structures or de-
form others. Varying intensities of light can alter the viewer's per-
ception of the bird's color as well as its shape or size. Visual
obstructions like leaves and branches can interfere with the recognition of identifying marks. In sleeking or fluffing its feathers,
stretching and contracting its neck and torso, or raising and lower-
ing its wings a bird can cause the bird-watcher all sorts of confusion. The posture of the bird can temporarily make it look larger,
smaller, thinner or fatter and certainly the angle at which the bird
is viewed can cause misperceptions as my berry-in-a-beak experience proves. Compounding these potential impediments the field
guide you trust to resolve such questions may not always be definitive. That is because field guides provide a drawing, painting or
photograph that represents what the author considers the most
common or average characteristics of a species.

In nature there is some variation in the appearance of individual birds within a species or even between geographic regions for that same species. Sibley tells us in *The Sibley Guide to Birds* that substantial coloration differences in the plumage of the Red-tailed Hawk, for example, predominate in western, eastern, and southwestern areas. He dedicates two full pages with more than forty illustrations to depict differences not only between and within regions but also among the sexes, adults and juveniles. In comparison he needs just one page and only fourteen pictures to highlight the variations that occur in Red-winged Blackbirds.

A species can also look extraordinarily different in and out of breeding season. When some species molt they change their appearance to a greater degree than others. An extreme example of this is the Scarlet Tanager. In the nonbreeding period of August through March the male Scarlet Tanager is not scarlet. It has a greenish yellow head, yellow throat and underparts and black wings and tail. In the breeding period of March through August the male maintains those black wings and tail but its head and torso feathers are a brilliant red. A first time birder could have a tough time identifying this bird if his or her field guide only illustrates the dramatic red and black plumage of the breeding season and does not include an additional illustration depicting it out of breeding season.

Remember too that a rare bird is, as the word implies, highly unlikely to be in your region. So, before you rush to tell all your friends and neighbors that you saw a bird with a red spherical beak, like I might have, stop to think it over. Then take an even longer look and think again to be sure what you observed is not just another berry-in-a-beak situation.

Part of my parent and child itinerary today included the newest Green Heron nestlings I have been hearing about through the bird-watchers' grapevine. On the way to their breeding ground I stopped at the site of the former Red-bellied Woodpecker cavity commandeered by a European Starling. I parted the low branches and looked up at the tree cavity. The face of a European Starling looked down at me. I backed away and gingerly let go of the branches. I know it is silly but it remains hard for me not to feel a twinge of resentment toward that particular starling.

At Bank Rock Bridge I stopped to watch the local male Red-winged Blackbird. He was busy chasing a female only to change gears and chase a competing male that kept slipping into and out of his territory. I met Ned here. Together we tried to get a look at the second Green Heron nest of the season but saw nothing. We decided to split up and look for the chicks from two different angles. Ned crossed to the paved path on the western side of the swampy cove and I went to the dirt trail above the eastern side. With aid of binoculars I located an adult Green Heron with two chicks. I called to Ned and he joined me. Later I heard talk that there are three, not two, nestlings in the nest. I was thrilled to see any chicks at all but dismayed to find myself one chick short again.

At George's Pond the Baltimore Oriole parents were making frequent trips to and from their nest. I did not see the nestlings today but every day they grow significantly larger, as chicks will, and I hope to see at least one tiny beak reaching up to receive a delivery of food from a parent. Beletsky, writing about Red-winged Blackbird chicks, says they "undergo a 700% increase in mass during their first 9 days of life."[1] Since Baltimore Orioles and Red-winged Blackbirds are both in the *Icteridae* family I suppose those oriole chicks will develop as or nearly as quickly. The basic shapes of the two species are similar except that the oriole is smaller ranging from seven to eight and one-quarter inches in length. I imagine if you colored a Red-winged Blackbird in the same tones and pattern as the Baltimore Oriole both species would be very close in appearance. Consult your field guide for pictures of both birds. Then try making a mental image of George wearing an orange-yellow sleeveless wet suit and judge for yourself. Do you see the similarities?

I found George, sans wet suit, perched at the dock overseeing his domain. I stayed for nearly an hour but saw neither his mates nor his chicks. I could not find them on my last visit either. Where were they? I did not find out.

When George turned his attention to collecting food from his

---

[1]Les Beletsky, *The Red-winged Blackbird: The Biology of a Strongly Polygynous Songbird*, p. 61.

admirers he became involved with a Club George charter member who shall remain nameless. This individual, who knew better, fed George from a freshly opened bag of Goldfish crackers. George loved the crackers but I could barely contain my disapproval about giving him junk food. Processed cheese, salt, trans fatty acids and refined carbohydrates are not the things to feed a wild creature or, in my opinion, any other kind of creature. Those who distribute this stuff lend support to those who disapprove of supplementing wild birds' diets in any way.

Where human alteration of the landscape limits the amount, quality or type of food available I believe some supplemental feeding is beneficial but only if it is wholesome, nutritious and promotes good health. In some instances supplemental feeding actually makes the difference between survival and disaster. One commonly quoted example involves the Mallards that concentrate in city parks. *The Birds of North America* makes the case that "in winter, urban Mallards often rely entirely on human-provided food, such as bread or seeds."[2] Would it be better to allow these park dwellers to perish? I do not think so but at the same time I would never advocate feeding them junk food.

Speaking of Mallards I saw only the family with five ducklings on the pond. I did not see the Canada goslings until they, with Mama and Papa, clambered up onto the flat rock where they would later sleep. There were Chimney Swifts and few of the House Sparrows, Common Grackles and European Starlings I expected to see and hear. Together they can make a substantial amount of noise, but just then the pond was nearly silent except for George and two tiny but mighty vocalists, the Song Sparrows.

I had given up hoping to catch a glimpse of George's kids but I stayed on the dock with Mark and Ned to see if the Black Skimmer was going to come. Mark left at about 10:00 PM, Ned and I remained. It must have been close to 11:00 PM when we gave up our unsuccessful vigil. This was the latest I stayed in the park and if you think that late departure indicated I have gotten fanatical about bird-watching you will not get an argument.

[2]Nancy Drilling, Rodger Titman, and Frank McKinney, *Mallard*, p. 9.

Chapter 34 · June 12

International Coalition

At George's Pond I stood on the northern peninsula across from where Mel, George's neighbor, perched dexterously with each foot clasping a separate cattail. His attention was riveted on the leisurely but relentless progress of a Great Egret stalking along the green wall of stalks with Mel and Mary's hidden nest site inside. The Great Egret appeared more interested in catching a fish, amphibian or bug but a helpless nestling could not be ruled out as a meal. The hunter stood motionless for several minutes at a time staring into the water, not into the plants where the Red-winged Blackbird nestlings were hidden, waiting

Mary came out of the phragmites where her nest was hidden to help Mel after he was unable to dislodge the Great Egret alone. A moment later George came to his neighbor's assistance.

for the ideal moment to strike. The ideal moment came twice in fifteen minutes but the Great Egret failed to score on either lunge. After each failure the Great Egret came a few steps closer toward where Mel was poised to make a strike of his own. When Mel decided that the Great Egret had come close enough he leapt from his perch with a shriek. "SEER," he screamed and dived within a few inches of the Great Egret's back. He came to full stop hovering in the air, turned and made another pass over the egret's back while screaming his head off. The Great Egret showed no hint that it was aware of Mel and continued in the same direction. A few inches farther along his route Mary came out and joined the attack. She dived at the back of the Great Egret's head while Mel crashed into its back and bounced off only to smack into his target again and again. The Great Egret continued to ignore them and kept on walking.

All this must be familiar to the reader by now since I have described similar scenes before but there was to be something new about this episode. As I watched Mel and Mary's pelting of the Great Egret I did not immediately notice George hurtling across the invisible boundary separating his realm from theirs until he had joined forces with his two neighbors. The Red-winged Blackbirds had formed an international coalition. While Mel and Mary smacked into the invader's rump George smacked into the back of its head. A barrage of shrieks and screams, a form of psychological warfare if there ever was one, accompanied the attackers' physical blows. George's military intervention proved to be the deciding factor in the battle. The Great Egret pushed off into the air and retreated to the far eastern end of the pond. Mission accomplished, George unceremoniously flew back across the invisible boundary line into his own territory. At once all three Red-winged Blackbird combatants resumed civilian activities as if nothing had happened. The international coalition of Red-winged Blackbirds that had successfully "mobbed" the enemy had formed, fought, won and dissolved within a minute.

A short time later, Mel and George perched close to one another each remaining on his side of the invisible boundary line.

George sat atop the Weeping Willow to the west and Mel sat atop a Weeping Willow to the east of the border. The emergency situation had passed and the two male Red-winged Blackbirds clearly had resumed their customary territorial behavior.

Reflecting on the possible explanations for this occurrence my first thought was to attribute it to altruistic motives: George perceived the danger confronting his neighbors, he determined their efforts were failing to meet their objective and he made the decision to come to their assistance. Together three Red-winged Blackbirds succeeded where two could not. I have since learned that this type of behavior is not unusual among the Red-winged Blackbird population but behaviorists judge it with a more critical eye. There is no question that George risked physical harm by aiding Mel and Mary but his reasons may have been more selfish than selfless.

One explanation for George's behavior may be that it is more advantageous to confront an enemy in a neighbor's territory rather than your own. In helping his neighbors eject the Great Egret from Mel and Mary's nest site George simultaneously increased the security of his own nest site, or sites, by driving the Great Egret farther away from his own territory. In this view, by helping his neighbors protect their nest George turned the situation to his personal advantage by getting their help to launch a preemptive strike to push the predator farther away from his own juveniles. The juveniles, I am sadly reminded, that I did not see again today.

Field studies provide evidence of a more complex explanation. Les Beletsky explains that Red-winged Blackbirds increase their survival and breeding success by returning to the same breeding ground every year for more than one reason. The advantages are that they do not have to spend time and energy searching for a suitable spot; they already know where the sources of food are and the location of the best perches and hiding places. Birds that must spend time and energy to first acquire this knowledge are at a disadvantage from those that already have it. Additionally, says Beletsky, and this is the key point, "Familiarity with their neighboring males reduces aggression during annual territory re-establishment and over boundaries. It may also lead to improved reproductive success because long-term neighbors are quicker or more efficient mobbers of nest predators."[1] So, as a consequence of returning to the same breeding ground the Red-winged Blackbird males get to know their neighbors and that fraternization, for lack of a better term, reduces conflicts and creates allies.

Ken Yasukawa raises the possibility of one more explanation stemming from the polygynous nature of the species. In Ken's view it is likely the male Red-winged Blackbird is motivated to help protect his neighbor's nests because he may have fertilized one or more of the eggs in them. You will remember how often I describe George's efforts to keep other males out of his territory but it may well be that Mel was unable to keep George entirely out of his, although I have no proof that it is the case. It remains a strong possibility that George surreptitiously coupled with Mary. If that is true George may have gone to the defense of his neighbor's nest to protect his own offspring. Professor Yasukawa gives us an idea of how prevalent this situation can be among Red-winged Blackbirds.

> On my study area, 33 of 100 nestlings were sired by a neighboring male, not the territory owner. There is some evidence that males have some knowledge of where their "extra-pair" young are located. Males have been observed to defend nests on other territories when all of the nestlings are theirs.
>
> Both of these lines of evidence (and others) suggest that male redwings are acting in their own self-interests when they join neighbors to mob predators on other territories.[2]

How about that? These explanations, whether by themselves or taken together, present a behavioral complexity I would not have predicted.

Besides the drama of the international coalition George's Pond would have one more treat for me this day. The Black Skimmer arrived at 8:50 PM while the sunlight was sufficient for me to see it in great detail. Its long red beak was the most impressive feature because under more typical low lighting conditions I see its color so rarely.

[1]Les Beletsky, *The Red-winged Blackbird: The Biology of a Strongly Polygynous Songbird*, p. 191.

[2]Ken Yasukawa, e-mail message, March 19, 2004.

Chapter 35 · June 13

One Chick, No Photo

A light rain had begun to fall when I met Ned. He told me he had been able hear the chicks vocalizing inside the Baltimore Oriole nest near George's Pond each time one of their parents arrived. I wanted to hear them as well. Ned led me to the spot on the path beneath the nest where he had heard the nestlings. The moment the mother oriole landed near the opening of the nest we heard the babies' excited calls although we could not see them. After a brief interval we moved a respectful distance away to continue to watch as both parents made trips to and from the nest. By now you must be wondering about the fate of the Orchard Oriole nest

George puffed up his feathers to keep out the cold and damp on this late spring day. Shortly after taking this picture I had to put the camera in its case to keep it out of the rain. That would lead to one more addition to a long line of missed photo opportunities.

that had been built in the same tree. The birder grapevine reported that a flock of House Sparrows, from a communal nest in an adjacent tree, had been seen attacking them. The House Sparrows, I am told, succeeded in forcing the Orchard Orioles to abandon their nest. It has been documented that House Sparrows sometimes drive birds out of tree cavities, nests, and even nest boxes. Why these sparrows picked on the Orchard Orioles and permitted the Baltimore Orioles to remain is a mystery.[1]

On the dock we found Gordon, without an umbrella, alongside George who was standing atop the fence. The rain did not appear to inconvenience either of them. When George's mate Ruby flew by he took off after her but he did not rush. This particular flight was for demonstration purposes only. He slowly glided with his wings outstretched and did not pump them to increase his forward momentum. The red epaulets on his wings looked as if they were standing straight up. I had never seen them so elevated. I know that the epaulet feathers are attached to specialized muscles that provide the Red-winged Blackbird with a considerable range of movement depending on what signal the bird wants to send. Obviously George was signaling a very specific message to his mate. She landed on the island. So did George. She walked away. He followed. She turned to face him. I have seen this all before. It looked like we were about to witness an amorous display but the sudden appearance of one of their fledglings jarred both adults out of their romantic mood and into one of parental responsibility. Surely you parents can sympathize with these two thwarted adults?

George left Ruby's side to instead slip into the tall grass. He emerged with a small dark object in his beak. Whatever it was, it was to the fledglings' liking. It disappeared down the eager baby's gaping mouth. I had been denied an observation of Red-winged Blackbird mating behavior but I did not care because not only did I get to see his offspring after a long absence but also I saw him

---

[1] Peter E. Lowther and Calvin L. Cink, *House Sparrow,* ed. A. Poole and F. Gill, no. 12, Philadelphia.: The Academy of Natural Sciences; Washington, D.C.: The American Ornithologists' Union, 1992, p. 10.

feed it. I once wondered what kind of father George would be. I was certain he was the feeding kind after seeing him make repetitive trips to the hidden nest site to deliver soggy bread and other goodies to unseen nestlings. Really it was no surprise to see him feed the baby but it was a delight. It gave me visual proof that George is a nurturing parent. Did I obtain photographic evidence of this event? Alas, I had stashed my camera in its case to keep it dry. I did not get a photo of the baby and I had to end my session early because the rain was too intense but I was happy as I could be to have seen George interact with one of his progeny.

Chapter 36 · June 15

Adaptor Snapper

Through the bird-watchers' grapevine I heard two reports about the newest Green Heron nestlings. One story was that three Green Heron chicks had been seen standing up inside the nest. Another version was that all three chicks ventured out of the nest and had walked a short distance along the thick bough supporting it. I was unable to locate even a tiniest smidgen of the nest or bird behind the layers of leaves. I had hoped to reduce my chick deficit today by finding the third chick, but as you may recall, I still have only seen two to date.

At George's Pond, Julio informed me that only minutes before I arrived George had been at the dock and there had fed one of his

I could identify this as a Snapping Turtle and the base of the lamppost but I could not identify those little black balls on its shell? Can you?

fledglings. Timing, as they say, is everything. I had missed a chance to photograph father and child at close range. George and the baby, said Julio, had since gone to the island together. I could not find the fledgling but instead saw George chasing a Common Grackle. Immediately after dealing with the grackle George dislodged two male Red-winged Blackbird intruders from his territory. That intraspecies conflict went on for more than fifteen minutes until a victorious George perched at the top of a birch tree on the island and sang out a few choruses of "konk-la-ree." He stayed there keeping a lookout for repeat offenders or new intruders.

I visited the Baltimore Oriole parents but periodically looked back to the island to see if George might be with his offspring. He remained firmly planted alone on his perch. The Baltimore Oriole parents were in near constant motion as they took turns ferrying food. The sound of chirping chicks coming from deep inside the nest had increased to the point where many passersby who had no knowledge of the nest stopped to look up over their heads trying to figure out where all the noise was coming from. Six picnickers on two blankets directly beneath the nest however were oblivious to the vocalizations and the busily commuting adult orioles. When I moved to view the orioles from a different angle a woman among the picnickers asked me, "What are you looking at up there?" After I explained to her what was going on above our heads all conversation ceased and all eyes turned upward. A male picnicker expressed the group's incredulity with a common expletive I will not repeat here. However their initial disbelief soon evaporated. During the next few minutes they watched Papa and Mama Baltimore Oriole as if mesmerized. When the picnickers concentrated by blocking out the extraneous noises they could hear the excited babies chirping inside when their parents poked their heads into the nest to deliver a meal. By the time I got on my way all the picnickers were standing, their voices silent, heads tilted back at the same sharp angle and their eyes fixed on the birds at the nest. From the impact these Baltimore Orioles had on the picnickers I would not be surprised if a bird-watcher or two may have been created during that experience.

I had tickets for the 92nd Street Y's Lyrics and Lyricists program, a traditional New York experience, at 8:00 PM. Consequently I had planned a short birding session but I had dawdled and was a half hour behind schedule when I started for home. Along the winding path at the northeast end of George's Pond a stranger stopped me. He had concluded from the binoculars around my neck and camera on a monopod that I was a naturalist of sorts. He was in need of one. The fellow said, "Do you know anything about turtles because there is a big one digging a hole in the ground over there." He pointed to a group of ten or so people standing in front of a street lamp. I could not see a turtle of any size but was curious to see what had caught the crowd's attention.

I have only a smattering of turtle knowledge, but I recognized this specimen as a fair sized Snapping Turtle. Its hind legs were slowly and methodically excavating a hole two or three inches deep at the base of the lamppost. Members of the crowd freely expressed their personal opinions and impressions about the turtle and made suggestions about possible actions that might be taken. "I think it's sick," one said. "Someone should go for help," said another. One young fellow found the presence of the reptile disconcerting. He asked no one in particular though with a great deal of urgency, "Maybe we should call the police?" "It might be lost and we should put it back in the water," another said to which a more knowledgeable observer added, "That's a good way to lose a finger." I wondered if these onlookers had watched one too many disaster movies to come up with these negative appraisals of the turtle's situation. The creature was exhibiting a benign and quite natural behavior. I surmised that this Snapping Turtle, a female, had exited the water, crawled through the thick shore vegetation, crossed a patch of open lawn and had chosen this heavily trafficked spot in which to dig a nest and lay her eggs. While the crowd deliberated the turtle paid no attention. It continued to laboriously burrow unaffected by the presence of the opinionated

New Yorkers. Like generations of Snapping Turtles before it this individual has found a way to adapt to a world in which humans are inescapable. The turtle had decided this was a reasonable location for the job at hand and was determined that the onlookers would not deter it. Of course the metal wire mesh fence between it and the crowd helped make that possible. I advised the group of my assessment of the turtle's behavior and that no action on their part was required. I explained that while this was not an everyday occurrence in Central Park it was quite natural and not an aberration of some kind. The turtle would dig a hole, deposit eggs, cover them over and return to the pond. My words were heeded. The crowd dispersed. I wanted to stay to offer the turtle whatever protection I could from further curious passersby but I had to hurry away. I hoped that newcomers would have the good sense to leave it alone but I had more confidence that the turtle knew what it was doing and had the situation under control, or so I told myself.

I have heard stories that Snapping Turtles have been found in other unusual places in the park during breeding season. There is one story that is told and retold about one large snapper (it gets larger with each retelling) that had crawled onto the Central Park West Drive where it was hit by a car. Its shell was damaged but the turtle survived. A kindly person promptly contacted the park authorities. They captured the turtle and brought it to an individual who specializes in the care of such casualties. The turtle was nursed back to health and released into the park where one hopes it would be more careful in the future when crossing the street. A policeman, pounding a park beat, told me that over the years he has encountered similar situations. Though the turtles are rarely seriously injured they do get into predicaments. However I have heard of one fatality that occurred on the Central Park East Drive. I guess that is inescapable unless the turtles learn to avoid active roadways or the roadways are closed to traffic. (Hint, hint.)

One might deduce from those anecdotes that Snapping Turtles are incorrigible. I do not have sufficient information to form an opinion on that score but I can tell you what is known about their general disposition. They are, if you did not know, tough omnivorous predators. Throughout the year they consume fish, amphibians, insects, small mammals and even ducklings. It is entirely possible that the turtle digging at the lamppost was responsible for one or more of the missing ducklings on George's Pond. Perhaps even more ducklings would be missing if Snapping Turtles did not supplement their diet in spring and summer with large amounts of vegetation. I assume they have healthy appetites because they can grow to considerable size. The length of the shell alone can extend to eighteen inches and they have been known to reach seventy pounds though they average thirty-five. Their heads, jaws, legs, claws and tails are larger in proportion to the rest of their bodies than other species'. That makes them easier to distinguish. They inhabit ponds, shallow streams and rivers from southern Canada to southern Ecuador. I have read that they do most of their hunting and egg laying at night but Central Park Snapping Turtles, if the ones I have encountered are examples, appear to march to a different drummer. On warm days it is not strange to see one or two in broad daylight in George's Pond or the Lake. However it is a fairly rare occurrence to see a female digging her nest here in the afternoon and in a place one might prefer not to encounter a Snapping Turtle at all. In the water they are known to avoid confrontations with humans but on land they are more inclined to bite or claw if they feel threatened. That is because they are much more maneuverable in the water. On land, out of their element, where their range and speed of movement are limited they are more likely to fight than flee since they cannot get out of harm's way quickly. Besides jaws and claws this species has another rather curious defense mechanism. When provoked Snapping Turtles may emit an extremely unpleasant odor from the opening at the end of the digestive tract. I have not been bitten, clawed or perfumed by a Snapping Turtle. By maintaining a respectful distance between us I hope to keep it that way.[1]

[1]Chesapeakbay.net, *Common Snapping Turtle: Chelydra Serpentina Serpentina*, Chesapeake Bay Program, 2003.

Chapter 37 · June 16 and 17

A Chick off the Old George

Yesterday, June 16th, I found George with both fledglings. Hooray! To be precise I actually heard them for a much longer period than I saw them. The vocal trio moved around the island and the pond's western shoreline where the frantic begging of one baby or the other was silenced by George's well-aimed insertion of a beak full of food. Every few minutes George broke away from the fledglings to chase male Red-winged Blackbird intruders. Once they were routed George rushed back to the fledglings. I have seen

At long last I was able to get a photograph of one of George's juveniles. Both female and male juvenile Red-winged Blackbirds strongly resemble the adult female. This plumage helps to camouflage the juveniles from would be predators and signals adult males that they are children and do not pose a threat. Male juveniles will gradually attain their black plumage and scarlet epaulets in about a year.

George display great energy before but never quite like this. The scene has answered any doubts I had about the total number of offspring but raised questions about the females. First of all, where are they? Secondly was Ruby the mother of both fledglings or was one the child of his other mate? There were no immediate answers to these questions.

The Baltimore Oriole parents were much in evidence too. They were actively shuttling sustenance to the nest. Although I could not see them the nestlings could be heard from a farther distance than before and they have added something to this nest watching experience. When the hidden chicks vocalize the entire nest shakes. The motions are a consequence of their vibrating wings, which cannot be seen but I assume to be part of their begging behavior. Shoving one another to get into the best feeding position may have even more to do with it. The vigorous way the chicks move the nest makes me suspect that it will not be long before they have the strength to fledge and leave it forever.

Back on the dock I settled in to observe George with his family and enjoy a sampling of the other birds that were present. There was a bonus sighting of two Green Herons and two Great Egrets all appearing at the same time on the island. On the water the Mallard ducklings foraged with their mothers and the Canada Geese goslings maintained their trademark single file line while crossing the length of the pond. After sunset most of the birds had retired except for one Black-crowned Night Heron that gave two barks before falling silent. But the surrounding area was anything but quiet. Tens of thousands of people were on the Great Lawn listening to an outdoor performance of Gaetano Donizetti's *Lucia di Lammermoor* by the New York Metropolitan Opera. When the Black Skimmer showed up at 9:15 PM to systematically work the pond very few in the opera audience noticed it because they faced in the opposite direction toward the stage. Think of what they had missed. If they had turned around an audience of hundreds if not thousands would have enjoyed watching the skimmer to the music of *Lucia di Lammermoor*. That is not something you can do every day, not even in New York.

Today, June 17th, the sunshine was exceptionally bright. I was keen to take advantage of the light for viewing birds and shooting photographs but by the time I got to the park clouds had rolled in and the brilliant glow was replaced with a dull diffused luminosity. Sigh. I got over my disappointment when I saw George accompanied by both his offspring. At last I was presented with the opportunity to photograph the fledglings where they stood with their father on the top of the fence at the dock. I should not have been surprised to see George taking seeds from two Club George charter members and redistributing them into the beak of one excited fledgling and then the other, but I was. The fledglings really did not need George's assistance. They have already progressed to the stage where they are able to take nourishment on their own but with limitations. Their tiny beaks cannot break up relatively large or hard pieces of foods like a bit of peanut, for example, but they went to town on bread crumbs, wild birdseed and sunflower seeds. It impressed me that George allowed his chicks to be close to us but I was bowled over to find him content to leave them alone with the Club George charter members at least for short periods. While he raced off in pursuit of a male Red-winged Blackbird and later a Common Grackle the two fledglings remained behind on the fence. I thought surely the little ones would flee and hide when George left them but they stayed put gobbling up the bounty placed at their feet. It was evident that these youngsters are a "chick off the old George," so to speak. Like their dad they exhibited a degree of trust of humans; at least of those providing a free meal. In contrast their mother (or is it mothers?) are shy and wary of even the most loyal and familiar Club George charter members.

I had altered my itinerary to visit George's Pond in the hopes that by arriving at a different time of day than I normally do I might find George's fledglings. My route change had paid off and I had the opportunity to photograph the youngsters but now I felt the need to at least make a quick survey of my other favorites. I was able to see Morton Downy and many of the usual suspects around his watering hole. When all the birds scattered and were quickly out of sight I knew a predator of some sort had prompted their reaction but I never did locate the creature responsible for the evacuation.

On the way back to George's Pond, for the second visit on the same day, I turned a corner and found myself about five feet from a Northern Flicker with its beak jammed into a pencil thin hole in the ground where it was collecting ants on its sticky tongue. I froze. I have never been this close to a Northern Flicker before. I had always found them to be shy and evasive. They typically scram when they see me coming. So you will understand why this was an especially fortuitous encounter. Ever so slowly I began to raise my camera into position but with each fraction of a movement the Northern Flicker stopped to look up as if considering whether it would flee or continue to eat ants. Each time the bird resumed its movements I resumed mine. Finally I had my camera in position. All that there remained to do was put the image into focus. The Northern Flicker had tolerated all my actions up to that point but when I twisted the manual focus ring on the camera lens the bird took great exception to it and bolted. Oh cruel but beauteous Northern Flicker! I vow to get your photo even if it will not be today.

Back at the Baltimore Oriole nest I did not see or hear activity. Later I learned through the birders' grapevine that the oriole chicks were said to have fledged earlier that morning. I had guessed this was about to happen from the violent way the nestlings had begun to shake the nest. If they remained inside any longer I feared they would be in danger of dislodging it from its moorings. Now that they were gone I no longer feared the hanging nest was in danger of crashing to the ground though it probably never was. Knowing the chicks had fledged I will pay more attention to the birds foraging on the ground in the area surrounding the nest site. With luck I hope to find the oriole fledglings with their parents foraging there together.

George, during my second visit, guided his fledglings around his island headquarters eventually leading them to a pinpoint landing on top of the fence at the dock. Once the three were assembled there George began singing, calling and displaying while Club George charter members paid rapt attention and made offerings of food. When his kids started to join in it began to look as if George were instructing them in the art of interspecies communication. The two emulated parts of George's vocal presentation but jazzed it up with their fledgling wing vibrations that used to consistently motivate Dad to feed them but was only working sporadically today. George fed them every so often but more and more they had to fend for themselves if they wanted to eat. I realized George was not being neglectful but instead had begun to wean the fledglings. The babies picked up seeds people placed on the fence but after a while they were not satisfied to wait for the food to be delivered. They made loud "chek" calls to demand our attention like their father before them. Their vocabulary did not include George's nuanced variations of the "chek" call, they did not sing the "konk-la-ree" song or display their as yet indistinct epaulets but their efforts got the desired results nonetheless.

Other family activities were on view around the pond. The Mallard ducklings were paddling with their moms. The Canada Goose goslings with both parents were doing likewise. I took note of the palpable signs that the ducklings and goslings are maturing at a ferocious rate. The goslings, for example, are showing the growth of primary flight feathers on their developing wings. They have lost almost all the greenish yellow down that had covered them from birth but retain a hint of it on their heads and their necks.

While Ned and I examined the goslings more closely a birder I did not know came to the end of the dock to stand beside me. She introduced herself as Joanna and was also fascinated by the goslings but for different reasons. She reminded us that in many communities Canada Geese are considered pests. Putting it bluntly Canada Geese are widely disparaged, especially in suburbia, where they range over fields, lawns and parking lots, like that one in Mahwah, New Jersey, where I learned firsthand about their nesting behaviors, nibbling grass in flocks of ten to one hundred or more where they poop all over the place. Parents have justifiable concerns about the prodigious amount of organic waste material the geese deposit on playgrounds and backyards where children play. Canada Geese are also perceived as pests in agricultural areas because they devour a

considerable amount of commercial crops. Significantly reduced in
numbers by hunters they have made a terrific comeback since the
1970s. There are so many that the population can absorb the loss of
two million in the United States and six hundred thousand in
Canada during hunting season every year and still total about five
million individuals in the breeding season.[1] Governments supposedly control the numbers that can be hunted but every now and
then I read about a community making a special effort to trim down
their local Canada Goose population for one reason or another. On
George's Pond I have watched these geese devour grasses and
flower stalks right down to the roots. At times they eat the roots as
well. On a small pond like George's Pond eight Canada Geese
could do measurable damage to the plants and unasked they spread
organic fertilizer over the meadow where folks like to picnic. I
would not be surprised to find that the park's administrators take
action to discourage their continued presence here. For now, at
least, the Canada Goose family remains for all to enjoy despite what
some consider their unhygienic and destructive habits.

As most folks drifted out of the park I remained with Joanna
and Ned discussing the pros and cons of Canada Geese behaviors
while we waited to see the Black Skimmer. I ran out of patience and
gave up my watch but when I stopped on the rock at the east end of
George's Pond for a last look a Black Skimmer glided by and one
word popped out of my mouth: "Excellent."

[1]Thomas B. Mowbray, Craig R. Ely, James S. Sedinger, and Robert E. Trost, *Canada Goose*,
pp. 28–31.

Chapter 38 · June 18

Replay or New Play?

did not see many birds as I entered the park. Such a poor beginning often gives me the feeling that I will have a completely uneventful walk but I tried to push aside feelings of negativity and reminded myself nearly every day brings something new and noteworthy: it may be subtle or it may be startling but it is guaranteed to be neither if one is not receptive. But when I saw three Blue Jays, a Red-winged Blackbird and three Northern Cardinals at Morton's Pond I thought to myself, "Oh, those guys again." I had the feeling that my bird-watching was becoming routine. That was before all of those birds came together in the same shrub at the same time. The juxtaposition of their colorful plumage and the amazing coinci-

Was this the same Snapping Turtle demonstrating the maxim, "If at first you don't succeed, lay, lay an egg"? Or was it another turtle?

dence that they would all choose to perch there at once was, and there is no other word for it, stunning. This is an important lesson that I learned and I hope to pass on to beginning birders and even some of you that have been at it a while. As you gain experience be on your guard not to become jaded. A jaded bird-watcher is an inattentive one. An inattentive bird-watcher is sure to miss something wonderful right under his or her nose and one should always know what is happening under one's nose regardless if one is a bird-watcher or not. Who could argue with that?

On the path leading to George's Pond I found something right under my nose that I might have missed if I had only been looking up instead of all around. Alongside the same lamppost where a crowd had gathered on June fifteenth to watch a Snapping Turtle dig a hole I found another turtle doing almost precisely the same thing. The difference was that the previous turtle dug on the east side of the pole. This turtle dug on the west. Her posterior was at the bottom of a shallow but wide hole cut through the turf and into the muddy earth below. The first question that came to mind was if this were the same female I had seen before or a different one. Could this be a replay or a new play with a different player?

Snapping Turtles lay one clutch of eggs a season. If this was the same turtle her reappearance implied that her earlier attempt to lay eggs had not been successful and she had come back determined to get the job done. That theory did not entirely appeal to me because it seemed more than a small coincidence to find a Snapping Turtle three days later digging a nest virtually in the same spot.

Might it be a different turtle? I examined this specimen to see if I could find any recognizable features to distinguish it from the previous one. Instead of a difference I found a slight but peculiar similarity. Both Snapping Turtles had small mysterious black balls attached to their shell. The first turtle had three of these but they, if memory serves me well, were positioned differently. Scrutinizing the small objects on this turtle's shell more closely than I had on my previous encounter I thought that the black balls were a wild fruit or berry, possibly a cherry of some sort. I imagine that as the turtle traveled between the pond and the lamppost it passed under a tree where the fruit, if that is what it is, fell and stuck to it. Come to think of it the turtle could have been eating the fruit. They do eat vegetable matter after all. I concluded that there really was no way for me to resolve whether she was the same or a different turtle. I watched her dig a while longer before deciding to give her some privacy in which to get her job done.

Farther along the same path I heard chirping coming from the Baltimore Oriole nest that I had been told and had believed had been deserted. Could another species have commandeered the nest or were the Baltimore Oriole nestlings still inside? I backed away to get a better viewing angle and presently the adult female Baltimore Oriole arrived to make a food delivery. When Mama leaned over the opening of the nest it began to shake and I could hear what sounded like whining. There had to be baby orioles inside. Mama made more deliveries. So did Papa but more often he stood on a branch high above keeping a lookout for predators. There could be no doubt about it. This was one time that the bird-watchers' grapevine had it all wrong.

George like his Baltimore Oriole relative was on guard duty. He however did more than simply watch; he fought. I watched George summarily repel several intruders but his assault on a Black-crowned Night Heron was a standout. When the Black-crowned Night Heron came unnervingly close to one of George's fledglings foraging in the phragmites George pounced. The ferocity of George's screams, lunges and one well positioned energetic dive into the heron's back drove it away within a few seconds. Rarely have I seen one of George's attacks produce positive effects so quickly. Good job Georgie boy.

Later in the evening I was with two frequent companions and a few unfamiliar birders who, having read my reports via the Internet about Black Skimmer visits to the pond, came to see them. Time passed and when the skimmer did not arrive these newcomers began to joke that my stories about sightings of the Black Skimmer were exaggerated. One of my companions interpreted these jests as jeers. I withheld judgment but when the jests careered past jeers to become taunts I grew defensive. If I ever needed the Black Skimmer to make an entrance it was at this moment but, alas, that was not to be.

Much of what bird-watchers report to one another must be taken on faith. Mistrust about sightings is reserved for those considered to be inexperienced or unreliable observers. This was the first time that others had not only doubted the level of my skill but my veracity as well. Their cynicism was hard to bear but there was little I could do about it. The others would only believe their own eyes. The only proof they would accept was in the form of the Black Skimmer itself.

Beginning bird-watchers be prepared to stick to your story when you are absolutely sure you are right but you may find on occasion that it helps to have the bird show up in the nick of time, and sometimes it won't.

First Club George Charter Member

found George chasing a rival male after which he resumed patrolling the perimeter of his realm occasionally stopping to display his epaulets and sing a chorus of "konk-la-ree." When he touched down on the top of the fence three Club George charter members were waiting in line vying to be the one to feed him. George had his pick of this smorgasbord. He chose sunflower seeds over bread crumbs and birdseed much to the delight of one and the disappointment of two other Club George charter members. It's the little things in life that make some people happy. Of course, I speak from experience on that score.

I did not see either of George's fledglings, but both his mates

I created the Club George Charter Member cards as a token of appreciation and fellowship. But who would be the first recipient?

came to the dock. I recognized Ruby and the other female with the brown epaulets and wondered why, after all this time, her fans had not settled on a definite name for her. Some who cannot tell them apart refer indiscriminately to either female as Georgette. That is a fine name and surely the combination of "George and Georgette" is appealing but I have resisted adopting it myself because it does not differentiate between the two females. That not only bothered me because it was inaccurate but also it seemed, to diminish their individual importance. I considered this as the two female Red-winged Blackbirds walked on the dock. A young mother with her eight-year-old daughter was watching them too and they asked me about the two birds. Neither the woman nor her daughter was a bird-watcher but they both had keen powers of observation. Unlike some experienced birders they recognized subtle differences about the two birds and could tell they were not the same species as the House Sparrows with which they intermingled. I explained to the woman and her daughter that these particular Red-winged Blackbirds were George's mates and I used the named Ruby to describe one of them. The little girl wanted to know the other bird's name. I told her she did not have a name and asked her to suggest one. Without hesitation she said "Claudia" with feeling and conviction. I found her instant enthusiastic response irresistible. As of that moment I would call this particular female Red-winged Blackbird Claudia and I would encourage other Club George charter members to use it too. Surely you would have asked the little girl why she had chosen the name Claudia just as I did? She gave a classic eight year old's rationale: "Because I like it." That was good enough for me.

Comparing the two birds side by side I noted that Claudia's throat is noticeably more peachier in color than Ruby's. In the future Claudia's more peachier throat will be an aid in helping me to identify her just as Ruby's red epaulets have been. The more time I spend in a specific territory like George's or Morton's Pond the more I want to be able to identify individual birds that regularly appear. To get to know more about them I must first be able to physically distinguish them from others of their species. In the case of

Ruby and Claudia, I have gone through a lengthy process looking for ways to tell them apart. I have finally found definitive markings that will be useful going forward. I would hope it would not take me nearly as long to accomplish this with other birds like the Blue Jays at Morton's Pond for example, but that may just be wishful thinking. The physical differences between individuals of a species can be too small to be meaningful if they can be detected at all. This is why ornithologists studying in the field tag individual birds with color-coded leg bands or dye a feather or two. It is the only way to do an accurate study of an avian community.

When Kim, a Club George charter member, arrived at the dock she asked me to fill her in on some of my recent sightings not the least of which was that of the Snapping Turtle digging at the base of the lamppost. She was intrigued by this story and asked me to show her the spot. The turtle was absent, as I expected, but the hole was much in evidence. It did not appear to have been filled in. I wondered if any turtle eggs had been laid in it after all or if its uncovered state meant a raccoon or another predator had feasted on them during the night.

All along I have been referring to various people as Club George charter members but actually I have shared this designation only with my closest bird-watching associates. As a group New York City bird-watchers, in my experience, are not easily given to expressions of solidarity. While they may willingly share factual information (e.g., the location of an interesting bird) they are less likely to share their feelings (e.g., saying they are fond of George) unless it is to complain (e.g., dogs should be kept on their leashes). Relatively speaking complaints are freely expressed. For weeks I had been thinking about finding a way for these independent bird-watchers, many of whom are strangers, to come closer together to share their feelings about George in particular and all birds in general but in a casual noncommittal way. One of my photographs of George gave me the inspiration for a way I might do it. With the use of George's image I created a token of appreciation and fellowship that could be distributed to enthusiasts I recognized to be Club George charter members even if they themselves were unaware they belonged. Standing with Kim over the muddy hole in the ground that either currently, had never, or had at one time contained Snapping Turtle eggs, I could think of no one who better exemplified the qualities of a Club George charter member than she. So, it was a pleasure to select Kim as the first recipient of a wallet-sized full color Club George charter member card. She loved it, as I knew she would.

Returning to the dock Kim and I found several bird-watchers gathered to look for the Black Skimmer. I handed out Club George cards to them. They each responded with the identical response: a hearty laugh and a sincere thank you.

The cards proved to be an excellent icebreaker. The now smiling, laughing, joking birders lingered on into the evening to maintain a Black Skimmer vigil for about forty-five minutes. There was growing edginess however and one bird-watcher decided to leave but before he did he told the group, "I volunteer to be the sacrificial birder. As soon as I'm gone the Black Skimmer will show up." We chuckled in recognition of the times we each had been told that others had seen an elusive bird after we ourselves had given up waiting for it and departed. The skimmer however was not in tune with this concept, as far as I could tell. After waiting another fifteen minutes I too gave up waiting and headed for home. Three intrepid bird-watchers remained behind. As I walked away I silently wondered if my departure would be the decisive factor in summoning the Black Skimmer. The three birders who stayed behind were from out of town and only visiting for the day. I never did find out if the Black Skimmer made an appearance and whether or not they found the sacrificial birder theory had any validity.

Chapter 40 · June 20

Oriole Rescue

A Tufted Titmouse asked me for a tidbit upon my arrival at Morton's Pond. The little guy buzzed around my head until I responded to its actions with an offering. Many of the neighborhood birds watched statuelike as the titmouse carried on. These other birds seemed unusually attentive. I felt as if dozens of tiny eyes were drilling into me. When the titmouse left some of the observers went into action. No less than ten House Sparrows took food from my hand over the next half hour. I have known these birds to do this now and then but this was the first time they vied with one another to get to my palm first. Other pond aficionados included a male and female Northern Cardinal, three Blue Jays, a

This is Charlie the Red-winged Blackbird who has a unique peanut snatching style. It's not as sophisticated as George's but it gets the job done.

female Red-bellied Woodpecker, several Common Grackles and eventually Morton, the Downy Woodpecker. A Red-winged Blackbird came screaming "seer-seer-seer" through the trees and made a beeline toward me. He bounced off my hand three times, grabbing a morsel each time he made contact and then disappeared into the woods. This was the unmistakable peanut snatching style of Charlie, the Red-winged Blackbird. His companion Squeaky arrived with him but behaved in his more reserved and cautious manner.

The sky was heavily overcast and occasionally a fine drizzle fell. It was unseasonably cool for a late June day and consequently very few people were in the park. I was having great fun with the birds at Morton's Pond but I planned to go on to conduct a shortened version of my routine because I feared the unattractive weather might turn ugly. I saw few people as I moved briskly along until I came to the northern shore of George's Pond where I met two bird-watchers, Betsey and Ralph. They were deliberating what to do about the plight of a baby Baltimore Oriole. The fledgling chick had tumbled from a low branch into a patch of phragmites, sedges and flower stalks at the edge of the water. The chick had been swallowed up by the thick vegetation and could not make its way out. The frantic Baltimore Oriole parents zigzagged over and around the vicinity where the frightened chick called out but they took no action to rescue their child. Betsey had to leave the scene but Ralph and I remained considering what to do. Ralph was conflicted. His dilemma was whether or not he should interfere and rescue the chick or leave it to its fate. Even if he did rescue it there was no guarantee it was not injured or that it could or would be cared for by its parents. I had no ambivalence whatsoever. In my mind there was no question of what to do. I would try to recover it. The positions of the two adult orioles gave me a general idea of where the chick was stranded but Ralph gave me a more precise idea of its location. Then I climbed over the three-foot high wire fence and began to search. That was all it took to change Ralph's mind. In fact he assumed control of the rescue mission. Leaning over a second wire fence he began to systematically part the plants looking for the baby. After a nerve-wracking two minutes that seemed like ten he turned toward me with a huge grin on his face. In his cupped hands he held up the tiny bird he had brought to safety and what a cutie pie it was. Ralph placed the chick on the lawn under the tree where it originally took its fateful tumble. After we backed away its parents sped to its side. Mercifully after much manic chattering and gyrating the three birds flew off together. The baby seemed unharmed by its harrowing ordeal as far as we could tell. The fact that it could fly was a sign that it was in good condition.

From the path behind us we heard the motor of an approaching vehicle. It stopped and a park employee spoke to us as he rolled down a window. I knew what was coming. He admonished us not to interfere in this way again because in these situations we should "leave it to nature" to decide an animal's fate. I understand the reasons for that position but it is not one I personally can support. I mean just consider if it had been a person and not a bird that had fallen down. Why wouldn't I try to be of assistance? Wouldn't you? Similarly if it had been someone's pet I would have done the same so why not for an oriole? I was proud of our response and delighted that Ralph had reunited this hapless baby with its parents.

When I later told my friends about Ralph's rescue of the baby oriole it dawned on me that I had passed up a rare photo opportunity. While engaged in the performance of the rescue mission I had not thought of taking a photo of either the chick or its parents. I had been utterly absorbed with the fate of the fledgling and did not have the presence of mind to take my camera out of its case. This was to become one more story, albeit a dramatic one, about the photograph that got away.

An unanswered question presented itself on further discussions about this incident. We had found one baby from the Baltimore Oriole nest but how many chicks were there in total? The grapevine had it that there were two that had survived and fledged. If the second had perished and a sole chick had survived it was one more reason to consider Ralph's rescue the right thing to do. If Ralph had not saved this chick the parent's efforts to breed for the season would have been a total failure as Baltimore Orioles only have one brood a year.

My planned short walk lengthened considerably when I decided to stay with a few others to wait for the Black Skimmer. An unfamiliar bird-watcher introduced herself as Isabel, a Portuguese surgeon, oncologist and amateur naturalist participating in a seminar at Sloan Kettering Hospital. This was Isabel's second attempt to see the skimmer, her first being unsuccessful. The Black Skimmer made Isabel's day by putting in an appearance and giving her a unique New York story to tell the folks, in Portuguese of course, back home: "Hello, Mom? You won't believe what I saw in Central Park today."

To top off this bird-watching session one of our group in the know took us to the site of a Cedar Waxwing nest. I had heard of its existence but did not know its precise location. It was after sunset but there was still enough light for us to see the nest situated between the outer branches of a Weeping Willow Tree. This nest site will be one more treat for the coming weeks. As I looked at it I silently hoped that the Cedar Waxwing family would escape any unfortunate situations like the one that befell the Baltimore Orioles and I remembered Ned's repeated warnings about the pitfalls of becoming attached to nesting birds. All birders, not just beginners, must keep in mind that there is always the potential for accidents, like the one involving the baby oriole, threats from disease, predators or some unpredictable environmental change that can prove fatal to breeding birds and their progeny. Clutches of eggs, brooded nestlings or new fledglings are all vulnerable.

Chapter 41 · June 22

The Masked Duck

This afternoon I visited friends, of the human species, on the Upper West Side of Manhattan. I brought along my binoculars and camera because after my social call I would be in a convenient location to explore the northernmost third of Central Park where I seldom venture. The middle third, an area of about three hundred acres, is the section I visit most often because it is closest to home. I try to visit different areas when I have reason to travel to other neighborhoods adjacent to the park but an opportunity had not

This is the domestic Muskovy Duck with its lox colored mask. The wild Muskovy is an even more exotic looking creature. They are mostly black but with a metallic green sheen. The only white coloration on the wild Muskovy is a small patch on the wings. They range in size from twenty-five to thirty-five inches in length. In comparison the average Mallard is about twenty-three inches long. This Muskovy is a big duck.

presented itself for a while. So I was very enthusiastic about a chance to enter the park at West 106th Street even though it was cold and drizzling. I carried an umbrella and my camera was mainly kept in its case. My binoculars did not get much use either. I tucked them under my jacket where they remained most of the time. When I first took my binoculars out they became completely fogged over. My body heat trapped under my jacket had warmed them. The moment they came into contact with the cold damp air water vapor condensed on the lenses. After I carefully wiped the lenses dry I raised the binoculars into position against my eyeglasses and, to my consternation, my eyeglass lenses fogged up for the same reasons. At first I was not sure how to cope with this complication but the solution was simple if not awkward. I had to wait and allow my binoculars to cool in the open air to the same temperature as my eyeglasses while keeping both sets of lenses dry before my next attempt to bring them into contact. This annoying episode illustrates how unexpected problems can arise and how the intrepid bird-watcher must be resourceful and ready to overcome them in the field. In this case I probably should have quit and gone home, but I can be quite determined if not downright stubborn as if you did not know by now. As it turned out if I had allowed my two sets of fogged up lenses to drive me indoors I would have missed an encounter with an unexpected critter.

At the entrance on West 106th street I had climbed a long steep staircase cut into the side of a hill. I was not familiar with the terrain at the top and did not know where the more scenic spots might be. My unfamiliarity of the area became a nonissue as I found myself beside the Pool, a small pond that had just undergone extensive renovation. The fresh landscaping looked too organized to be natural, but I was sure by the end of this growing season it would lose its manicured appearance after the plants spread out in unpredictable directions. The birds did not betray any reservations about the landscaping.

Over the water Northern Rough-winged Swallows and Barn Swallows swirled about conducting their aerial bug collecting business. I could only estimate the quantities of them because they were rapidly crisscrossing paths while racing through figure eights and tight loops but I estimate there had to be more than twenty-four individuals. As hard as it was to count the swallows I was at a loss to identify a bird on the shore nibbling vegetation and slowly working its way in my direction. This creature looked a bit like a duck but its size suggested it might be a goose. Its most arresting feature was a fleshy salmon colored mask on its face. The mask looked like a thick lumpy slice of lox as might be carved by a first day novice at a New York delicatessen counter. Later I identified this bird as a white form of domestic Muscovy Duck that had either escaped or had been abandoned. They are bred for the dinner table and not for the wild or for public parks. Precisely how did it get here? Who knows, but I imagined it was enjoying its freedom, the lush if a bit too symmetrical landscaping, and the wet weather more than I. After all, it was in its "natural" element and the originally intended fate for this creature was a far less attractive alternative, don't you agree?

The drizzle began falling harder and there were fewer birds to see or hear as I moved east. Some American Robins, Common Grackles, European Starlings and House Sparrows were to be seen, but only fleetingly one or two at a time. Unfortunately the weather kept me from taking full advantage of my location as I sought more familiar territory to the south where I knew I could find shelter from the rain in a hurry should I need to. When I reached the reservoir I was more at home with the landscape but it too was sparsely populated with either birds or people. I spent some time trying to photograph a Double-crested Cormorant but the hyperactive waterfowl repeated its dives so speedily that after it resurfaced it would dive again before I could get my camera lined up on its new position. On the opposite shore there was a Great Egret and Ring-billed and Great Black-backed Gulls along with a gull species or two floating on the Reservoir that were too far away for me to identify.

I had been walking for about two hours by the time I came to the dock. I heard George calling from a distance and soon found him sitting in his Weeping Willow Tree on his side of the invisible boundary. His neighbor Mel was sitting in his Weeping Willow Tree on the other side of the dividing line. The inclement weather had convinced the other neighborhood birds to seek shelter but these two Red-winged Blackbirds were undaunted. Despite the rain it was business as usual for George and Mel though it did seem they were taking time out to consort with one another rather than forage or patrol.

Four bird-watchers I did not recognize joined me on the dock. One began waving a piece of bread in the air and calling out, "Larry, Larry." "I call him George," I said understanding at once that he was looking for the famous Red-winged Blackbird. I assured this fellow that he did not have to call out and wave a bribe of food in the air because George would be along soon enough. And so he was. The four birders took turns feeding George taking obvious joy in it. Before they left I gathered from their conversation that one of them was a science writer for a major New York newspaper. I kept an eye out for his column in the paper for months afterward but I never discovered if George had been the subject of his writing.

When these four were gone four more familiar bird-watchers replaced them. Their mission was not to see George but to see the Black Skimmer. Throughout the duration of our group skimmer watch, dress rehearsals for Shakespeare's *Henry V* were progressing in the Delacorte Theater. More precisely I think this was what might be called a technical rehearsal. The director and crew were working on synchronizing sound effects simulating an explosion of considerable magnitude for a battle scene. The director was obviously displeased with the results because the explosion was repeated over and over again. I started to count but soon lost track of how many times it recurred. At first all the birders ignored the noise but that was short-lived. The noise came to dominate our consciousness and the topic of our conversation. Curiously some of the pond's inhabitants were not as distressed by the sound effects as much as the birders were. The Mallard ducklings and their mothers were preening along the shore. The Canada Goose goslings and their parents were doing the same on the flat rock that is remarkably close to the rear of the Delacorte stage. The waterfowl did not seem to care about the boisterous booming that was making the bird-watchers increasingly crabby. The play's director was either finally satisfied with the sound effects or reached a point where he could not stand it either. In any event the crashing crescendos ceased and the pond became serene but the bird-watchers had lost their enthusiasm somewhere between the bouts of natural drizzle and those of special effect explosions. By 9:30 PM the Black Skimmer had not arrived and all the birders departed not having the collective patience of a single solitary waterfowl to remain.

Chapter 42 · June 23

The Art of Bat Detection

Yesterday's rain pushed the total June precipitation to a record high in New York State. The low temperature was not a record but a maximum of sixty degrees was nonetheless uncharacteristic for a late June day. Today the clouds were gone but the humidity remained and the temperature rocketed into the high eighties. Summer made a powerful move to reassert itself.

I thought the birds would be conspicuously taking advantage of summer's restoration but my initial observations and those I heard from the bird-watching community indicated that was generally not the case. At Morton's Pond however the usual suspects acted independently. There I found myself in the company of a dozen Com-

George paused to choose what he would peck next. It was a bit of food. Not the hand.

mon Grackles, even more House Sparrows, two Mourning Doves and a few Rock Pigeons. Morton Downy came along and soon after so did a Tufted Titmouse and a Blue Jay but the image that stayed with me for hours afterward was that of a male Northern Cardinal gingerly placing food inside his mate's beak. No matter how many times I have watched this, and with my newfound awareness it has become an increasingly common sight at this time of year, I never cease to be entertained and, I freely admit, touched by it. I have not been successful photographing one cardinal feeding another though I have tried many times. I have always caught them in the act where branches and leaves shield them from predators and photographers. If I could learn to identify any signs they make to hint the cardinals were about to exchange food I may gain the few seconds needed to get into a position to photograph it. In my readings on this subject there is one particular twist I have witnessed that I have not found reported by others. On that occasion I saw a female Northern Cardinal give food to a male. The texts describe the male as the one to pass food to the female and not the other way around.

Ned came along amid this flurry of bird activity at Morton's Pond but too late to witness Northern Cardinals feeding one another. He expressed the widely shared complaint about the scarcity of birds but here, though he had already seen most of the species present, he could at least add a Tufted Titmouse to his daily list. How many species had Ned seen so far? He had identified twenty-one different species and thought that was disappointing. How many had I seen? I counted up the species I had recognized and could only come up with thirteen. Comparing my daily count to Ned's drew my attention to the fact that my bird-watching skills still need upgrading: big-time.

Ned had come directly from the Green Heron nest where he saw three nestlings. That was not startling, but his next bit of news was. A third Green Heron brood is being raised in their breeding ground. Ned volunteered to return with me to the area and show me where to find the newest nest. When we reached our destination we could account for only two of the older nestlings in the earlier or second nest. An adult was sitting on the latest or third nest. If there were nestlings inside we did not see them. At this point if you cannot keep track of how many nests there are and how many birds are in each I cannot blame you. It is getting rather difficult for the bird-watchers to keep it straight when they discuss these nests among themselves.

On my way to see George I looked for an easier nest to discuss: the Cedar Waxwing nest. I quickly found it because it is in a prominent spot but I failed to find either of the adults. I had no trouble finding George. He was harvesting food from a dozen admirers on the dock and repeatedly carried the edibles to the island where I presumed he was feeding his offspring behind the thick vegetation.

This evening eight people including a newcomer with an unfamiliar electronic device gathered in hopes of seeing the Black Skimmer. Brad was the fellow holding the intriguing gizmo. It was a small rectangular white box with two large black knobs. The box periodically emitted a series of clicks, whirrs and buzzes whose meaning I did not comprehend. My unfamiliarity with the apparatus will be understandable to most readers when I explain that when I asked Brad what it was he described it as a bat detector. How does it work? The device converts the bat's ultrasonic calls into lower frequencies that the human ear can hear. Each time a bat came near, and there were a total of three, the bat detector's speaker announced its presence before we could actually see it. Brad compared the frequency reading of one bat's ultrasonic signature with a chart in the bat detector instruction booklet. He informed us, "A reading of 40kHz is most likely from a Small Brown Bat." Well, how about that? For those of you who covet the potential entertainment and/or scientific value of a bat detector be advised that they do not have widespread distribution in retail outlets. This particular model was manufactured in England. Brad found an ad for it in the classifieds at the back of a bird-watcher magazine. So please do not think you can rush down to the local electronics chain store to buy one as I am fairly certain you will be disappointed. With considerably less difficulty you can track down a bird-watching magazine and scan the advertisements. Happy bat detector hunting, nature lovers.

Chapter 43 · June 24

Red-winged Blackbird Nest Too

We have gone from two months of unseasonably cool and wet weather into subtropical-I-want-to-go-home-and-take-a-shower-right-now weather. I slowed my pace in an effort to avoid the effects of the ninety-one degree heat and nearly one hundred percent humidity but it did no good. When I reached Morton's Pond my visage did not paint a pretty picture. I was hoping no one I knew would see me in my present condition but Harry was sitting in his usual spot. Mercifully if he noticed I was a soggy mess he did not let on. Harry himself looked as cool as the proverbial cucumber even though I could see the telltale signs that he had been

Here is a double dose of Double-crested Cormorants drying and cooling off on a log jutting from the shore of George's Island. The blurry white object behind them is a Great Egret.

physically exerting himself before I arrived. Scattered clumps of his homemade mixture clung on the bark of a Cork Oak Tree. He explained that he applied a generous amount to the tree but the usual suspects had quickly descended on it leaving behind the meager remnants I saw.

It became increasingly quiet around Morton's Pond. At first I thought that was because Harry's homemade mixture was all but gone but then I saw evidence that the usual suspects were likely to be taking a siesta to escape the heat and humidity. The condition of a dozen House Sparrows told the whole story. I do not exaggerate when I tell you that these sparrows all had their beaks wide open and they were panting. This behavior is not something I have often seen but I have observed it on equally brutal days like today. Birds do not have sweat glands but they they can achieve thermoregulation by perspiring and by panting. In the process of perspiration cooling is achieved as water evaporates from the skin but during panting it evaporates from the surface of internal air sacs, which in addition to lungs, are part of the bird's respiratory system. Some species have developed a more sophisticated form of panting. The first time I saw a Double-crested Cormorant rapidly vibrating its throat I could not imagine what purpose that activity served. Another beginning birder, as clueless as myself, suggested it might be part of a mating ritual. Another was sure it was ill. Wrong. It was actually what is known in ornithological circles as gular fluttering. Never heard of it? Me either. For example, cormorants and pelicans, two birds that have large throat patches, rapidly vibrate them to speed the process of expelling excess heat from their bodies.[1]

I left cool-as-a-cucumber Harry and the panting House Sparrows behind and headed for the Green Heron breeding ground where I watched chicks moving around in one nest and an adult female heron sitting on the other nest. The next stop on my itinerary was the Cedar Waxwing nest site. Their presence has eluded me but I knew my luck had changed when from a distance I saw four

[1]David Allen Sibley, *The Sibley Guide to Bird Life & Behavior*, p. 31.

bird-watchers with their binoculars trained on the same spot. They were looking at a male Cedar Waxwing standing guard duty high in the branches of a tree adjacent to the nest tree. Presumably, the male was watching over the female Cedar Waxwing that was sitting on the nest, but the Weeping Willow leaves covered her and this could not be confirmed.

Walking up the cliff to the castle I was on my way to check out what Bruce had told me about another Red-winged Blackbird nest with chicks belonging to Claudia, George's other mate. From the cliff Bruce had watched George repeatedly coming and going with food to a specific place on the island. That kind of repetitive behavior is a strong clue that a nest is the destination for those visits. On my first look down at the island I saw the behavior that Bruce had described. George collected food from a human admirer at the dock and immediately conveyed it to a point on the southeast section of the island. He repeated this several times in the course of fifteen minutes. On each trip he came to a stop on the same branch of a particular bush and then disappeared behind the leaves. Although I could not see or hear them I am certain there were one or more chicks concealed there.

Later when I stood on the dock I saw George refusing people's offerings of seeds and nuts. He examined palms lined with them but rejected them jumping on those holding bread instead. Not only was he being picky about what he pecked but also he processed the bread after he collected it. George carried the bread to a small opening on the shore surrounded by tall sedges that partially concealed him. Here he soaked the bread in the shallow water. When the bread was waterlogged he collected the pasty goop in his beak and took it to the hidden nest. Watching this I recalled the only other occasion I remember seeing George soak bread in water and that was for his first brood of chicks earlier in the spring. I know from that experience he will favor bread for a short time and then revert to his usual food preferences.

The audience for George's performance was larger than usual today. I have not kept records but I believe the number of Club George charter members has steadily grown since his reappearance on the pond in April. During the late afternoon while I was at the dock people came and went but about a dozen were consistently present to either watch him or inquire about him. Roughly a quarter of them were young children. They mainly came to see the turtles and ducks but some were on a mission to find the increasingly well-known Red-winged Blackbird.

On the periphery of the pond three Black-crowned Night Herons were beginning their evening hunt while a Great Egret was finishing up its workday. Two Green Herons were disagreeing about which of them was going to stand on a log poking out into the water from George's Island. At the foot of the dock a gang of molting male Mallards and the Canada Goose family were gobbling up handouts. The pieces they missed were gobbled up by a school of small fish and about three dozen turtles. Now and then a Large-mouthed Bass gobbled up one or more of the minnows. Then from the depths a shadowy figure about the size of a dinner plate slowly rose toward the surface. It was a large Snapping Turtle. I assumed its arrival would ruin the party but it did not. This predator ignored the ducklings, turtles and fish and instead came to claim a share of the free eats the crowd was distributing to the other animals. The scene resembled a living bouillabaisse with creatures so consumed with consuming that even mortal enemies, at least those on the surface, did not attack or flee from each other.

Chapter 44 · June 25

The Importance of Being Repellent

The temperature hit ninety-one degrees and the humidity hit ninety-one percent for the second day. In the Ramble birds were scarce but at Morton's Pond a number of the usual suspects had been coaxed out of their torpor by the lure of Harry's homemade mixture. Morton Downy and one of the Tufted Titmice were temporarily working in the trees surrounding the Cork Oak waiting for a Gray Squirrel to finish taking a share of Harry's concoction and leave so they could get at it themselves. When the squirrel descended that is just what they did. A couple of Mourning Doves and several House Sparrows, panting as they were yesterday, were not as energetic. They foraged instead in heavily

I had not deliberately set out to memorize one of the Northern Cardinal's songs but without consciously making an effort to do so I have.

shaded areas closest to the water's edge. I imagine it was a little cooler there.

When I heard a bird singing loudly I guessed that it was a North-ern Cardinal but for practice I left the pond to follow the music and find out if my identification was correct. It was a male North-ern Cardinal singing. I watched and listened to him for nearly ten minutes. He was still singing "whoit, whoit, cheer, cheer, cheer, cheer, cheer" when I left him. I had not deliberately set out to memorize this particular bird song but without consciously making an effort to do so I have. I once despaired of ever being able to rec-ognize bird vocalizations but now I find that I am slowly building a repertoire of them. Beginning bird-watchers may fret that they will never learn to recognize calls or songs. They should stop worrying and start stalking instead. That's right, if you hear a bird you do not recognize follow the sound to its source. When you confirm both the audio and visual information in this way, presuming you find the bird, it will make a stronger impression on you than any recording or book can. It just requires practice. Alas I know there are a few bird-watchers that are "tone-deaf" and cannot differenti-ate bird vocalizations in the same way they cannot tell one musical note from another. On the other hand many experienced birders pride themselves on how well they can identify bird calls and songs. Some who list the different species they find each day include birds they identified solely from their vocalizations.

After leaving this singing male Northern Cardinal I walked down a path, rounded a corner and met another male Northern Cardinal. This one was standing on the ground. He picked up a bit of food in his beak and took it to another bird completely ob-scured in the shadows inside a small shrub. I could see the male leaning forward and touching the beak of the other bird. He re-peated this action five times but still I could not see the recipient. I assumed that the male had been giving a female a present of food. But wait a minute. When I later described this scenario to Viviene she suggested that the repetitive nature of the male's actions might indicate it was not his mate that he was feeding but a fledgling in-stead. That was a possibility I had not considered. I do not remember hearing the characteristic excited chirping that juveniles make when they are about to be fed so I am not sure if this was a youngster or not. Regardless of whether it was an adult female or a fledgling I never imagined Northern Cardinals would become the source of such demonstrative behavior almost on a daily basis.

Checking the Green Heron nests was not as rewarding. I was unable to find any chicks, but I could see an adult sitting on the newest nest. Checking on the Cedar Waxwing nest I came along as one of the adults stood on its rim. As I watched the bird disappeared into it but when the breeze blew it uncovered a view of the adult's tail poking out. That tip of a tail was all can I tell of my tale about Cedar Waxwings, at least for today.

George collected bread again, soaked it and made nearly continuous shuttle flights carrying it to the newest nest site. A few times he paused to eat but when he did he consumed seeds, bugs and nuts rather than the mush he made for the chicks. This business about food preferences and George's participation in feeding the chicks raised a few questions not just about parental care but about intelligence too. Not mine, George's. You may have read in a number of sources, as I have, that female Red-winged Blackbirds feed the nestlings much more often than the males but that, I have since discovered, is a misleading notion. Research shows that the amount each sex feeds the offspring differs in geographical regions. Les Beletsky's influential fieldwork in the Columbia National Wildlife Refuge in Washington State found that most males did not feed their nestlings but that is not the case in other areas.

All male redwings probably *know* how to feed nestlings but in some populations few do so. West of the Rocky Mountains, few males feed nestlings, whereas in the East and Midwest a much higher but variable proportion of males do so. Productivity of breeding habitat, harem size, and breeding season length may all contribute to the pattern. (Orians 1985, Muldal et al. 1986). In particular, the highly productive marshes of western North America permit females alone to raise their broods successfully, freeing males to exercise their options of prolonging advertisement and aggressively guarding their fertilizable females far into the breeding season.[1]

In short Beletsky says when conditions are optimum the males may not help feed the nestlings but when they are less than optimum they may tend to do so. Additionally there is also evidence to suggest that broods fed by both male and female adults have a statistically higher survival rate than those fed by the female alone.[2] If that is the case George is making a maximum effort to ensure that his children are well fed and have the best possible chance of survival.

While I now know it is not that unusual for male Red-winged Blackbirds to help feed nestlings it does not explain how George came to select bread for them, how he came to soak it in water or how he learned how to collect it from humans. I have come across other stories about Red-winged Blackbird behaviors that are equally as intriguing. One particularly interesting story comes from Robert W. Nero's observation of a resourceful Red-winged Blackbird's behavior that displays a provocative degree of specialized intelligence as distasteful as it may seem to some readers.

I saw birds at the Vilas Park Zoo in Madison, Wisconsin, regularly use their bills to tip up or push over dung in the animal pens in search of prey. One day, however, I observed one do something that astonished me: a first-year male Redwing, confronted with a large, dry buffalo or bison patty, grasped the nearer edge with his feet, flew up with it still held in his feet, and thus tipped it over! He then searched for food on the newly exposed ground. When, I wondered, did he learn that unusual technique?[3]

Indeed, when did he learn it and how did he learn it?

I think the buffalo patty-flipping bird's behavior and George's

---

[1] Les Beletsky, *The Red-winged Blackbird: The Biology of a Strongly Polygynous Songbird*, p. 198.
[2] Ibid., p. 201.
[3] Robert W. Nero, *Redwings*, p. 36.

range of interactions with people are evidence of an underrated intelligence in his species and perhaps birds in general. If these examples have not convinced you I have another one from Les Beletsky that may.

> Redwings are smart. In our work we catch most of them with "funnels" traps, which are made of wire netting and into which birds drop through wire "funnels" to get at seed bait. The funnel area occupies only a small portion of the main body of the trap, so the birds cannot locate the funnel again to exit. Several males had territories near to one of our main trapping locations, and I knew from watching that the banded owners of those territories regularly went to the large trap to gorge on sunflower seeds. However, to my surprise one year, as I inspected our trappings records, I found that we rarely captured these males. Suspicious, the next time I set the trap I watched it from afar with a telescope. Sure enough, some of the males who frequently visited the trap not only knew how to enter, but had also learned how to exit through the funnel.[4]

Still not convinced that birds that can figure out how to escape a trap are pretty smart customers? Here is one more example I find remarkable. Beletsky also tells a story of a researcher that bought an expensive custom-made shotgun that fired a net to capture birds at a lake for study. The first Red-winged Blackbird he tried to catch with the contraption easily evaded the net while the other birds fled as soon as they heard the shotgun blast. The second time the researcher attempted to use the gun all the Red-winged Blackbirds on the lake left the area before he could even get it out of its case. Beletsky believes that after only one exposure to the net firing shotgun the Red-winged Blackbirds had learned to recognize it on sight and to get away from it as quickly as they could.[5]

There were no dry buffalo patties, funnel traps, or custom-

---

[4]Les Beletsky, *The Red-winged Blackbird: The Biology of a Strongly Polygynous Songbird*, p. 6.
[5]Ibid., p. 6.

made net-firing shotguns at George's Pond but there was much more bird activity here than elsewhere on my walk. I found Roger Egret, two Green Herons, a fourth and new Mallard family with eight ducklings and a separate group of ten adult males, the Canada Goose clan and around the periphery several American Robins, European Starlings, House Sparrows, two Song Sparrows I could only hear singing, and as the sun began to set, three Black-crowned Night Herons.

About the time the night herons arrived the air was seemingly at once filled with dozens of dragonflies. There may have been one hundred individuals, or maybe more. They were flying in a specific area over the water where they were hunting insects so small I could not detect them. The dragonflies carried on for about fifteen minutes and then all but two of them disappeared. Those two appeared to be mating. Where was Stan, the bug guy, when I needed him to explain what it was I was watching?

I wanted to wait for the arrival of the Black Skimmer but I was involuntarily forced into an interaction as unwanted as it was unpleasant. Quite suddenly I felt unseen creatures biting my hands and forearms. Perhaps they were the same ones the dragonflies had massed to attack earlier. I did not stay to investigate that hypothesis. The biting was so savage I bid my companions a hasty farewell while I rushed from the pond. Twenty-five feet from the water the attacks stopped. My hands and forearms were smarting and I cursed the bugs but I knew it was really my own fault. I have a supply of insect repellent spray at home and though I have been diligent in applying it for the past week I had imprudently failed to apply it today. It is not that the concoction is ineffective. In fact it works well, but it has an unfortunate side effect on me. Put politely the spray's chemical aroma is not to my liking. I made sure to purchase the so-called "scent free" formula but my nose still detects one and it is not of roses. Maybe this is also my fault. Could I be misinterpreting the advertising copy on the packaging? Since the product surely has an odor should I take the "scent free" statement to mean there is indeed a scent but I have not been charged for it? Just kidding folks but the odor is no joke. I guess I'm just going to have to get used to it. Sigh.

Later when I examined my wounds in the mirror I found a small raised red lump on my left hand and one on each arm. Judging from the vehemence of the attack I thought I would be in worse condition but there still was the concern that I might have been injected with an insidious microbe like West Nile virus or something even more diabolical. Only time would tell on that score, but those three welts had served as a wake-up call for me to be more disciplined. I only hoped my vow to take future precautions had not come too late.

Reading my e-mail after applying alcohol and calamine lotion to my bug bites I learned that the Black Skimmer had paid a visit to the pond about twenty minutes after I had fled. I consoled myself for missing the skimmer with the knowledge that I had summoned the will to overcome my aversion to the scent of insect repellent. I would be prepared to face another insect onslaught and be repellent on my next bird-watching walk.

Chapter 45 · June 27

Cedar Waxwing Magic

I found Viviene sitting on a park bench opposite the Cedar Waxwing nest. Lately I find her there nearly every day. That is because Cedar Waxwings are one of her favorite species. She loves their physical beauty, their high-pitched calls and their gentle behavior in or out of breeding season. I stopped to chat with her and get an update on the nest's status from her. Ned came along and joined us. While we chatted both adult Cedar Waxwings perched together on a branch high above their nest in an adjacent tree. We trained our binoculars on them and got, as they say, more than we bargained for. I cannot tell the sexes apart in this breed but Viviene can. She was certain the male sat facing away and the female to-

Papa Goose resumed his lookout duties over his goslings after our unintentionally close encounter.

ward us. We watched him lean toward her and place something, we could not see what, in her beak. She swallowed it. The act was repeated. Then the male turned around. As if by magic a brilliant red berry appeared at the end of his open beak. It was these same red berries, we reasoned, he had twice fed his mate when his back was turned. He gave her more until he had fed her five. We were thrilled to witness this but were baffled when trying to imagine where and how this little bird (seven inches from its beak to its tail) was storing all those berries. The male produced them from somewhere deep inside with such apparent ease that it looked as if he were some kind of berry dispensing machine. Watching his actions reminded me of the plastic Pez candy dispensers that I was crazy about when I was a child. You must have seen them, had one or have one now especially if you have children of your own. They are small colorful plastic gadgets that deliver one small lozenge-shaped candy when you press the button, often in the shape of a cartoon character, on top. Personally, I never cared as much for the taste of the candy as much as I enjoyed pressing the button to watch it pop out.

I might have stayed to see if the waxwing would produce more berries but the overcast sky reminded me it would become dark early. I had priority locations to cover so I left Ned and Jane with the berry dispensing bird and hurried to the dock to see George before he retired for the evening or the weather changed for the worse. George was ferrying a variety of food that included soggy bread to a hidden nest. He deviated from this chore only to chase a territorial invader. Both Claudia and Ruby were visible collecting bugs in the reeds along the water's edge. Disappointingly the fledglings I believe to be Ruby's were nowhere to be seen.

Viviene and Ned rejoined me and a small group of Club George charter members that were going to watch for the Black Skimmer. Lucky Ned had seen three Black Skimmers here at the same time the previous night. This night at about 9:35 PM during the intermission of *Henry V* playing in the Delacorte Theater, a solitary Black Skimmer sailed into sight. At about 10:00 PM a second skimmer arrived and there was a confrontation between the two birds.

We heard a few notes of high-pitched barking as the skimmers snaked about one another twenty feet above the water. Then the arguing birds turned and headed straight toward us at the end of the dock. They flew directly at us clearing the tops of our heads at such a short distance that we had all instinctively ducked. I had always hoped to get a truly close look at the Black Skimmer but this was never what I had in mind. After sharing our mutual reaction of terror we all shared a laugh. I recalled when Great Egrets and bats had flown directly over my head as I stood on this same spot. I wondered if there might be a common denominator in each of these occurrences. One came to mind. It was the presence of Bruce. While Bruce protested I asked the group if it were possible that he possessed some form of animal magnetism that could account for these too close encounters but when someone reminded me that I was present at each event myself I dropped that line of questioning. Maybe there are some questions a bird-watcher should not ask?

Chapter 46 · June 29

Distress Calls

The temperature dropped to a high of eighty-two degrees and the humidity was marginally this side of clammy. Comparatively speaking it was a lovely day. Thank you Mother Nature.

The improved weather attracted noticeably more visitors to the park than yesterday. The Ramble was especially peopled. The benches at Morton's Pond were full. Someone sitting there got the idea to wedge a whole peanut, still in its shell, between a metal post and the wire mesh of the fence with the hope of enticing a Blue Jay to come down from its perch to take it. The idea worked as planned. The Blue Jay swooped down, grabbed the peanut, carried

Some birdwatchers do not get excited when they see a Blue Jay because it is one of the usual suspects. I do. No matter how many times I spot them they always impress me.

it to a much closer perch, opened the shell and swallowed the contents in one gulp. Blue Jays could be described as almost inhaling their food as we might describe some people we may know. Statue-like this Blue Jay watched and waited to see if another peanut would be placed on the fence. It was. The bird pounced on it, took it to the same perch, ate it and waited for another peanut that was soon forthcoming. A small crowd that gathered applauded each time the Blue Jay repeated this feat. What most impressed me was how readily the bird had sized up the situation and rather than go elsewhere to forage after it snatched the first bit of food, as I have seen other species do, it anticipated being able to collect more. Only when the peanuts ceased to be replaced did the Blue Jay move along to search somewhere else for a meal.

Most new birders are surprised to learn that Blue Jays, and jays in general, are in the family *Corvidae* as are ravens and crows. That is because the jay's physical appearance is at least superficially different. For example Blue Jays have crests, relatively smaller beaks and are colorful whereas ravens and crows do not have crests, have stouter beaks and are predominantly black except for the Tamaulipas Crow from Mexico that is mostly shinny blue and the Eurasian Jackdaw with its mixture of gray, black and blue coloring that to my eye combines the look of a jay with a crow. Sibley notes that jays, crows and ravens have the capacity to "learn and take advantage of new situations and especially the corvid ability to exploit human activity for their own benefit."[1] The Blue Jay collecting peanuts on the fence had quickly figured out how to exploit this activity by waiting, observing, taking action and finally recognizing when the party was over.

Admittedly this Blue Jay's behavior was not terribly sophisticated, but other corvid species are capable of taking actions and making choices of much greater complexity. Crows, for example are well-known to deliberately drop nuts from a height onto paved roads in order to break them open. Some are said to wait by the roadside for a red light, place a nut in front of the stopped vehicles

[1]David Allen Sibley, *The Sibley Guide to Bird Life & Behavior*, p. 412.

and hurry out of their way to wait for them to be run over and opened after the light changes to green.

Sibley describes an experiment involving the Common Raven that is an uncommonly clever species whose behaviors have been compared to certain kinds of intelligence exhibited by monkeys.

> Experiments with Common Ravens, on the other hand, have demonstrated that they can show true insight when solving problems, without prior trial-and-error learning. Ravens faced with a novel task, such as getting food that is dangling on the end of a string, were able to assess the problem and use their feet to hold the string and pull the food up. They performed this action without mis-steps the first time they attempted it.[2]

The bird activity around Morton's Pond increased after the Blue Jay left and Harry came along to apply five patches of his home-made mixture on the Cork Oak Tree. As if by wizardry the birds began to gather there. As is often the case House Sparrows were the first to arrive. Then came the neighborhood's pair of Red-bellied Woodpeckers, followed by a few Common Grackles, after which Rock Pigeons got in on the deal and finally one male Red-winged Blackbird, the one I call Squeaky. I wonder how the House Sparrows are able to find Harry's mixture so quickly and once they had did they summon the rest of the flock or did the other birds find it on their own? A new bird-watcher might wonder if the House Sparrows were alerted to the food by its smell but most songbirds supposedly have a poor sense of smell unlike, say, a Turkey Vulture that has keen olfactory powers to help it locate carrion. I imagine at least one House Sparrow might have watched Harry apply his homemade mixture and the other birds found the tree by playing follow the leader. That makes sense but how were the other species alerted that Harry's mixture was being served? It did not seem to me that the other species were physically close enough to see Harry apply it or the sparrows feeding on it. Could it be they heard

[2]Ibid., p. 412.

their vocalizations and came to investigate? I suppose it is likely a combination of sight and sound that clued them in but I still would like to know if the sense of smell played even a small part in the process.

When a Downy Woodpecker joined in I assumed it was Morton but there was a significant though tiny difference about this particular specimen. Instead of sporting a bright red patch on the back of its head this woodpecker had a red patch on the front of his head. A female woodpecker, I assumed to be Mary Downy, perched beside this unfamiliar bird and placed something inside its open beak. This could not be a courtship behavior or could it? My speculation was put to rest when a more experienced birder arrived and explained that the bird with the red patch on its forehead was a juvenile Downy Woodpecker. You may be wondering if the juvenile was a female or male. There is no easy way to determine its sex unless one could examine its most intimate parts and then one would have to have a very good idea of what it was one was looking for. Let's just say identifying the sex of juveniles is a challenge even for experts. I was satisfied enough to know that I had seen a female Downy Woodpecker, possibly Mary, feed her fledgling. I was glad to have that much cleared up but it was immediately followed by an even more ambiguous episode. Two adult female Downy Woodpeckers drew close together on the same tree trunk and one presented the other with a beak full of food. Even the more experienced birder, that had identified the juvenile woodpecker for me, was at a loss to explain this action. "Well'" he said, "it looks like one adult female is feeding another. These are New York woodpeckers and anything is possible." We never did figure this behavior out.

Neither could we comprehend the next observations we made. An adult male Downy Woodpecker joined the two adult females. I was not sure if the fellow was Morton because he did not act as I expected the territory owner to act. I thought Morton would not tolerate a second adult female on his turf but she remained unchallenged both by the first female I presumed to be his mate and himself. My assumptions about woodpecker territorial behavior were now officially in a state of confusion. In the past I have seen male Downy Woodpeckers fight aggressively to stake out or defend borders but those confrontations had always been between males. The relationships among these three birds were entertaining but baffling.

Soon after my encounter with confusing woodpeckers Gordon confounded me with more befuddling bird behavior. He told me that he had come from visiting George's Pond where George had been extremely agitated, shunned the dock and people, and had stopped bringing food to his chicks. Gordon did not elaborate further but his terse report was enough to trouble me. I hurried to see for myself. When I found George I saw justification for concern. He was perched on a branch over the hidden nest on the island. Over and over again he loudly repeated a piercing single syllable "seer" distress call. Periodically he swooped off his perch to chase one or all four Common Grackles that were arranged in the branches of the same birch tree a couple of yards below him. I analyzed what I could observe and came to a disturbing hypothesis. I felt that George's aggressive actions, his alarm calls, the close proximity of the Common Grackles to the nest site and the fact that he had stopped feeding the nestlings suggested that it had been attacked. I could not know with certainty that this was so but I knew enough to be filled with a sense of dread that the worst had transpired.

More than disease, parasites, or accidents, predators are the major cause of danger to nestlings. Summarizing eight studies on the subject Yasukawa and Searcy say that a "mean of 41% eggs and young were lost to predators (*Searcy and Yasukawa 1995, see also Martin 1995*). Predators vary over species' geographic range. Principal nest predators include raccoon, mink (*Mustella vison*), Black-billed Magpie (*Pica pica*), and Marsh Wren (*Cistothorus palustris*). Marsh Wrens may puncture eggs or kill young without eating them (*Picman 1977*). Hawks and owls take adults (*Orian 1980, Nero 1984*)."[3] Although Common Grackles were not included in their list of likely predators Ken Yasukawa confirmed to me what I had

---

[3]Ken Yasukawa and William A. Searcy, *Red-winged Blackbird,* p. 11.

read elsewhere, that grackles are well known to take the eggs and nestlings of a wide variety of birds.

I tried to get the scene on the island out of my mind. I would reconsider it later when I had additional information. To distract myself I had a long look at the adult Cedar Waxwings. When I was told someone had seen two Northern Rough-winged Swallows feeding their fledglings while they flew in midair I went to see them. These things would normally have cheered me but they did not now. After sunset when George had ceased to call out and presumably had gone to his roost I stayed on the dock. I was fortunate to see the Black Skimmer but that sighting and the camaraderie of the other birders sharing the experience did not lift my spirits. I could not stop worrying about the fate of the Red-winged Blackbird nest.

Chapter 47 · June 30

The Molting Has Begun

Viviene said she saw Northern Cardinal parents feeding a fledgling at Bank Rock Bridge earlier in the day. I had heard about this family unit before and had searched for them twice without luck. Viviene's report inspired me to try to find them once more. As I approached the area I recognized the call of an adult Northern Cardinal and the rapid high-pitched chirping of a bird I did not recognize, but its call had a lot in common with other baby birds I had heard. My guess was that these vocalizations were of the cardinal parent and fledgling Viviene had described. Moving toward the sounds I came upon a male Northern Cardinal standing on the ground. Just above him on a low branch stood his mate. The

George was anxious. He spent most of his time calling, displaying and anxiously scanning his domain.

male carried a morsel of food not to his mate, as I thought he would, but to another tree where a third bird sat. When the adult male came alongside this smaller bird it became very excited. Its rapid-fire chirping and fluttering stubby wings identified it as a fledgling. The two birds stretched their necks toward each other and the male passed the food to the fledgling. How delightful.

Conveniently this Northern Cardinal breeding territory coincides with the Green Heron breeding territory. In the newest heron nest I could make out what I assumed to be a portion of an adult Green Heron. If I did not already know what it looked like I might not have recognized it as a Green Heron's back.

At Morton's Pond I saw Morton Downy and one raspingly vocal Tufted Titmouse but few of the other usual suspects were around. I was in a much better mood than last evening but my mind involuntarily revisited the ominous scene I had witnessed on George's Island. I vacillated between wanting to know for certain if the Common Grackles had raided the nest and wanting to avoid all thoughts of it. I put off my usual visit to George's Pond for a while but inevitably went there, as I knew I would. Once in the neighborhood I started stalling again. Instead of going to the dock I first checked up on the Cedar Waxwing nest and was lucky to arrive just in time to see one of the parents slip inside it. There was no further activity there but nonetheless I stood staring at the inactive nest rather than visit George and face learning the fate of his nest. Finally with no small amount of trepidation I proceeded to the dock. George was energetically coming and going from his favorite perch but once there spent most of his time calling, displaying and anxiously scanning his domain. Seldom did he take food from Club George charter members. Neither did he attempt to acquire sustenance elsewhere. Most tellingly he did not carry food to the nest site on the island. He did not travel to the island at all while I was watching him. His mate Claudia made a couple of lengthy forays on and around the dock and she sometimes went to the island but she did not enter her nest. There was no sign of Ruby, his other mate. I thought the visual evidence I found was consistent with the theory that the nest had met with a disaster.

Around George's Pond I noticed for the first time that here and there the grass has turned brown. It has gone dormant from the sustained heat and lack of rain over the last few days. Today was sunny with a comfy eighty-five relatively dry degrees. It is ironic that we had a record rainfall during June but at the end of the month one would think we were in the midst of a severe drought. Looking at the wilted vegetation I incongrously found myself in the position of wishing it would rain when I have so often complained about the frequent precipitation.

There were fewer of the usual suspects around the pond than yesterday and those present seemed subdued. There was no sign of the Great Egret and none of the Green Herons either come to think of it. The number of birds on view has begun a diminishing trend for the balance of the season. This is the time of year when I start to hear some birders who should know better attribute the dwindling number of birds to hypothetical adverse environmental conditions or an imagined calamity of some sort. The explanation is a lot more simple and benign.

At this point in the breeding period a majority of nestlings have fledged and the parents have their beaks full, so to speak, feeding, protecting and keeping up with the rapidly growing and increasingly active offspring. The parents may try to keep the family hidden because the fledglings may not yet have the necessary skills or the physical maturity to escape or evade predators on their own. Parents often act secretively and take circuitous paths to their offspring so as not to call attention to them and accidentally alert a predator to their hiding places. It makes sense then that the birds may be seen less often. However the onset of molting can make them even harder to find.

All birds molt at least once a year. Some molt more frequently but whenever it occurs the process requires a lot of the bird's energy and resources. Acquiring an understanding of the molting process intricacies can be complicated if not downright daunting. According to Sibley, for example, a bird in its first year could undergo a primitive basic, modified basic, simple alternate and a complex alternate molt. There are even more stages possible in a bird's second year. I recommend *Sibley's Birding Basics* to the beginning birder for a comprehensive overview of this subject that I will refrain from attempting to explicate for fear of creating permanent and debilitating confusion.[1] What you really need to know is that bird's feathers wear out and the process of replacing them is called the molt. Generally crucial flight feathers drop off in an orderly sequence so that enough are retained to permit the bird to fly well enough to escape danger if not at its optimum level. Molting birds are vulnerable and sometimes go into hiding relying more on stealth and experience to help protect and feed them until they can once again rely on their full powers of flight. Got it?

[1]David Allen Sibley, *Sibley's Birding Basics*, pp. 123–36.

Chapter 48 · July 1

Barnstorming Skimmer

This was a perfect summer day. The temperature did not climb over eighty-five and I did not care to know what the relative humidity was because it was a nonissue. The usual suspects were conspicuous at Morton's Pond but Morton was not. There had to have been two dozen House Sparrows, a dozen Common Grackles, multiple Rock Pigeons and a few Mourning Doves all foraging together on the south shoulder of the pond. Above me were one buzzing Tufted Titmouse and two shrill Blue Jays. When I heard soft "chip" calls I recognized them as coming from Northern Cardinals.

Harry had plastered the Cork Oak Tree with his homemade mixture before I arrived and in a burst of culinary creativity he, or

A glamorous George was soon to be an amorous George.

someone else, had embedded a dozen shelled peanuts into the deep grooves of the bark of the same tree. It had transformed the stuff into Harry's "chunky homemade mixture." The House Sparrows were industriously prying it loose after the bulkier Common Grackles and Rock Pigeons in their more laborious attempts had given up. The gurgling sound of the Red-bellied Woodpecker announced its arrival. It was the female that descended to get a taste of Harry's offerings. The Northern Cardinals, Mourning Doves and Blue Jays did not attempt to extract the mixture from the tree bark. It occurred to me that I have never seen those breeds attempt it. I am only guessing but maybe they do not have the ability to cling to vertical surfaces as the other species do.

All this avian activity was cheering but my thoughts kept returning to George and the fate of his newest nest. To get a different perspective on the situation I decided to go to the Castle on the cliff above his island to look down on the scene. On my way I caught sight of an adult Gray Catbird feeding its fledgling in the undergrowth. I thought how strange it is that this season I have seen catbird adults with their babies often when last year it seemed a rarity. The sight served as another reminder that my charter membership in Club George has opened a new world to me.

From the cliff I did not collect any new information about the suspected crime scene on the island. In fact I saw little from up there. When I came down from the cliff to the dock I found George pursuing one of his mates. Each time she fled him he followed her while repeatedly performing his slow speed display flight and ostentatiously showing off his red epaulets. George's transparent courting behavior was, of course, normal for a male Red-winged Blackbird but its timing intrigued me. Were George and his mate attempting to start another family at this point in the breeding season? If so will they be trying to replace the nest I believe was destroyed? It is well documented that many birds, not only Red-winged Blackbirds, will try to breed again if their nest has failed but there has to be sufficient time to do so. In this region George and his mates have until the end of July to raise one more clutch of chicks. If my calculations were correct they would have just enough time to do it if they started right away. I based that on the absolute minimum of eleven days to incubate the eggs and another eleven to brood them until they can fledge. The process usually takes twenty-one to twenty-six days. Theoretically there may be just enough time for them to pull it off. We shall see what we shall see.

Chapter 49 • July 2

Northern Flicker Sitter

This had been another lovely summer day and what could have been a better way to enjoy it than to have Morton Downy make a two-point landing on my palm? Why having him repeat it two more times, of course. After his third visit Morton encountered a rude guest awaiting his return to his perch. A Blue Jay snatched the peanut right out of Morton's beak. Morton shrieked in a manner amazingly vociferous for such a diminutive creature, but his vocalizations could not alter the outcome and he hastily retreated to join his spouse at a farther and safer distance.

I have expressed my admiration for Blue Jays. I am also aware that they can be opportunistic bullies. The observation of this par-

I marveled how this Northern Flicker could nonchalantly conduct his hygiene routine while vertically hanging onto a tree twenty-five feet in the air.

253

ticular Blue Jay stealing little Morton's food is just a hint of how aggressive they can be but at Morton's Pond I have come to see that
Blue Jay personalities can vary. Of the two seemingly identical Blue
Jays that frequent the area around the pond one is clearly more aggressive than the other. This bolder bird has no compunctions
about coming closer to people if it senses the possibility of a free
meal or of stealing one from another bird. It was, I believe, this
same aggressive Blue Jay taking the peanuts wedged in the fence as
described in an earlier chapter. The relatively shy Blue Jay of this
duo is less likely to act in these ways. In fact I have seen this bird allow itself to be intimidated by the histrionics of a single and significantly smaller House Sparrow. The relationship between the two
Blue Jays is unclear. I have no clue to their sexes but recent events
suggested they are female and male adults. Lately the presence of a
third Blue Jay led me to think that it may be their offspring. For
some time I had toyed with the idea of referring to the adults as the
Blue Jay Brothers, an allusion to a movie entitled *The Blues Brothers,*
despite the possibility they may well be a mated pair. Regardless of
their proper relationship I decided today to call them the Blue Jay
Brothers from this point on solely because it amuses me to do so. I
know it's not scientific but I cannot resist a good pun.

After the number of birds thinned around Morton's Pond I followed the adult Northern Cardinals in the hopes they would lead
me to one of their fledglings so I might get the parent-and-child
photo that keeps eluding me as much as the male-feeding-female
photo does. I wandered a good distance before I had to admit the
cardinals had given me the slip but I found something equally as
captivating.

Ned was standing at the bottom of the ravine beneath the Rustic
Arch looking up at a male Northern Flicker clinging to the side of
a Honey Locust Tree. Beginning bird-watchers take heed: whenever possible politely inquire of other birders as to what he or she is
watching lest you miss something wonderful. In this case Ned had
come upon a woodpecker and its circular cavity cut into the tree
trunk. As I came upon the scene the Northern Flicker popped its
head through the opening, disappeared for a few moments, and

then emerged to perch beside it. This bird, a male, began preening himself. I marveled how he could nonchalantly conduct his hygiene routine while vertically hanging onto a tree twenty-five feet in the air. When this male flew off his mate took his place but she quickly entered the cavity and remained inside. What was this activity all about? These Northern Flickers were breeding. Presumably these two birds had carved out the hole in the tree. There were three possible conditions inside the cavity: eggs were about to be deposited, eggs had been deposited or eggs had hatched. Presently I could not say which was the case but I knew I would be here as often I could until I found out.

Checking up on three other nests did not offer as much immediate gratification. The Green Heron fledglings were either hiding or have gone elsewhere. The newest Green Heron nest was nearly impossible to see through the dense vegetation. Near George's Pond I could not see any activity at the Cedar Waxwing nest but Viviene was there keeping up her daily observations. She told me she had seen the adult waxwings earlier and all seemed to be going well.

At the dock Julio filled me in on some of George's activities during the afternoon. He told me that he had watched George soaking bread in water that he subsequently conveyed to his nest site on the island. How was that again Julio? I asked Julio to repeat it. In complete contradiction of my dire scenario of doom Julio's observation strongly suggested that at least one of George's chicks was alive. I wanted more details but that was all he could recount. It was more than enough to give me hope and I was extraordinarily happy to know I had been wrong. I wanted very much to confirm Julio's story with my own observation but I could not. Sunset arrived without my having witnessed the behavior Julio described or anything else that would support the notion the nest was still viable.

The gathering of Black Skimmer watchers was larger than it had been in a while. Among the group were Viviene, Mack, Bruce, Mark, Alice, Terrence, Sam and five or six others I had not met before. Hopes were high that the Black Skimmer would arrive while the sunlight was bright like it did on a prior evening at 8:35 PM. That time passed and the skimmer did not skim but at about 8:50

not one, but two Black Skimmers glided over the water in tandem. They made a few circuits around the western end of the pond and once barnstormed the Canada Goose family, over their strenuous vocal objections, as a solitary skimmer had done the other night. All too soon the Black Skimmer pair, still in tandem, flew away to the north over the Great Lawn. I assumed the presence of the Canada Goose clan and the many Mallards on the water's surface interfered with the skimmers' work habits. On a small pond like this the Black Skimmers do better to wait for darkness when the majority of waterfowl retire to the shore or the rocks for the night. That would benefit the skimmers, but not their admirers who were so pleased to have had a clear view of them in the evening light.

At home later on I was amused to read someone else's emailed story about an aggressive Red-winged Blackbird. A male Red-winged Blackbird in Quogue, Long Island, it was said routinely attacks the author whenever he attempts to get into or out of his car. The author's parking spot in his driveway is in close proximity to the bird's nest. Characteristically this bird only attacks when the author's back is turned. The bird targets the back of his head as it swoops down coming so close he hears the "whoosh" of the air made by its wings. If the author looks directly at the bird it appears aloof or distracted and pays scant attention to him but once he turns around the blackbird attacks again. The Quogue bird exhibits a typical Red-winged Blackbird behavior that contrasts sharply with George's behavior in dealings with people. How is it that the majority of a species attack virtually any animal that comes near its nest while an individual of the same species actively attracts people to come close and provide food for its offspring? I have discussed other Red-winged Blackbirds that exhibit curious behaviors but here I am suggesting that some, George in particular, have a set of distinct behaviors that define a unique personality. Les Beletsky concluded from his own research that Red-winged Blackbirds are not little automatons that always react in identical ways in certain situations. Instead he suggests that these birds learn from experiences and are capable of making choices, albeit in a limited way, about how they might act or react to their best advantage.

This investigative method assumes that, within certain limits, breeding behavior, although influenced by genes, is modifiable by individuals and that decision-making behavior has been acted on by natural selection so that decisions are geared to increase lifetime reproductive success.[1]

Both George and the Quogue Red-winged Blackbird are in breeding mode but, as Beletsky suggests, they have each chosen to pursue a different strategy where humans are concerned. One bird sees people as a threat to be driven away while the other sees them as a resource and interacts with them. Vive la différence.

[1] Les Beletsky, *The Red-winged Blackbird: The Biology of a Strongly Polygynous Songbird*, p. 144.

Chapter 50 · July 4

A Paper Trail

ot and humid weather returned with a vengeance on July 4th. Initially at Morton's Pond I found exactly one Rock Pigeon and no other birds. After considerable waiting a few House Sparrows, Common Grackles and additional Rock Pigeons gathered to forage together in the shaded ground close to the water. When I provided some seeds Morton Downy and a Tufted Titmouse added a livelier element to the scene but it was not sufficient to hold me there. My thoughts kept returning to the Northern Cardinals at Willow Rock and George.

Yesterday at Willow Rock when I heard the male and female making "chip" calls to one another it was nothing new but when

This Northern Flicker does not need a shave. The "mustache" identifies it as a male.

they began to whiz inches past my head and shoulders they captured my full attention. The female repeatedly dived into the same spot inside an opening in the leaves of a Wisteria vine while her mate shot up to the tree above to perch and sing. I realized what they were engaged in when the female emerged from the cove holding a strip of brown paper in her beak that was longer than she was. As she moved away from me I saw more of the paper than I did of her. So I could say I followed her paper trail to the Wisteria. Slight but distinct clicking sounds emanated from the spot in which she disappeared. It took a moment but I understood what both birds were doing. She was weaving the paper into a network of twigs and grasses that were being fashioned into a nest while he kept a lookout.

Today when I peeked through my binoculars at the Northern Cardinal's nest at Willow Rock it looked like they had made considerable progress, but the builders were not there. I listened for their calls, but I did not detect them. I began to worry that maybe my presence had caused the Northern Cardinals to abandon their work. A wave of guilt washed over me. It lasted until I recalled I had not seen a cardinal anywhere on my walk. Later, I found information that could explain why the Willow Rock nest builders were absent and perhaps why I did not see other cardinals. Generally Northern Cardinals work on their nests in the morning and midafternoon. They do not obsess on getting the job done but take time off to eat, drink, bathe, and rest. The weather has an impact on the process as well. Their work can slow significantly if the temperature is high. Today's sweltering conditions easily justified a temporary work stoppage. Generally Northern Cardinals take three to nine days to finish a nest. Sometimes they may abandon it for a number of reasons (e.g., predator too near, lack of cover, too far to water source, etc.) and build another in a different spot.[1] I thought it likely if the Willow Rock Northern Cardinals were busy nest building then it was a good bet other adults in the Ramble were doing the same and perhaps they were all taking a break because of the heat and that's why I did not see any of them.

[1]Sylvia L. Halkin and Susan U. Linville, *Northern Cardinal*, p.16.

The location of this particular nest, I must say, seemed a less than optimum choice because it was a mere eight feet or so from a frequently traveled footpath and in a popular spot for viewing the Lake, Bethesda Fountain and the city skyline to the south. It is a favored destination of birders, sightseers, tourists, picnickers, dog walkers and lovers. Though it is rarely crowded a few representatives of one or more of these groups can almost continuously populate the place especially on a weekend or holiday. If the Willow Rock Northern Cardinals chose to finish their nest here they could not be birds that shunned the company of people. In this location avoiding people would be impossible.

I decided not to give up on the nest but to periodically monitor it in coming days. I then moved on toward the Northern Flicker nest. On the way Mack joined me and I was delighted to be able to give him his very first look at both a Northern Flicker and a Northern Flicker nest. The male flicker was standing guard next to the tree cavity. His position afforded us a great view of his intricate plumage. Every new bird-watcher should see this bird firsthand because most field guide illustrations do not do it justice. Northern Flickers look as if an artist had designed them. Henri Matisse comes to mind. The various geometric shapes and contrasting colors give its plumage a fauvist look. It has a light brown back with black "ladder stripes" not unlike similar species but that bold red "V" on the back of its gray nape, black crescent at the base of the throat, light cream-colored breast studded with smaller black spots sets it apart. The male has a prominent black line on its face, a red line in the western variety. To my eye their most dazzling plumage is the least likely to be seen. Here in the northeast the Northern Flickers are described as "yellow-shafted" because the feathers under the wings are a brilliant yellow. Out west the "red-shafted" breed have, as the name implies, red feathers on the underside of their wings. It is hard to get a look at the underside of the wings unless you see them in flight or you are positioned under a perching bird. Beginning bird-watchers are reminded that standing directly under any bird can have unpleasant consequences so if you attempt this approach I can only advise you to be careful and, to be safe, wear a hat.

Mack and I continued on together to see the Cedar Waxwing nest. A tail was sticking out of it. We could not see other bird parts or whole birds for that matter so we went to George's Pond. Finally I saw what Julio and Mack had told me. George was again ferrying food to the nest but he mainly concentrated on patrolling his territory. After George retired for the evening I waited with Mack, Nick and three or four other birders for the Black Skimmer. I found myself conflicted. I wanted to wait with the others for the skimmer but the desire to go home and take a shower nearly overwhelmed me until a cooling breeze came up. The air suddenly was filled with the sweet smell of whatever plant it is that has been smelling so pleasantly around George's Pond for the last week. The next thing I knew twenty minutes had passed and Mack was pointing toward the water saying, "There's the skimmer." We watched the bird hunt for about a half hour while alternately chatting and listening to the occasional line of Shakespeare's *Henry V* wafting from the stage of the Delacorte Theater. When we left the Skimmer was still working the pond with grace, ease and seemingly limitless energy.

Chapter 51 · July 7

Cedar Waxwinglets

All day I heard ominous predictions about imminent severe thunderstorms from the Weather Channel. When I was ready to make my foray into bird land, the sky was completely overcast and the air was heavy with moisture. It looked like the dire forecasts were going to be proven correct. I repeatedly checked the local weather report on the Weather Channel when the clock was "on the 8s" as they advertise. The Doppler radar picture showed a storm approaching each time I looked so I remained inside working and occasionally tuning in "on the 8s." My prime-time late af-

If you do not recognize this species it is probably because it has retracted its long narrow neck. This usually stoic Great Egret would later jump from a lofty perch and fly erratically over our heads trying to escape the explosions of sound and light.

ternoon bird-watching period came and went, but still it did not rain. I had to accept the fact that I had been misled, no matter how well meaning, by my faith in the Doppler radar image. I had missed my chance go birding for the day but I itched to get outside, especially on this summer evening. That was because the New York Philharmonic Orchestra was scheduled to play on the Great Lawn at 8:00 PM. The Great Lawn is adjacent to George's Pond.

At 7:30 PM I listened to WQXR radio, the classical station, and heard an announcement that the concert would go on despite the predictions of rain. I thought to myself, "Who am I to disagree with the decision of the New York Philharmonic?" I had no adequate reply to that question. I mustered the will to override my faith in the infallibility of Doppler radar and set out for the park. Just in case I had a folding umbrella with me but as I moved along so did the clouds. The sky had lightened considerably by the time I reached the park. I took this to be a good sign

On the Great Lawn there were fewer people assembled than usual for the outdoor New York Philharmonic concerts that have become a New York summer rite routinely attracting 50,000 people more or less. Sometimes a lot more than that. This evening many New Yorkers had been dissuaded from attending by the negative weather forecasts. I am certain many had accepted the Doppler radar images of an approaching storm as gospel. I was glad I had taken the chance but in truth the entire assemblage was plain lucky it did not pour.

That I would listen to the concert from the dock at George's Pond was a given. The sight lines are not the best but the sound is good if the wind is not too strong and there is the possibility of finding a seat on a wooden bench if one gets there early enough. I was in a hurry to secure my spot on the bench but I stopped at the Cedar Waxwing nest for a quick look. When I stood on the path across from the nest one of the adult waxwings faced me. I have debated whether or not to take a photograph of a Cedar Waxwing sitting on the nest, but each time I found an adult there its body was hidden. The most I ever saw was a tail sticking out. Tonight this waxwing was positively photo-friendly, but alas, I was not prepared.

I left my camera home as a precaution against the predicted storm. Maybe it was for the best. I would not want to unduly stress the wax wings with a camera flash.

I got to the dock in time to secure a seat and even managed to save a spot for Michael who arrived with reading materials, his take-out dinner and a printed program of the music to be played. He came prepared to enjoy himself and did.

Near the end of the concert at about 9:55 PM I spotted a Black Skimmer. Michael quickly spotted a second skimmer at the same time as the customary and popular fireworks display at the concert's end commenced. The human spectators spontaneously expressed their approval en masse. The birds had a contrary response. The Mallards squawked leaping from the water's surface and fleeing to the tallest thickest reeds on the north rim of the pond. The Canada Geese parents also sought a more secure spot but, keeping in character, the family calmly slipped from the flat rock on the edge of the island and paddled in straight line formation across the pond toward the eastern shore. An upset Great Egret jumped from a lofty perch and flew erratically over our heads trying to escape the explosions of sound and light. The two Black Skimmers had differing reactions to the fireworks. One raced off to the north at the first boom. The other continued to skim along the water as explosions echoed across the water but then it slowly rose and elegantly disappeared into the dark.

Jane and a friend came looking for the Black Skimmer. She was confounded when I told her she had just missed not one but two of them. Jane had a much more compelling story to tell herself. My observations of the waxwings that evening had not been sufficient to discover what Jane had. There were little "waxwinglets" in the nest. Jane had seen two chicks earlier in the day. This was welcome news to all the birders not just because there would be more adorable babies to observe but also because their arrival was taken as another sign that the park had become a little more hospitable to all species in general and this species in particular. The conversation then turned to speculation about how the nesting waxwings had reacted to the fireworks. We had witnessed the reactions of the

Mallards, Canada Geese, Great Egret and Black Skimmers but there were many other unseen species of birds that had been subjected to the same frightening flashes and crashes. I imagine that many of the usual suspects took it in stride having had experience with their occasionally rude and inconsiderate human neighbors. Perhaps migrants with less knowledge of people had more difficulty coping, but that is only speculation.

Some birders remained on the dock in hopes the skimmers might return but quickly lost interest due to the late hour but not before Michael reminded the group that the New York Philharmonic Orchestra was going to play their second and final outdoor concert of the summer on Thursday. We would all be back to enjoy the music, another obligatory fireworks finale and with luck a Black Skimmer or two.

Chapter 52 · July 8

Hawk on a Lamppost

Very few birds and even fewer people were around Morton's Pond. Excessive heat and obscene levels of humidity kept them away. I could mostly hear and occasionally see a few of the usual suspects like the Common Grackles and American Robins. These birds congregated in a shallow section of the Gill and on the shores

The incongruous juxtaposition of a wild raptor using a lamppost as a perch is inescapably symbolic of the admirable ability of some wild animals to adapt to a once natural landscape that has been radically transformed by humans. This particular Red-tailed Hawk happens to be the famous Pale Male. He has thrived in Central Park and successfully bred offspring for several years from a nest built over a window on a co-op located at 927 East 74th Street and Fifth Avenue. Pale Male has been the subject of innumerable amateur and professional photographs, the star of a documentary, a public television show and is a biographical subject in Marie Winn's, *Red-tails In Love*.

of Morton's Pond where they bathed, bathed some more and then bathed again. I do not believe these birds were just sprucing up. Their repetitive and lengthy dips looked more like a way to find relief from the weather. I wished I could join them but this is not possible in any of the seven bodies of water in the park that cover a total of 157 acres. They are off-limits to human bathers. Never say I did not tell you.

George's departure from his breeding territory will take place at the end of the month. Contemplating the inevitability of this was all the motivation I needed to skip all other points of interest and go directly to George's Pond. The shortcut I selected took me through the Maintenance Meadow, a spot I mainly visit at the appropriate times of the year to look for migrant birds. As I passed hurriedly over the grass my forward motion and my good intentions were arrested by the figure of a large Red-tailed Hawk standing on the open ground. This was none other than the world famous celebrity hawk, Pale Male. Opposite him three people sat on a park bench. Two more sat with their backs up against a tree. They and I had an unobstructed view of the hawk but the others seemed utterly oblivious to his presence or else they were among the most nonchalant New Yorkers this observer has ever encountered. I watched the hawk for a while before beginning a cautious approach. I was afraid I had startled Pale Male when he leapt into the air but he did not leave the area. He only moved a short distance to a branch on a tree beside the fence that marks the boundary with the sunken roadway known as the 79th Street Transverse. Once he perched there American Robins began to vocalize their extreme displeasure. I figured they were defending their nests in the same or a nearby tree. Baby robins, I have heard, are not an uncommon snack for a hawk. The angry American Robins' noisy commotion did not draw the attention of the people any more than the Red-tailed Hawk standing on the grass had. In a curious parallel the hawk paid no attention to the robins either. He sat aloof amid the hollering and hopping for a while. Then the hawk was on the move again. Pale Male glided over a chain-link fence to come to rest on the top of a street lamp anchored into the shoulder of the 79th Street Transverse below. From this vantage point the hawk continued to survey his surroundings.

I was amused to casually come upon this Red-tailed Hawk in this way and have the opportunity to watch him in action at such close proximity. The nonreaction of the other people present made it doubly entertaining. It seemed absurd that these folks took no notice of a bird about twenty inches in length with a wingspan of forty-eight inches standing on open ground in front of them. I wondered too what effect the sight of the raptor looking down on them had on the drivers speeding along the 79th Street Transverse and hoped it did not distract them with potentially fatal consequences. The hawk remained for several minutes on the lamppost and then flew a short distance to a tree beside the East Park Drive. A mere ten or twelve feet off the ground he perched above dozens of joggers, strollers, dog walkers and bicyclists that continually passed by and a line of customers waiting to be served by the hot dog vendor on the sidewalk. None of these people seemed to be aware of the Red-tailed Hawk in their midst either.

While Pale Male stood over the path I decided to detach my camera from the aluminum monopod so I that might take a picture at a different angle. Clumsily I dropped the monopod. A loud "CLACK, CLACK, CLACKITY, CLACK, CLACK, CLACK" rang out as it bounced down the side of the boulder upon which I stood and above which the raptor perched. I thought to myself, "You've done it now, klutz. The hawk is history," but instead of bolting Pale Male's head swiveled around and he gave me an intense look. A faint but undeniable shiver ran through me as I found myself at the business end of his sharp hooked beak and large expressive eyes, but there was no cause for alarm. The hawk stayed put, turned away and resumed its surveillance. He paid no more attention to me.

Chapter 53 · July 9

A Controversial E-mail

Did you ever pat yourself on the back for producing a good piece of work and then have a friend tell you it is too controversial to touch with the proverbial fork? My story about yesterday's close encounter with the Red-tailed Hawk provoked a wholly unexpected and downright disheartening response. I had sent an abbreviated version of it in an e-mail to a bird-watcher newsgroup. I expected that the newsgroup moderator would enjoy the story but instead it caused him apprehension. He argued against offering it

People should keep a reasonable distance away from nesting birds but these American Robins made that difficult. Instead of hiding their nest the adults (the male assists the female who does most of the work) built it alongside a well-traveled path more or less at human eye-level. This is not a good example of effective nest concealment.

to the network subscribers. He explained his misgivings in the following e-mail message with a few of my editorial additions placed in brackets to make the meaning more transparent.

> Unfortunately your post [e-mail] puts photographers in a bad light, which many individuals on the list are more than happy to use against photographers.
>
> This post [e-mail] will cause many to write and a battle may ensue over the rights of photographers and the rights of birds. This has happened before [with the members] on the list. Even though the RT [Red-tailed Hawk] didn't seem to mind you being there this same behavior could be used on a Mourning Warbler or more rare and skittish bird.

I decided not to argue the point and withdrew the story. While I knew that the moderator was correct in saying some would have objected to it I had a hard time accepting the notion that the episode would be perceived as a call to arms. This prompted me to reexamine my bird-watching behavior and ethics. After considerable thought and discussion with others I decided that I had behaved within acceptable limits. Instead of coming away from this self-examination chastened I had a greater awareness of the range of thought and feeling within the birding community and the existence of some unattractive intolerance of differing ideas among portions of it. Sometimes I think the impulse to protect and preserve birds can go so far as to make all but the most passive behaviors unacceptable. There is a continuum of opinion on how much interaction is permissible in the field. I deliberately use the word "interaction" to describe even the most unobtrusive actions of bird-watchers. Standing still and silently watching a bird from a distance of thirty feet may not fit everyone's definition of interaction but it does mine. The mere presence of the human observer in the field makes an impact no matter how miniscule or difficult it may be to measure. Once the bird is aware someone is watching it is no longer precisely the same bird it was before. As many a researcher understands, when you change the way you look at things the things you look at change. For me the issue then is about the appropriate limits of interaction. To put it another way when does interaction become intervention? That is the question every birder must answer.

What issues did my story about the hawk raise that others would find objectionable? First and foremost was my closeness to the hawk. I was within twenty feet of it at times. If some say I was too close should the same be said of the other people on the scene that were just as close? After all before I got there this hawk chose to stand out in the open within twenty feet of five other people. The difference between this observer and the others is that though they were physically present they did not pay attention to the hawk. If the hawk had a problem being close to any of us he did not show it. Second there was my clumsy dropping of the metal monopod that prompted the hawk to turn toward me. Objections to this overlook the fact that it did not result in the hawk's departure. The falling monopod was only a distraction. His hunt was not troubled by the sights and sounds coming from extremely active surroundings filled with people and all manner of noises produced by bicycles, baby carriages, park vehicles and conversations. Third some may say I was "stalking" the hawk with my camera. I say if the hawk felt threatened from any source it would not have remained in the same position long enough for my companions to search for and find it exactly where I left it some fifteen minutes later.

The moderator raised another issue about how birders must take care not to frighten skittish creatures that are considerably more timid than an adult Red-tailed Hawk like Pale Male. He might have chosen a different example than a Mourning Warbler. While usually secretive these birds are well-known to be attracted to birders who make a noise that sounds like "pish" and, I am not joking, this practice is widely referred to as "pishing." I have heard recently of how a Mourning Warbler, admittedly rare in Central Park, took so little notice of a group of birders that it wandered around their feet and nearly "climbed onto my shoe" in the words of one witness. Still I agree there are truly shy birds and nests that should be left alone.

Migratory species that spend a few days or weeks before moving on are in a different class. As a group they are more likely to react negatively to human presence. Most tiny migrating birds like warblers, or vireos, that hide in vegetation have a shy disposition. The message their stealthy behavior conveys is easy to read and must be respected by catering to the bird's shy disposition first and the bird-watchers' curiosity second.

In the environmental movement there is a conflict between those who would conserve nature and those who would preserve it. The difference, in very broad terms, is that conservationists allow for the interaction of people with the wild but the preservationists would diminish or, in extreme cases, deny it. A similar conflict exists in the bird-watching community but people draw distinctions between the concepts of interaction and intervention that change when applied to different situations. For example I came across a passage in John Shaw's *Nature Photography Field Guide* where he strongly advises photographers not to take photos of nesting birds because the risks of causing the birds to abandon the nest are very real. Says Shaw, "Nesting birds have been photographed over and over, and I doubt if any new or unique pictures are to be had. No photograph whatsoever is more important than the welfare of the subject."[1] I have no objections to this. I have taken photos of nests, but not many, and only in situations where I was assured I was not causing a problem for my subjects. My pictures of the American Robins that nest in heavily traveled public places are a good example. Mr. Shaw's decision draws a line where he believes the photographer crosses from interaction to intervention. However on another issue Mr. Shaw draws the line in a different place. He sees sees no reason to refrain from feeding wild birds and says he maintains more than one wild bird feeder year-round on his Colorado property. His position on feeding wild birds puts him at odds with those bird-watchers that think that feeding of birds is as undesirable as photographing nests. There are in fact large numbers of bird-watchers that believe providing food for birds diminishes their self-reliance by making them dependent on humans. Some also caution that when birds congregate at bird feeders they come into

[1]John Shaw, *John Shaw's Nature Photography Field Guide*, p. 144.

increased contact with droppings of other birds, which exposes them to possible infection or disease. My point is not to bemoan an inconsistency in Mr. Shaw's viewpoints, though some would say it does, but to demonstrate that individuals have different perceptions of what is interaction and what is intervention on a broad spectrum of related issues. Devoted nature lovers like Mr. Shaw make personal choices based on their own experience, knowledge and, whether they will admit it or not, emotional investment in the creatures they observe. I happen to agree with Mr. Shaw on both points. I might add that both the Audubon Society and the Humane Society, to name two authoritative groups, agree with Mr. Shaw as well.

There is at least one more potentially divisive issue running throughout *Club George* that some may find provocative. Among bird-watchers there is disagreement about where appreciation ends and anthropomorphizing begins. Anthropomorphism is bad, they argue, because animals are erroneously attributed with human abilities, feelings and thoughts. The false expectations of the observer may result in danger to both the object and observer. For example, albeit an exaggerated one, say an observer sees a Grizzly Bear cub. He or she might ascribe human traits to its behavior. It is playful. Its awkward juvenile movements and curiosity about its environment are reminiscent of a human infant's. It looks cute and furry too. The observer decides to touch it. This action could result in accidental injuries to either party should the cub be frightened or worse if one or both of its parents are present. Common sense says it is a really bad idea to play with a wild bear cub. How can any logical person argue with that? Let's consider another less extreme example. More than one bird-watcher I know vigorously opposes assigning nicknames to individual birds because they see that practice as going too far down the road to anthropomorphization. They argue that when one names a wild creature one begins the same process of attributing human characteristics to it that could eventually lead someone, as in my example, to touch a wild Grizzly Bear cub. Naming a wild bird, they believe, is not an interaction but an intervention. They draw the line in a far different place than I do. I

did not name George and do not know who did but many others
and I started using the name the moment we heard it because it
amused us and because it made it a lot easier for us to share information about this specific bird of whom we often speak. It is far
simpler and clearer to say "George" instead of "the male Red-
winged Blackbird at the pond near the Castle" every time we want
to talk or write about him. There are birders who object to this and
think it unethical. Needless to say there is a wide variation in what
bird-watchers believe is appropriate and responsible behavior.
Common sense, book learning, your own field observations and experiences will help you decide where you stand on these issues.

Chapter 54 · July 10

George Is off His Feed

I t had rained in the morning and because I feared it was going to rain again I was undecided if I should or should not take my walk. In the early evening an e-mail message from Viviene informed me that she had defied the weather reports and gone to the park where she had seen the two Cedar Waxwing nestlings in their nest again. She also described how a pair of adult Barn Swallows had been feeding two fledglings in the air while flying several feet above George's Pond. Reading her account made me feel a little envious and more than a little antsy. I discounted the threat of more precipitation, consciously avoiding a peek at the Weather Channel Doppler radar image lest it dissuade me, and went outside.

This Great Egret was perfectly agreeable to share its vantage point with two humans. The bird was not camera shy either.

When I reached the east end of George's Pond I climbed on to the rock for a panoramic view of the area. In front of me also surveying the pond stood a Great Egret. A male stranger sat not more than six feet from this egret that seemed perfectly agreeable to share this vantage point with two humans.

On the north side of the pond I spied Thelma and Viviene. Thelma waved to me then began pumping her arms as if she were flapping wings. She was trying to call my attention to something special. I thought she might have been referring to the stoic Great Egret at my feet but I was unsure. I decided to go ask her precisely what her arm flapping meant. Along the way to her I passed the Cedar Waxwing nest. I got there just in time to first see the profile of a parent standing on the edge of the nest putting food in one of two tiny upturned beaks. Another parent landed facing me on the opposite side of the nest. I saw this adult literally cough food up into its beak and then deposit it into one of the gaping mouths below in another display of Cedar Waxwing magic.

My first objective had been speedily accomplished. The content of the Cedar Waxwing nest had been revealed to me almost effortlessly. Immediately thereafter my second priority was met. I spotted the Barn Swallow family flying not over the water but above the Great Meadow in their acrobatic aerial feeding mode. I felt satisfaction having duplicated Viviene's sightings of the "waxwinglets" and the swallows but I did not know she and Thelma were way ahead of me. The two women had been watching three Black Skimmers flying in tandem over George's Pond as the New York Philharmonic Orchestra was warming up for the evening's outdoor concert with a rendition of Leonard Bernstein's *Symphonic Dances from West Side Story*. The three skimmers were what Thelma had been trying to alert me to with her arm flapping. I had missed them while concentrating on the Great Egret, the Barn Swallows and Cedar Waxwings. Oh well, I consoled myself with the thought that three out of four sightings was not bad but I would have loved to see the three Black Skimmers in the strong late afternoon light and flying in tandem no less. Beginning birders must accept that even the most keenly aware observer is going to miss something terrific some of the time.

Thelma had to leave, but Viviene and I returned to the Cedar Waxwings. Viviene has observed the Cedar Waxwings' behavior so closely that she knew the nestlings were fed at thirty to forty minute intervals. About thirty-five minutes had passed since I had seen the adults feed the chicks. As Viviene predicted the parents soon were back with another load of food. Viviene remained at her Cedar Waxwing observation post and I went to visit George. I only saw him once. He landed on his dockside perch, belted out a "konk-la-ree" song and displayed his red epaulets. I held out my peanut laden palm for his inspection. He cautiously approached then hesitantly placed one foot on my palm. Keeping the other foot on the fence he snatched a morsel and hustled several inches away on the top of the fence. This was not the George that exuded confidence and decisiveness but a somewhat timid and guarded George. Club George charter member Lena informed me she also thought George was behaving out of character. As Lena put it, "I think George is off his feed," not intending to make a pun as much as to make a point, though she did both neatly don't you agree? She went on to say during her observations the normally perky Red-winged Blackbird seemed far less energetic, was generally inactive and made noticeably fewer trips to the dock.

We conferred about George as if we were discussing the health of a family member. Could someone have frightened or hurt him? I did not think so but he had begun to show signs of having started to molt. A few contour feathers on his head and shoulders were gone. Lena noticed that too but she suggested his condition might indicate that he was ill. "He looks a little ratty," she said. I had to concur on that point but not necessarily that he was ill. We postulated this or that theory but there was no way for us to explain the change in George's behavior.

It could be normal and appropriate for George to look and act this way at this point in the season. It might be that he has entered a new phase in preparation for his departure from his breeding ground in about three weeks and his probable migration after that. This might explain his perceived lethargy and timidity but it does not illuminate the possible destiny of his last brood.

What is the fate of his newest chicks: where are they? While I am at it what happened to the first two fledglings? Why had no one seen George bring food to the new nest site for days, then they did and today we did not? If these nestlings had recently fledged some-one surely would have reported seeing them. I kept thinking back to the day George was making distress calls and chasing the four Common Grackles on his island. I suspected then that the nest had been attacked but later came to believe the chicks had not been in-jured. I was no longer sure of what had really transpired.

George, if only you could talk.

Lena and I continued to ruminate on these matters while we waited with Viviene, and later Michael, to see if the Black Skimmers would return to hear the performance of the New York Philhar-monic Orchestra as opposed to the rehearsal that the birds at-tended earlier. The skimmers did not reappear. The concert was wonderful, especially the Bernstein piece, but then I have always been partial to it. The obligatory fireworks display at the end of the concert thrilled the crowd but distressed the waterfowl. The Mal-lards exploded in erratic flights and calls but the Canada Goose family, as I anticipated, remained calm and orderly as they tra-versed the length of the pond searching for a place to escape the cacophony I knew they would not find until the fireworks ended.

Chapter 55 · July 11

Genuine Infectious Excitement

I devoted all my bird-watching time to George today. My thoughts keep returning toward the inevitability of his looming departure. After he is gone I would not want to feel I missed opportunities to make whatever final observations were possible. I want to know that I spent "quality time" with him while I had the chance and that I did not waste it. I had to wait about twenty minutes until he came to his perch at the dock. Upon arrival he sang a chorus of his "konk-la-ree" song and then hustled to my upturned palm filled with sunflower seeds and peanuts. He seemed like his old self again until, as he did on the last occasion, he hesitantly placed one foot on my hand and kept one on the fence while he grabbed a beak

The Common Raccoon was not possessed. The light in its eye is the raccoon equivalent of "red-eye" caused by the camera flash.

full. Then he retreated a few inches to devour it hurriedly and rushed off. He was energetic but still in an insecure mood.

There still have not been any reported sightings of Red-winged Blackbird chicks at the pond and I have not seen them or either of George's mates in a few days. Watching George head toward the island and work his way between the reeds I realized he had entered this same spot a little earlier. Over the next hour he spent significant amounts of time in the same clump of vegetation at the water's edge. Although it was not far from it, this was not the location of his last known nest, but it was precisely the type of place in which Red-winged Blackbirds favor nest construction and an excellent place for a newly fledged baby to hide. Could it be George had a third attempt at family production in the works? If a nest had escaped my detection and was a couple of weeks old there would be just enough time left for the Red-winged Blackbird adults to raise one more brood before they left the pond. The other possibility was George was not attending to a new nest but tending to fledglings from the last known nest. Oh brother! I need more observations and more information. Right now I am utterly puzzled by this behavior.

Meanwhile over the pond two elegant adult Barn Swallows with their two equally elegant fledglings arced and swooped as only swallows can. Twenty or more feet above the swallows, four loudly chattering Chimney Swifts were hunting in a style as reminiscent of bats as it was of birds. Still keeping an eye on the doings of the swallows and swifts I arrived at the Cedar Waxwing nest. An anonymous bird-watcher told me I had arrived between feeding intervals. The nestlings, she said, continued to be fed at thirty or forty-minute intervals and I had about ten minutes more to wait. The returning Cedar Waxwing adults proved her to be correct.

As George's Pond was my only planned destination today I could not gather firsthand knowledge of my other current prime viewing locales like Morton's Pond, Willow Rock, the Northern Flicker nest at the Rustic Arch or the Green Heron breeding ground, the latter having been neglected for too long. Luckily, Ned filled me in with his observations. Morton's Pond, he said, was nearly devoid of birds. He saw little at Willow Rock but he had big news about the Northern Flickers. Ned saw one baby inside the tree cavity as it poked its head out to take food from a parent clinging outside to the tree trunk. The Green Heron nesting area was, as disappointed birders often put it, quiet.

At about 7:00 PM the sky precipitously precipitated catching this startled bird-watcher unprepared. For all my indulgent self-congratulations for defying yesterday's weather forecast to find the Cedar Waxwing nestlings and the Barn Swallow family I had miscalculated big-time today. Without an umbrella, hat, or jacket I was soaked before I could get under the Willow Oak Tree at the dock entrance that has sheltered me on many occasions. Hoping to minimize the damage I still sought shelter there and for a short time the Willow Oak did a splendid job but when the wind began to drive the rain perpendicular to the ground I was sunk. My shirt became so heavy with water it clung to me like plastic wrap. My shoes were so filled with water that my feet made sucking sounds when I wiggled my toes. I stood with two companions under the tree. They shall remain nameless, because neither offered to share their umbrella with me. I was embarrassed to ask either of them if I might get under one. My mind raced trying to remember if I had done something that had so thoroughly displeased them they would withhold their assistance in this soggy situation but while I was working toward a diplomatic way to broach the subject the rain stopped. The sky cleared. I slogged my way to an open spot where the sun warmed me and I began to dry off. It was then that I discovered that my binoculars were water resistant but not waterproof. Looking through them was like watching a scene in a romantic movie where the image of embracing lovers is hazy and has a kind of halo around the edges. If my binoculars do not dry out overnight I know where I will be tomorrow. I will be digging through my files searching for the warranty I saved against the day just such an event might occur.

My hair and clothing dried off much more quickly than I could have predicted but, even after taking off and emptying my shoes, squishing noises continued to accompany my smallest movements.

Most people, whether they were rain soaked or not, wandered away at sunset. I waited with a couple of dedicated birders to see if we could spot the Black Skimmer. We did not see the Black Skimmer, but we did have an intriguing visitor. From the midst of the vegetation on the north side of the dock came a short series of thrashing sounds. I peered over the railing to find the source and found a Common Raccoon peering up at me.

This creature moved closer to the dock and was not at all concerned that a small crowd had gathered to watch it. While keeping both eyes on us the raccoon used both front paws to feel for something under the water. Whatever edible this might have been was impossible to determine because it was conveyed to the raccoon's mouth and swallowed in an instant. In the meantime a father with a young daughter and son had come onto the dock. I thought the kids would appreciate a close-up-and-personal look at the Common Raccoon so I called their attention to it. Father and son were enthusiastic about seeing the animal but the daughter was positively ecstatic. The little girl, five or six years old, could not stop repeating out loud that this was the first raccoon she had ever seen. I kept it to myself but I felt satisfaction having introduced her to it. Her excitement was genuine and infectious. It came closest to approximating my own.

A Very Sad Story

The quiet perfection of this sunny eighty-two dry degree day was disturbed by a brief but intense disagreement between two female Northern Cardinals over food at Morton's Pond. This was the first time I saw this behavior in the females of the species. They leaned toward each other until they were virtually beak-to-beak. Their bodies were held parallel to the ground. Their wings were raised up and away from their torsos. A sound that was part hiss and part growl emanated from both of them. It was over quickly when one gave up and fled. The one who stood her ground got the food.

Oblivious to this drama Morton Downy was hammering away at something on a thick branch. Mary Downy was working a series of thin branches below him closer to the ground. Beneath her in de-

Digesting her food, the victorious female Northern Cardinal kept her eye on me.

scending quantities were House Sparrows, Common Grackles, Rock Pigeons, Mourning Doves and the Northern Cardinals that kept rushing in and out of sight. The Blue Jay Brothers eventually joined in but remained overhead and mostly obscured behind leaves.

I considered if my next destination would be the Willow Rock Northern Cardinal nest and having failed to find the cardinals there for days I rejected the idea, but I found them hard to put out of my mind. The hope of finding them again resurged and I decided to try one last time. The moment I arrived I heard the "chip" call followed by a "whoit, whoit, cheer, cheer, cheer, cheer, cheer" song of a Northern Cardinal. A male with his crest standing straight up was singing flamboyantly on a branch above the nest. He twisted to the left and right and his chest heaved with deep breaths as he went on with his vocal performance. Knowing the male was here I suspected the female would be close to him and began to search for her. I looked at the nest site and found nothing but on second inspection I detected a small bright spot of coral peeking through the leaves. I suspected the coral color was from the beak of a female Northern Cardinal. Not wanting to inhibit the cardinal, I moved to the observation post behind the tree across the path I had used when I first watched the nest being constructed. From there I stared at the coral spot. I reasoned if the coral spot moved it meant there was a female cardinal hidden there. Several minutes passed and it did not change position. I began to think I had misinterpreted what I saw but then the spot moved. It stopped but then it moved again. The nest I assumed had been abandoned had not been abandoned after all. What was going on? The female Northern Cardinal was incubating her eggs while the male stood guard and warned off any potential intruders letting his mate know he was on the job with his song. I felt a combination of relief and excitement at having made this discovery. I was relieved that the nest was intact and excited that I would have a new destination on my agenda for days to come but I was still mystified that the cardinals had chosen this location. The human foot traffic was considerable. Several people passed between the nest and myself, for example, in the course of the few minutes it took to make these observations. Then again, as you know, I have seen nests in even more unlikely places. You will recall that American Robin's nest between the bronze breasts of Juliet and her Romeo, no doubt. After seeing that location I should not be surprised to find birds nesting anywhere.

The Northern Flicker nest site is in a less heavily traveled though by no means deserted area on a hill that is one of the highest in the park. These adult birds had made a greater effort to hide their activity than the cardinals but even they had uninvited company. I came here today specifically to look for the Northern Flicker nestling that Ned had told me about. As soon as I relocated the cavity I found the baby male poking his head out of it. Sometimes he called out and sometimes he fell silent. Mostly he stood in the opening as if he were waiting for something or someone. He was doing both. He waited for a parent and a meal. Mom and Dad were taking turns delivering food. They did not enter the cavity but remained outside holding on to the rim of the entrance with their claws and then leaned inside to feed junior. This kid apparently eats a lot and often. I watched several feedings during the next fifteen or twenty minutes and probably would have seen more had I remained.

Instead I found Viviene at the Cedar Waxwing nest where I told her the happy news about the Northern Cardinal and the Northern Flicker nests. She had already discovered them for herself but she had her own story to tell. Hers was a sad story, a very sad story.

Another bird-watcher had reported that a Brown-headed Cowbird had been seen tossing two chicks from the Cedar Waxwing nest to the ground. Viviene was visibly upset as we waited and watched together hoping to find proof that the story was wrong. For several minutes we saw no activity. It seemed that the nest might be empty and the disastrous story correct but when one of the Cedar Waxwing parents perched on the rim of the nest it bent over and planted food into an open beak that sprang up to meet it. Viviene was afraid that her own wishful thinking had caused her to misinterpret what she had seen. She was so unsure she asked me to tell what I thought I saw. I assured her that we had both witnessed proof that at least one chick was alive. Viviene and I reconsidered the evidence and tried to reconcile it with the story she had been told. It was possible that a Brown-headed Cowbird adult had placed her egg in the Cedar Waxwing nest, that it had hatched and when the nestling was strong enough it had tossed out one or two waxwing nestlings. Brown-headed Cowbirds do not build their own nests but instead deposit and then abandon their eggs in the nests of other species where they count on the parental instinct of the "host" birds to incubate, brood, and feed their deserted offspring. When they hatch the Brown-headed Cowbird chicks are larger and stronger than most of the songbird nestlings they compete with. The cowbird chicks will muscle the others out of the way to get more of the food the parents deliver. Sometimes the cowbird chicks literally push the others out of the nest. Unable to fly back to the nest these unfortunate babies will perish from exposure or starvation unless they are killed outright in their fall. Amazing as it may seem the breeding adults of many species accept and nurture cowbird nestlings left in their care but Cedar Waxwings are not usually known to be so accommodating. Instead they typically damage or push aside cowbird eggs.

The behavior I have described, that of an adult Brown-headed Cowbird deliberately planting its egg in another species' nest, is referred to as "brood parasitism." It is a phrase for the beginning birder to remember because you will eventually come across it in your reading. The Brown-headed Cowbird, primarily a ground feeder, is thought to have originally restricted its range to the Great Plains where it followed herds of bison whose hooves turned over the topsoil exposing food sources that would otherwise be harder to reach. With the thinning of the thick forests that once covered a larger portion of North America, and the introduction of grazing livestock, humans have unknowingly increased the amount of suitable foraging areas for cowbirds and at the same time brought them into contact with more breeds that they might parasitize.[1] Even though we knew these facts Viviene and I hoped that the story

[1]David Allen Sibley, *The Sibley Guide to Bird Life & Behavior*, pp. 548–549.

about the demise of the two waxwing chicks was not valid. Thinking back we were probably in denial and really did know the truth. At the time we were only willing to say that we knew for sure that at least one nestling was alive. What we could not contemplate until later was the probability that the surviving nestling we had seen being fed might not have been a Cedar Waxwing baby. It might instead have been the cowbird nestling that the grapevine had described as having done away with the host nestlings and ironically was now being raised by the adult Cedar Waxwings. It was possible that the sad story Jane had heard was true.

I had plenty of time to visit with George but after waiting two hours on the dock he still had not come near. I heard him moving about. I caught a few brief glimpses of him going to or from the north side of his island headquarters behind the shrubs or in the birch trees. He did not visit the spot where I had reason to suspect a nest or fledglings were hidden yesterday. That seemed to rule out the likelihood of a new nest but not the possibility that fledglings were in hiding somewhere else. Julio told me that that Gordon had fed George earlier in the day, but he and others had not seen him since. Considering again why George stayed away from the dock I hypothesized that he might be deliberately reducing the amount of calories he obtains from the foods Club George charter members can provide in favor of a protein rich insect and arachnid diet. He may require a diet change because he has begun to molt or because he is preparing for a migratory flight or both. Also the fact that I did not see either of his mates Ruby or Claudia may be a significant clue as to what the pond's Red-winged Blackbirds are up to. It is known that the female Red-winged Blackbirds begin their migration prior to the males. Maybe George's mates have already left.

Those of us remaining saw a Black Skimmer in the evening. Later when I stopped on the pond's east side hoping to catch one more glance at the Black Skimmer I nearly stumbled upon an adult female Mallard, her three juveniles and an adult male. They had all been snoozing in the center of the rock where I had not expected to find them in the dark. No damage was done but they all had been inadvertently awakened. A chorus of faint peeping-muttering sounds came from them as if they were too groggy to give me a proper round of irate "quacks" and "qwecks." The halfhearted calls petered out rapidly; the Mallards resumed their reclining positions and went back to their slumbers. I decided not to stay to search for the skimmer but instead backed away quietly so as not to disturb the sleeping ducks again as I departed.

Chapter 57 · July 14

Triumphant Trio

Polite summer temperatures prevailed again today and though an increase in humidity was detectable a strong breeze mitigated its potentially rude effects. At the Willow Rock Northern Cardinal nest I heard the male calling high in a tree but the nest was unattended. The female stood several feet beneath him on a nearby shrub. I put a bit of food under the shrub and backed away. She dived on it, ate a smidgen but rushed the balance to the nest. I left more food for her in the same spot as I was leaving. Before I could take three steps she was on it. I heard her babies chirping as she slipped into the vine. The chicks fell silent, I presume, when she began to fill their open mouths with pulverized peanuts.

Polite summer temperatures made for a lovely day and an even lovelier evening at George's Pond.

At the Rustic Arch the Northern Flicker female adult, clinging vertically to the tree trunk, was preening herself outside the nest cavity. Her chick poked his head out and called but she made no response. No doubt junior was asking to be fed but his mother had nothing to give. She must have already handed over whatever food she had to offer and was waiting for her mate to return with a meal for junior. Once he came back she would set off to collect more food for this insatiable critter.

I have been downplaying news of the Green Heron breeding ground not because I have lost interest but because the thick vegetation has made it so hard for me to make observations worth sharing. I gave it a try today and found a spot from which I could see a Green Heron adult, or I should say, I could see a portion of one sitting on a nest. Both sexes incubate the eggs so I am not sure if this was female or male. Regardless of its sex this bird does not seem to have changed position since the last time I caught a glimpse of it a few days ago. I do expect this site to become livelier soon because enough time has passed for more chicks to hatch. "Where are the older juveniles from the previous nest"? I asked myself before leaving. I imagine they really have fledged and are gone, but they have fooled me before. They still might be here hidden behind the leaves.

Viviene has been questioning almost every birder she meets to find out what they know of the fate of the Cedar Waxwing nestlings. She was at her park bench observation outpost when she told me she believed one of the Cedar Waxwing nestlings was in fact alive. She had watched the parents periodically arriving and passing food to a small beak that thrust up from inside when they leaned over the rim. I did not ask her the question that was struggling to find my lips: was it a Cedar Waxwing or a Brown-headed Cowbird they were feeding? From her optimistic attitude it was obvious that Viviene believed at least one Cedar Waxing chick was alive in the nest. She was interpreting all her observations as proof of what she wanted to be true, that a Cedar Waxwing nestling was alive and well. I wanted to believe it too but in my heart I felt it was not so.

I waited twenty minutes, before George made an appearance at the dock. He arrived in style by sweeping low across the water from the Weeping Willow Trees to his favorite perch on top of the fence. George's red epaulets stood up and away from his wings as he glided head-on toward me. This view of George in flight is one I can never see too often but ironically have never been able to capture with my camera. The moment he touched down I recognized that he was his most energetic and confident self. He blasted out his "konk-la-ree" song and then lifted his wings to show off his epaulets in a very jazzy display. George looked to me to be in fine health though I noted those few tiny spots where contour feathers were missing. He was clearly not off his feed today.

When Ned told me that he had spotted a Red-winged Blackbird chick from the cliff I was thrilled but puzzled about which brood it could be from. It might have been one of the two chicks from his earlier brood that had seemingly vanished but there was also the possibility it could have emerged from the newest nest site. Either explanation was welcome but I really could not give an informed opinion about which was correct. My understanding of his off-springs' fates has been plagued with gaps, confusions and utter misunderstandings. I need more time to look and learn but time is running out.

While I was not close to unraveling the truth about George's progeny at least I got to enjoy an unexpected bonus along with this evening's other Black Skimmer watchers. Ned, Peter, Dennis, Mark and Alice and I watched a trio of Black Skimmers glide in formation over the pond. Unfortunately the Mallards and Canada Geese were scattered over the water at the time. We assumed that the skimmers were going to another venue where they would find the water's surface deserted when they rose up and wheeled away into the distance. We were all wrong. After a number of the other waterfowl moved away from the center of the pond and toward the shores one of the Black Skimmers returned. Five minutes passed and a second skimmer joined the first. Soon, a trio of Black Skimmers was again over the pond. Of course, it is possible these three skimmers were not the same three birds that were there earlier. As is too often the case without unique identifying markings, it is impossible to say with certainty which individual birds these were but it really did not matter. What was important to us was seeing the three of them together. Two flew in tandem while the third went its own way. At one critical juncture all three Black Skimmers were about to converge on the same spot at the same time. We thought a collision was unavoidable but the birds knew better. I was not the only one that gasped out loud believing the birds really were going to crash but we were once again mistaken. They steered clear of one another with a series of subtle maneuvers performed at the last possible second. The most accomplished precision flying teams like the Blue Angels or the Thunderbirds could never come close to the skill with which these creatures passed within inches of one another with seeming ease and undeniable grace.

Chapter 58 · July 15

Wafer Thin Gray Fuzzy Fringe

The last three rolls of film I had developed and printed were a sorrowful lot. So many opportunities wasted. So many unique sights left only to memory. Ordinarily even in a largely disappointing batch of photos there are a few of value but this time there were literally none. After an extended session of self-reproach and a shorter one of tooth gnashing I renewed my commitment to do a better job. Maybe I have been concentrating on looking to the exclusion of shooting? That works for the bird-watcher in me but not for the photographer. Both require practice as I, at times such as this, am painfully aware. I resolved to do better as I started my session today. Of course to take photographs of any quality one does

This Red-tailed Hawk was the motivation for the songbird's agitation.

require subjects. Few birds were visible at first. At Morton's Pond
even the reliable usual suspects were not in sight. Teasingly to the
northwest I heard the calls of two or more birds. Straining to identify them I began to think they were signaling distress. I followed
the sound and found four angry and animated American Robins.
The motivation for their agitation was a large Red-tailed Hawk in
their midst. After about fifteen minutes the Red-tailed Hawk
moved on, the irate American Robins quieted down. I began hearing the usual suspects as they returned to Morton's Pond. First to
be back on the scene were a dozen House Sparrows followed by a
few Rock Pigeons, then Morton Downy, an adult and juvenile
Tufted Titmouse, a male and female Northern Cardinal and one of
the Blue Jay Brothers.

Now that I felt all was right with the world, beginning at least at
Morton's Pond, I went to Willow Rock where a strong breeze periodically parted the leaves of the Wisteria to give me a view of the
female Northern Cardinal snugly situated inside her nest. Above
her looking spectacularly fiery red in the late afternoon light her
mate kept watch.

In contrast at the Northern Flicker nest I saw nothing at all for
the fifteen or more minutes I waited. I began to believe the status
of the nest had changed because I should have seen at least one
parent on the tree trunk or junior's head poking out of the opening during that time. The possibility of foul play comes to mind
more often when I do not see birds I have expectations to find especially after the debacle with the Cedar Waxwing nest and
George's here-again-gone-again juveniles. However in this case I
leaned toward the idea that the Northern Flicker nestling had
fledged and the family was off foraging together in another part of
their territory. Sufficient time had elapsed for that to be possible.

At the Green Heron's breeding ground I enjoyed a tantalizingly
contrary experience. An adult heron was not sitting as I have so often reported. It was standing. Its head and upper body cleared the
top of a branch so I could see it quite plainly. That was the largest
proportion of any adult Green Heron at this nest that I had seen in
a long while. Maddeningly a single large oak leaf covered the

opening of the nest but through my binoculars I saw what looked like a wafer thin gray fuzzy fringe protruding from behind it. What was it? I believed this barely perceptible wafer thin gray fuzzy fringe was a trace of down covering an otherwise completely concealed newborn chick. I hoped that the breeze would move the leaf blocking my view but it did not. I gave up looking after my arms began to ache from holding up my binoculars for too long. I will come tomorrow when I presume either the leaf or the wafer thin gray fuzzy fringe will have moved sufficiently to reveal its true identity but between you and me, I know it has to be a nestling.

I wished Viviene had been at her observation post so she could fill me in on the Cedar Waxwing nest's status but she was not there. I made a mental note to make my own inquiries along the birdwatchers' grapevine or the Internet newsgroup to get the latest information about it as I gravitated toward the dock. On my way I met Lena who was also on her way to visit George. Together we listened to him as he carried on around his island. He did not visit the dock but one of his mates did. Yesterday I had speculated that both female Red-winged Blackbirds had left the pond but that theory collapsed when Ruby showed up. It then occurred to me that Ruby might have been the bird Ned saw when he reported finding a juvenile Red-winged Blackbird on the island. It is unlikely Ned would confuse an adult female with a juvenile but no one else as yet has said they saw a fledgling. Certainly neither Lena nor I saw one today and we surely wanted to.

Swirling around us there was an almost constant turnover of parents with young children coming mainly to look at the waterfowl and turtles in the water at the foot of the dock but several strangers made inquiries of us about the status of the famous Redwinged Blackbird they had heard about. They may not have had a satisfying look at George but many of them got an uncommon look at the pond's big kahuna Snapping Turtle after it came up from the deep to take some of the food being offered the other creatures on the surface. As the sun went down the crowd lost its enthusiasm for the animals including the Snapping Turtle and drifted away. The animals too began to go to their resting places. Lena left before it got dark but Mark and Michael stayed with me to look for the Black Skimmer. We gave up waiting when our impatience grew to unacceptable levels and we went our separate ways but during my customary nightly peek at the pond from the eastern end a Black Skimmer flew past the edge of the rock I stood on. It was making repetitive tight circular sweeps over the cove at the extreme southeastern end of the pond. It would have been difficult if not impossible to see the bird in this position from the dock. The skimmer might have already been here unseen while my friends and I grew frustrated searching for it from our vantage point across the pond. Sorry fellas. Alone I watched the skimmer until it began widening its range over the water and when it chose to linger on the far western end I chose to do my own lingering even farther east, at home.

Chapter 59 · July 16

Blue Jay Blues

saw a Red-tailed Hawk near Morton's Pond less than fifty feet away from where the distraught vocalizations of American Robins led me to one yesterday. Here the chorus of screaming robins randomly dived perilously close to the back of the unflappable raptor. If there were other sights and sounds around me I did not notice them. My attention was riveted on this scene. In due course the hawk moved on and the American Robins calmed down and returned unscathed to their activities that had been interrupted when the raptor arrived.

I told Viviene about this robin-raptor confrontation and she told me about another that, unlike the one I watched, had a brutal outcome. I found her across from the Cedar Waxwing nest. She

The inspiration for my Blue Jay Blues.

told me that while she had watched both adult Cedar Waxwings coming and going from the nest she saw them feed the sole surviving chick. Then she abruptly broke off the conversation for reasons that were not apparent. Something in her manner told me she was upset so I did not question her. We both silently stared at the nest where there was no perceivable activity. When I turned back to Viviene her eyes were filled with tears and she could not speak. In a while she composed herself enough to tell me she had more to say but that she could not bring herself to talk about it. Instead she would send me an e-mail with an account of her observation in the evening.

WARNING: Look out. Here comes one more story of graphic violence.

Her e-mail told how she had watched an adult Cedar Waxwing clutching a bright red berry in its beak stand on the edge of the nest. Instead of passing the food to the chick inside the adult waxwing flew off with the berry still in its beak. Immediately a Blue Jay took its place at the nest. Viviene was shocked as she helplessly watched the Blue Jay bend over the nest and unceremoniously devour the living nestling inside. Considering her strong emotional attachment to the inhabitants of the nest it was no wonder she had found it hard to discuss without allowing for a reasonable amount of time to pass. Viviene's story leaves no doubt at all about the nestling's fate but questions still remain about what species it was. If the birders' grapevine story about the Brown-headed Cowbird nestling pushing two Cedar Waxwing chicks out of the nest is correct then it is likely that the sole remaining chick was the perpetrator itself. It was a Brown-headed Cowbird.

Piecing all the facts together I now believe that the Cedar Waxwing parents had in fact played host to a Brown-head Cowbird nestling. When it had reached a sufficient level of development the Brown-headed Cowbird chick had eliminated the competing Cedar Waxwing nestlings. Ironically the Brown-headed Cowbird nestling itself had been done in by a marauding Blue Jay. This nest site had more than its share of violence but most nestlings face stiff odds against their survival. Roughly fifty percent of songbirds do not survive their first year and smaller birds tend to have a shorter life expectancy than larger ones. In some diminutive species mortality rates may rise to seventy-five percent.[1] There are a number of reasons for this high mortality rate but one of the most common is predation. In Central Park there are a surprising number of predators. I have previously mentioned Red-tailed Hawks, Black-crowned Night Herons, Common Grackles, and Great Blue Herons but falcons, gulls and owls of various species exact a toll too. So do raccoons, Gray Squirrels and feral cats. Of the latter I have personal knowledge of three individuals actively hunting in the park.

Diseases caused by viruses, bacteria, fungi, and parasites assault birds but usually do not cause widespread damage unless environmental factors create a situation in which an outbreak afflicts a large population. The results can be devastating but stricken species typically make a comeback in subsequent breeding seasons. Competition for resources, including food, water, nesting sites and nesting materials, between individuals or between species can limit the numbers that survive in a given season. Weather is a powerful factor. People are not the only victims of hurricanes, tornados, deep freezes and floods. Fire is another threat. Loss of habitat in general is perhaps one of the most vexing dilemmas. Severe weather and fire are relatively short-lived threats but climate change can have a longer lasting effect. Natural changes in climate are arguably being exacerbated by man-made causes. Habitat loss is aggravated by civilization's pollution and territorial encroachment that are relentlessly increasing worldwide.[2] The introduction of non-native species is another contributing factor. My witnessing of the Red-bellied Woodpecker's eviction by a European Starling, for example, demonstrates how similar confrontations have led to

---

[1] Joseph Forshaw, Steve Howell, Terence Lindsey, and Rich Stallcup, *A Guide to Birding*, p. 33.
[2] Author's Note: I recommend reading a comprehensive summary on the topic of factors limiting the size of bird populations in David Allen Sibley, *The Sibley Guide to Bird Life & Behavior*, pp. 107–118.

a decline in several North American bird species since the starlings were introduced here.

A report from the National Audubon Society paints a disturbing picture for many species especially those whose prairie, grassland, forest and shoreline habitats are eliminated to make way for homes, industrial parks, parking lots, agribusiness megafarms and beachfront developments. "The State of the Birds," a report in *Audubon* magazine for October 2004, provides this sobering summary.[3]

> Almost 30% of North America's bird species are in "significant decline." The overall state of the birds shows:
> 70% of grassland species are in statistically significant decline.
> 36% of shrubland bird species are declining significantly.
> 25% of forest bird species are declining significantly.
> 13% of wetland bird species are declining significantly.
> 23% of bird species in urban areas are declining significantly.

Lest you dismiss these sobering statistics as being an exaggeration or that only birds are suffering consider this prediction, or warning if you like, from Edward O. Wilson, scientist, author, professor, and curator in entomology at Harvard University in 1992. He is widely recognized as the originator of the field of biodiversity or the study of how environmental changes have influenced the genetics of species. His studies led him to conclude that birds were not the only creatures in peril.

> Species are disappearing at an accelerating rate through human action, primarily habitat destruction but also pollution and the introduction of exotic species into residual natural environments. . . . In the world as a whole, extinction rates are already hundreds or thousands of times higher than before the coming of man. They cannot be balanced by new evolu-

---

[3]Greg Butcher, www.audubon.org/bird/stateofthebirds. "The State of the Birds," *Audubon*, October 19, 2004.

tion in any period of time that has meaning for the human race.[4]

No doubt Wilson's alarming analysis about widespread extinction of species puts my story of this single Cedar Waxwing nest into perspective. There are much larger issues at work in the world than this episode in Central Park. While it is indisputable that humans contribute to the demise of birds there is an epilogue to the story of this unlucky Cedar Waxwing nest in which this concept was carried to an extreme. A particular bird-watcher spread word through the birders' grapevine that Viviene was responsible for the debacle at the Cedar Waxwing nest. How so? This individual claimed Viviene's habitual presence near the nest site had alerted the Blue Jay to its location. In this interpretation of these events Viviene's behavior crossed the line from interaction to intervention with deadly results. I think that is an unfair judgment. Even if Viviene had been the only person in the vicinity the Blue Jay could have found the nest without her assistance just as Blue Jays have done for millennia. Raiding nests after all is part of what Blue Jays do for a living. In this case dozens of people sat on the particular bench that had been Viviene's observation post and adjacent benches for prolonged periods, weather permitting, every day. Others picnicked on the grass directly beneath the nest. Many more strolled past it. Some rolled by on skates, skateboards, or bikes. If a finger should be pointed to anyone that led the Blue Jay to the spot it would be hard to determine which one or which group was responsible since so many had been there.

I had other feelings to work through after this incident. Though I understood that the Blue Jay's action was all part of its daily effort to survive I was ambivalent about it. I was having a hard time separating my intellectual comprehension from my emotional reaction to the brutal killing of a defenseless chick. My feelings were further complicated by recognition of my own prejudices about the species

[4]Edward O. Wilson, *The Environmental Ethic*, quoted from "The Diversity of Life," in *Listening to Earth, A Longman Topics Reader*, Christopher Hallowell and Walter Levy, eds.: pp. 201–202.

involved. I felt it was less upsetting when the victim had been the Brown-head Cowbird and more so when it had been a Cedar Waxwing. The cowbird, I reasoned, had taken lives not in a direct effort to obtain food but indirectly through the elimination of its competitors. Was a creature that behaved that way somehow more deserving of a violent end than a seemingly less aggressive species like the Cedar Waxwings? Asking questions about the morality of these acts clouded my judgment and conflicted my interpretation about the essential facts.

My case of Blue Jay Blues reminded me of how I had been filled with negative feelings toward the European Starlings that evicted the Red-bellied Woodpecker from its home. It took a while but I got over it. Well, almost. On occasion I still visualize that episode when I look at a starling and again experience negative feelings, but that's the exception and not the rule. I have actively been trying to accept all birds as they are and not as I would have them be. I am not always successful but I do remind myself that it is fruitless to apply moral values to their behaviors. Birds follow an instinctive plan for survival that, as far as we know, goes unquestioned. Questioning is not a trait observed in most of the animal kingdom and sometimes is hard to detect in the creatures at the top of the food chain whose questioning nature is supposedly one of their defining characteristics.

I did get some uncontroversial news through the birder grapevine later on. I learned that others reported the Northern Flicker chick had not met a cruel fate but had fledged and was in the care of its parents. I also heard about the male Red-winged Blackbird called Larry that has been taking food from people at Bow Bridge. I had looked for this legendary creature before but had not found him. I decided to try again. As I began my search I met Harry, the fellow who applies his homemade mixture to the Cork Oak Tree at Morton's Pond, standing close to the southern end of Bow Bridge. The first thing he spoke of was the same male Red-winged Blackbird I sought though he did not identify it as the bird called Larry. A passing stranger who overheard him paused long enough to say, "Oh, you mean Larry the Red-winged Blackbird" then continued on his way. Without missing a beat the very bird under discussion, Larry himself, raced down the center of the path, made a dramatic two point landing on Harry's hand, messily snatched up some seeds and disappeared with them into the shrubs. "Amazing timing," I said, and we both laughed. What could possibly have constituted a more appropriate introduction to Larry? I cannot think of one.

There were many birds in this spot, another of Harry's favorite locations. The species included dozens of Mallards and House Sparrows, many White-throated Sparrows, two Song Sparrows and a male and female Northern Cardinal that were mates. I stayed with Harry and this colorful collection of birds until the urge to check up on the Green Heron nest grew too strong.

Inside the Green Heron breeding ground I assumed the same vantage point I had the last time. I discovered that my conjecture about the wafer thin gray fuzzy fringe in the nest was only partially correct. I found not one gray down-covered Green Heron chick in the nest but three. When I spread word to other birders about these nestlings I found my knowledge lagged far behind the rest. There was a report that others saw not three but four chicks and another report that one more had been spied in the Green Heron nest in the adjacent tree. Again I was chagrined to find that I was one chick short, possibly two in this instance. I will have to search for a better spot to view these nests but the lush foliage is a formidable obstacle. Looking at those substantial leaves I thought back to the beginning of the season when I could see straight through the branches to the adult birds at their nests. The leaves did not obscure them then but the birds must have known that by the time their eggs hatched the sites would be completely covered over. I assume it was instinct that instructed them and they did not learn the best places to build by trial and error, but let's not get into that chicken-or-the-egg and nature-versus-nurture debate now. We have already had too large a dose of philosophizing for one session.

My combined missions to find Larry the Red-winged Blackbird and my observation of the Green Herons had cost me considerable time. I arrived too late at George's Pond to see George. I heard him calling and singing from his island but he had already begun the process of roosting. A Club George charter member who had visited with him earlier filled me in as best she could. Basically all she could report was that she had seen George acting out in his aggressive and energetic manner. That was reassuring but I wanted to know more. No one could tell me more. I did derive some additional comfort listening to the strong but calm tone of George's voice as he settled in for the night. He sounded like he was in fine shape.

However there was something at the pond that did alarm me. A huge crop of algae had blossomed in the water seemingly overnight. Aesthetically speaking it is the pits but I do not think it is detrimental to the animals. It did not dampen the spirits of the various turtle species, the Mallards or Canada Geese on the water though technically they were already damp and you would be right in thinking I just committed a shameless pun for which I am unapologetic. I felt the need to lighten up the narrative at this point. Whether or not I succeeded I leave to your judgment. And speaking of the crowd of damp creatures at the foot of the dock, among them I recognized Daffy, the Mallard with the broken beak. He continues to survive in spite of his disability and the random persecution by his brother and sister ducks and puns, like water, roll right off his back.

Chapter 60 · July 17

Beaucoup de Rendezvous

I had promised to take Kim on a tour of my preferred bird-watching locales. I picked the right day. The weather and the sunlight could not have been better. We found the usual suspects at Morton's Pond plentiful and lively. Kim was especially taken with a male and female Cardinal couple that moved around us perching on a branch or fence where they studied us with what we interpreted as increasing inquisitiveness. What we found most fascinating was how the feathers of their crests rose partially, then fully and then collapsed into the contours of their sleek heads while they looked at us through one eye and then the other.

I believe that the Northern Cardinals around Morton's Pond are relatively tamer than others in the Ramble because of their

Peek-a-boo, I see you. A curious male Northern Cardinal checks us out.

more frequent exposure to people. I have a strong suspicion too that they can recognize individuals that routinely feed them. To demonstrate to Kim just how responsive these particular birds can be I held up a peanut with which I deliberately tried to attract the female Northern Cardinal's attention. Standing on the fence directly opposite me, the cardinal at once locked her eyes onto the peanut. Her head moved in sync with the food whether I moved it left, right, up or down. All the while the feathers of her crest moved oh-so-slowly-up and then oh-so-slowly-down. When I pulled back my arm to prepare to toss the peanut, the cardinal repositioned her torso parallel to the ground and leaned forward. Undoubtedly she understood my body English and was poised to spring forward the instant I launched the morsel. As the projectile hit the ground the female was on it. I had never done this quite in this way with this particular bird. I was even more impressed than Kim with the cardinal's response but I did not let on preferring to strike a nonchalant pose, as by now you know I sometimes do, just to get a laugh when I have a witness present. I know it's corny but I get a kick out of it.

The female cardinal that had retrieved the peanut resumed her position on the fence and continued watching us. Her male companion joined her. Now both sat intently watching my hand, their crests slowly rising and falling, and their bodies poised and ready to rocket to the food. They each in turn went after the food several times but their actions began to attract the attention of some of the other usual suspects. A group of House Sparrows and Rock Pigeons and two Gray Squirrels joined in. When the female cardinal lost out to a speedier House Sparrow she made a dramatic and unexpected display of anger. Rearing up on her legs, she stretched her body making herself appear larger than she really is. Then she hissed like a snake. None of this impressed the sparrow but it greatly impressed her two human observers.

For a while Kim found it hard not to talk about how expressive the Northern Cardinals had been. It was a revelation to her to see how readily she could read the bird's body language and vocalizations. I have found I can distinguish surprise, excitement, irritation and, though rarely, rage in their movements and sounds. I have seen the expression of these basic emotions in other species too but the cardinals' use of their crests communicates a wider and subtler range of information to me. If you think I have launched into a bout of excessive anthropomorphizing first consider the behavior of animals of which many readers have firsthand knowledge: domestic pets. For example, visualize if you will the body language and vocalizations exhibited by a dog playing catch. The pooch's eyes follow the thrower and the ball. The animal communicates its enthusiasm, or lack of it, by how and where it focuses its eyes, how it wags its tail or moves its head, paws and body and in the tone, volume and duration of its vocalizations. To the experienced pet owners these behaviors unambiguously signal the dog's emotional state. It is not, I believe, rampant anthropomorphizing for one to say that the pooch is excited, enthusiastic, playful and even happy. Cat owners know the same thing about their pets. In their feline way they exhibit similar behaviors that let their owners in on their emotional state. In my close observations of Northern Cardinals I have come to recognize signs and signals that communicate in a similar way. Okay, admittedly it is not at the same level of sophistication exhibited by dogs or cats but it is comprehensible.

On the periphery of Morton's Pond Kim enjoyed personal appearances by the Blue Jay Brothers and the Tufted Titmice. Disappointingly the peanut-catching Red-bellied Woodpeckers were out of sight. When Kim saw two long reddish feathers protruding from the nest at Willow Rock she needed to be reassured that they actually were attached to the end of a female Northern Cardinal snuggled inside. She was crestfallen to learn her back had been turned when Larry the Red-bellied Woodpecker landed in Harry's hand near Bow Bridge.

At Bank Rock Bridge, Bruce was looking through his industrial strength binoculars resting on a tripod beside a photographer looking through a five hundred millimeter telephoto lens atop a second tripod. A few yards away two Black-crowned Night Herons were standing close together in a tree. The herons, usually hidden during the day, made no attempt to conceal themselves. A passing bird-watcher told us these particular birds were likely to be mates because they had been seen in the company of a juvenile Black-crowned Night Heron earlier. As exciting as it was to get an unobstructed view of two Black-crowned Night Herons they were not what Bruce and the photographer were focused upon. They had found an opening through the trees that allowed them to peer directly into a Green Heron nest. Through Bruce's powerful binoculars we were able to see an adult Green Heron tending four chicks. Before moving on the anonymous but well-informed birder told us someone else had seen one newborn chick in the Green Heron nest in the adjacent tree. That confirmed the story I had recently heard. We indulged ourselves in the sight of the four down covered nestlings in one nest but none of us could locate the baby said to be in the other. This meant that I remained one chick short but, not that it was a consolation, so did my companions.

I had an insight about the two loitering Black-crowned Night Herons as we walked away that had not dawned on me when I first saw them. I have no doubt that the Black-crowned Night Herons were also watching the Green Heron chicks but for a very different reason. The herons were waiting for an opportunity to make a meal of them. They were not likely, I think, to raid the nest but stood by ready to take advantage of the situation should one chick step out into the open or fall from the nest as they sometimes do. The Black-crowned Night Heron's presence had served as another reminder how closely violence waits below the surface of all this natural beauty but I did not risk spoiling Kim's excellent mood by mentioning it to her.

I took Kim to the former Cedar Waxwing nest site. I am not sure why I did since I knew it was empty. Directly under the nest, a young woman and man were picnicking. They asked me what I was looking at, which was understandable, especially since I had mindlessly wandered so close to them that I was nearly standing on their blanket. Reflexively I recounted the violence that had been witnessed here. How a Brown-headed Cowbird had killed two Cedar Waxwing chicks and a Blue Jay had in turn devoured the Brown-headed Cowbird. As the words came out of my mouth grimaces grew on the faces of the strangers and Kim. I was sorry to have said them. I apologized and expressed my hope that my story about violent deaths on the spot they occupied had not ruined anyone's appetite or afternoon. I grabbed Kim's arm and we hurried away.

Our final rendezvous of the day was with George at his pond. Julio was there to fill us in on George's activities. He said he had seen George as early as 9:00 AM making several trips to the dock to hustle food from strangers and Club George charter members alike. In the afternoon his visits were fewer but Julio said he saw George hunting up meals from naturally occurring sources in various places around his territory. Julio's observations added exactly zero evidence to my hypothesis that George was deliberately limiting the seeds and assorted baked goods humans offered him to concentrate instead on increasing his insect and arachnid intake. Today he was evidently tapping all available food sources equally.

When George came to the dock Kim held out her hand filled with bread. Mine was filled with peanuts. On the top of the fence George wove back and forth studying the contents of the two hands. Decisions, decisions. He acted decisively choosing the peanuts in my palm. He lingered a moment after he ate his fill, looked me in the eyes and then left. Kim felt a little sad that he had not favored her hand. I felt a little sad because I was aware this would be one of my last encounters with George during this breeding season.

Mingling with the Club George charter members and assorted visitors were a photographer and a reporter from the *New York Post*. They were doing a story about the Great Egret (very likely Roger Egret) that frequents the pond. Someone had called the paper and said that "a big white bird" as he or she put it, "was seen flying over the stage of the Delacorte Theater during last night's performance of *Henry V*." They assumed the bird was a Great Egret but from their description of the bird and the circumstances I thought it possible that the "white" bird could have been a Black-crowned Night Heron or even a Black Skimmer. The reporters might have taken a photograph of any of these species had one been available but none were. They left saying they would return the next day hoping for a better "big white bird" turnout.

Chapter 61 · July 18

Squirrel Attack

Morton's Pond was the picture of ornithological inactivity. A lone male Northern Cardinal stood out sharply against a pile of freshly overturned earth. He had discovered a bug bonanza in the soil that had been freshly dug up by the crew repairing a section of drainage pipe. Flooding had plagued the area around Morton's Pond as long as I have visited it and, as others have told me, long before I came onto the scene. I am glad it is being corrected but it was an incongruous sight to see a backhoe parked in the Ramble. It reminded me that the wild birds and landscape I cherish are part of a fabricated wilderness. The illusion that it is natural is strong enough to convince the birds and myself to stay and that is all that matters.

The aggressor strikes an innocent pose. I won't be fooled again. I hope.

Betsey stopped by Morton's Pond and had a chance to tell me what she knew about the demise of the Cedar Waxwing nest. She said that she had heard a Brown-headed Cowbird chick had been responsible for pushing both Cedar Waxwing chicks out of their nest. Stan, she told me, had found the deceased nestlings on the ground beneath the nest. Betsey had confirmed my understanding of the events except the part about the Blue Jay later attacking the Brown-headed Cowbird. I have continued to avoid discussing this interpretation of the story with Viviene but now that I was certain it was accurate I thought she should know. I remained reluctant however because I did not want to upset her again.

Mama Northern Cardinal was still on her nest at Willow Rock where there were no overt signs of danger but when I could not find her mate I grew concerned. I began a systematic search for him in the surrounding area. As I walked along I paid scant attention to a Gray Squirrel closely following me but in hindsight I should have known better. I paused in my search to put some mixed wild bird seed out for the White-throated Sparrows but the squirrel got the greatest benefit. The rodent stood up on its hind legs munching away while keeping its eyes on me. I immersed myself in my search for the male Northern Cardinal and did not give the squirrel another thought. Suddenly something heavy was pressing against my right thigh. I yelled and jumped back acting instinctively to dislodge it but whatever it was would not let go. I jerked my head down to see what in the world it could be. For an instant my eyes were locked in a gaze with a furry creature. Then it sprang to the ground and scrambled to a point five feet away, and turned to face me. It was the Gray Squirrel that had been, I realized too late, stalking me. Sitting on its haunches, holding both paws against its chest, it thrust its tilted head forward and froze in place. The squirrel appeared unhurt by its fall but I was not so sure about myself. I examined my thigh with trepidation fearing I would find a gaping wound or at the very least a tear in my jeans. Finding neither I took inventory of my remaining limbs and was relieved to find they too were intact but the Gray Squirrel ominously stayed put, watching and waiting. I imagined it was prepared to spring upon me again the moment my guard was down. I walked away but try as I might I could not put much distance between this aggressive New York rodent and myself. I tried losing the squirrel by turning off one path and quickly ducking down another but the squirrel stayed with me. Fortuitously as I passed a stranger sitting on a park bench the squirrel transferred its attention to him, for no discernible reason, but by then I did not need an explanation. I just wanted to be free of the critter. When I was out of sight a twinge of guilt struck me. I wondered if I did not have an obligation to return and warn the stranger about this impetuous squirrel but then I supposed the fellow would just think I was some kind of a nut. I hurried away instead.

Despite having gotten the squirrel off my tail, or thigh to be precise, at least momentarily I was in no mood to tempt fate further. I forgot about my search for the male Northern Cardinal and put an even greater distance between the squirrel and myself. I proceeded to George's Pond where the squirrels, though of the same species, are not known to be nearly as aggressive. Julio gave me a pithy update about George's activities. The Red-winged Blackbird had been very animated in the morning. He lingered on his island during the middle of the day spending a conspicuous amount of time on its southern shore where Julio could not see what preoccupied his interest. Most recently George had been on his favorite perch on the dock.

A few minutes later George paid a brief visit before returning to the island for the night. Viviene came to the dock giving me a chance to speak to her about what Betsey had said about the demise of the Cedar Waxwing nestlings. On our last meeting Viviene could not speak about it. This time she was able to share her feelings. She expressed her sadness about the episode but also her determination to change her approach in the future. She was determined not to invest her emotions as heavily in the lives of wild birds. I know it is going to be hard for her because she cares deeply about them. I am sure I should follow her example and I will try but it is impossible where George is concerned.

Chapter 62 · July 20

Heroic Hawk Harasser

I had no luck finding the Willow Rock Northern Cardinals but then Sam told me he had seen the female sitting on her nest and later found male and female foraging together. I also could not find Larry the Red-winged Blackbird at the Bow Bridge but I made a fresh discovery. I located a Red-winged Blackbird nest lashed to the phragmites on the edge of the northwestern shore of the Lake in a discrete area adjacent to Bow Bridge. The nest is close to the edge of the reeds only inches from the water and three or four feet above its surface. This area is an ideal spot for many birds to for-

Just about anywhere else angry adult Red-winged Blackbirds would have, should have, and could have attacked these intruders but not in this area of Central Park. I was standing on the other side of the phragmites when I first saw the Red-winged Blackbird and her chick.

age, roost and, as I have just discovered, nest because its thick vegetation provides a supply of arthropods and seeds and protection from prying eyes like mine. This protected pocket slopes down toward the water and is shielded on one side by Bow Bridge, on another by the Lake, and on the third by an outcropping of rock. At first I felt rather special having found this nest. I assumed it was exceptional for anyone to catch sight of a hidden female Red-winged Blackbird feeding her nestlings deep in the reeds until a rowboat drifted by on the other side of the phragmites that separated us. The boat floated about a yard away from the reeds as I heard a woman say to her oarsman, "Oh look, there's a little bird's nest in there." The man steered the boat to get an even closer look until it came within a foot of the nest. Neither the adult nor the juvenile Red-winged Blackbirds showed the slightest concern about the boat with its two passengers or me. In fact I showed more of a response than the birds did. My research and my own experience had prepared me to expect the adult female Red-winged Blackbird would attack the folks in the boat and me but she did not. At the minimum she should have raised an alarm to summon her mate to defend her and the nest's contents but she did not do that either. Where, you might ask, was her mate while this was going on? He was perched directly above her and did not protest against these trespasses in the slightest way. I was doubly mystified. Why were these Red-winged Blackbirds positively passive? Why did they act contrary to what is known to be their instinctual behavior?

As I pondered these questions I thought of similar behaviors in other birds I have observed in Central Park. The list of individual Red-winged Blackbirds that act against type has grown. George and his mates, his neighbor Mel, Charlie and Squeaky at Morton's Pond, the male at Bank Rock Bridge and Larry at Bow Bridge are all demonstrably more tolerant of humans than Red-winged Blackbirds are widely known to be. In fact these birds, with the exception of Mel, deliberately interact with people though to varying degrees. There were other species I added to my list. The Willow Rock Northern Cardinals are unaffected by the continuous flow of human visitors at their nest site and take food I supply them to their nestlings. There is the bold Morton the Downy Woodpecker too and several of his neighbors like the Tufted Titmouse, Red-bellied Woodpeckers, Common Grackles, House Sparrows and even the Blue Jay Brothers that have displayed uncommonly tame behaviors at one time or other. I would not want to appear to make extravagant claims that Central Park is the embodiment of the peaceable kingdom where the lion lies down with the lamb but I can say with certainty that individual birds have adapted in their own ways to accommodate human presence and activities.

I finally saw a fourth Green Heron chick thereby reducing my chick deficit by one but the chick reported to be in the other nest evaded me. The brood of four nestlings, I confess, made it easy for me to find them. They frequently stood up and at times I did not need binoculars to see them. The general wisdom is that these babies will soon be mature enough to climb outside the nest and begin exploring their surroundings.

My visit to George first involved a climb to the cliff above his island headquarters to find out why, as Julio had said, he is spending a large portion of his time on its southern side where he cannot be seen from the dock. Looking straight down the face of the cliff I saw a low narrow rock shelf at the water's edge with a thick clump of phragmites and cattails growing out of one side. My attention was drawn to these plants when I saw Claudia, one of George's mates, entering the network of stalks. She worked her way between them and paused in front of a small dark brown mass that contrasted with the straw colored reeds surrounding it. Through binoculars I got just enough additional visual information to think the dark mass could be a nest. When the female Red-winged Blackbird leaned over the dark mass I was more confident that it was a nest. After Claudia repeated these actions several times I was certain it was a nest. I thought back to Ned's comment six days ago that he saw a Red-winged Blackbird chick when he looked down from the cliff. I had been skeptical at the time thinking he mistook an adult female for a nestling but now I knew that he had been right. I had not actually seen the chick but surely there had to be at least one inside the nest. Claudia's behavior proved that. I knew the chicks had to be a minimum of six days old and were probably twice that age. It was possible they are nearly old enough to fledge. If so they will have just enough time to hone a few essential skills before the adults must follow their instincts and leave the pond. The irony that I have been obsessing on George's looming departure, when I could instead have been enjoying the discovery of another brood I only found at the eleventh hour, was not lost on me.

As I continued to search the nest site a shadow sailed across the water in front of it. I looked up to find two Red-tailed Hawks turning in a tight circle overhead. I worried that the hawks had spotted the Red-winged Blackbird nest just as I had. Simultaneously George obviously had the same troubling thought. He launched from his island climbing almost straight up until he was directly behind one of the hawks. At first I was not sure I was processing what I saw correctly but it looked as if George had slammed into the hawk's rump. When he repeated the action I knew I had it right the first time. Having detected no tangible effect George tried another tactic. He dived into the hawk's back, ricocheted off, fell behind it, sped forward to catch up with his target and dived into its back again. He body-slammed the hawk three more times. While George pressed his attack the second hawk was only a couple of yards away but it did not come to the aid of its companion. I thought one or both of the hawks would retaliate. Neither made a threatening move but when the hawks made a beeline for the Ramble and quickly passed out of George's territory, I was certain they had more than enough of the relentless Red-winged Blackbird. As they disappeared behind the treetops George landed on the tallest branch and pumped out three defiant choruses of his "konk-la-ree" song. Then he ruffled his feathers from head to tail and preened a bit. When he took to the air again he was cool, calm and collected as he slowly glided back to his Birch Tree perch on his island. It looked as if the heroic hawk harasser had indulged himself in a self-congratulatory victory lap. If so it was well deserved.

I came down from the cliff to the dock but George did not go there. I continued to hear and see him patrolling his territory, but by sunset he had quieted down and remained out of sight. I marveled about the brave defense George had made of his breeding ground and no less at my confirmation that he and Claudia had a new brood. My imprecise observations from the prior year placed his departure dates between July 22 and July 24. It seemed improbable that he would leave during the same period this year. Surely, I reasoned, he would not abandon his breeding ground while underdeveloped offspring still needed his protection.

There was an important "first" at the pond, both for me, and for the Canada Goose goslings. The whole family rose together to fly from the western to the eastern end of George's Pond. Such a short flight would not be remarkable had it not been one of the very first flights the goslings had ever made. It is conceivable that I had witnessed their maiden flight. They flew low over water and landed safely if not as gracefully as their parents. I wondered how long they would remain on the pond after the goslings had perfected their flying skills. Would they linger in the park as a family or join others of their kind to forage in a flock through the fall and winter elsewhere in the region? Would they migrate instead? I had a partial answer to these questions. I was sure the geese would not remain at George's Pond regardless of their ultimate destination.

Chapter 63 · July 21

Bird Talk

George's infrequent appearances at the dock and his frequent visits to the southern end of his island now have a perfectly logical explanation. His behavior has little to do with diet, molting or migrating and much to do with raising a new clutch of chicks. Thinking back now I am ashamed that I did not come to this conclusion before. In fact there was one major piece of evidence I thought so insignificant that I did not even record it. George had spent a large percentage of his time perched on the cliff edge. Now that I knew the location of the nest I understood why. The cliff provides a bird's-eye view, so to speak, of the nest site and its surround-

This perch on the edge of the cliff provides an unobstructed view of the nest site, its immediate surroundings and the approach of a predator from any direction.

ing area. From the cliff he could see an approaching invader from all directions including one from above.

I have described how George drove off two Red-tailed Hawks yesterday. I have heard about similar attacks today. Julio, for example, told me he saw George chase a Red-tailed Hawk twice and Michael saw him do it once in the last two days. As I considered these stories of conflict I watched George serenely sitting in the birch tree enjoying a peaceful moment. He sped away in the next to direct the full power of his wrath at Roger Egret. The Great Egret had been stalking along the shore of the island where several yards of open water separated it from the Red-winged Blackbird nest directly opposite. George was not alone thinking the Great Egret was too close; so did Claudia, George's mate. The Red-winged Blackbirds coordinated a vigorous pelting of Roger Egret's back and rump. At first I did not think they were supplying sufficient pressure but I knew I was wrong when the Great Egret lifted off and floated to an uncontested bit of shoreline elsewhere.

After an hour of observations I began to recognize a pattern in Claudia's visits to her nest. She only approached it when George stood on his cliff edge or birch tree lookout post. When she entered or left the nest she sang "tee-tee-tee-tee-tee"; otherwise she was fairly silent. While he watched her from above George almost continuously vocalized. I have no doubt that he was deliberately keeping up a running conversation with her to maintain audio contact whether or not visual contact was possible at any particular moment. Mostly George used variations of his "chek" and "chuck" calls interspersed with his "konk-la-ree" song and an occasional display of his epaulets. At one point he let rip a stream of high-pitched "seer" calls that I assumed were meant as an alarm. I searched all around to see if I could identify what had disturbed him. I had given up when I saw George racing toward a tiny dot high in the sky to the northwest. I watched through my binoculars until the black dot came closer and only then did I realize it was a hawk. George had been able to identity it at a great distance whereas I needed binoculars and a much shorter distance to do the same. I have not read glowing praises about the Red-winged Blackbird's eyesight but if this is representative of the breed's visual acuity I think it is quite remarkable.

Throughout George's long-range hawk interception Claudia remained in the shrubs on the island. I knew for certain that the hawk was gone when George's voice trailed off in a diminishing series of "seer" calls and returned to a less frenetic slower paced stream of "chek" calls as he resumed his cliff edge perch. Only after George's switch to "chek" calls did Claudia leave the island and go to the nest. From these and other observations I came to understand that Claudia would not approach the nest unless George was watching her from one of his high perches on the cliff or the birch tree. Furthermore her decision of whether or not to enter the nest was also dependent on George's vocalizations. If he gave an alarm she stayed away. If he gave a routine "all-is-well" signal she went into the nest. When she got there she let George know by giving her own call and she used it again to let him know when she was leaving.

George left the cliff mainly when Claudia was away from the nest. The few times he took off when she was there were when he struck at an intruder. Among his other targets today were a Common Grackle, and a European Starling. The grackle received considerably more police actions than the starling no doubt reflecting the potential threat of each species. After each foray George returned to one or the other of his high perches where he ruffled, then sleeked his feathers before assuming a stoic posture that belied the violence of his actions only minutes before.

If this is news to you my conclusions might seem exaggerated but it turns out they are consistent with the Red-winged Blackbird's well-documented communication system and nesting behavior. Ken Yasukawa pointed out that not only is the coordination of actions between male and female roles important to the success of the nesting process but so are vocalizations and even the use of tall perches are key elements. George and Claudia are a textbook case as Ken described it.

I have studied alarm calling and anti-predator behavior a lot (as has Les Beletsky, who described the alert call system of male redwings). The following results support your description. (1) In response to a simulated predator (a plastic crow) placed near their nests, male Red-winged Blackbirds increased the amount of time they spend near active nests. (2) Nests near tall perches were more successful than nests far from tall perches or near short perches. (3) Female Red-winged Blackbirds prefer to place their nests near prominent perches used by males.[1]

As the sun went down George moved to a lower perch on the cliff side where he often sits just before he goes to his island roost for the night. The early evening light fell serendipitously on the nest site to create a silhouette of the female Red-winged Blackbird brooding her hidden nestlings.

I decided to remain on the cliff after sunset. If the Black Skimmer arrived I thought looking down on it would give me a different perspective on its movements. My plan was interrupted by an unforeseen development. Since I became a Club George charter member I have become more tolerant of rodents, with a few exceptions that I have discussed previously. Besides appreciating them for their own sake I have at times reflected on the importance of their position in the food chain as for example, their crucial role as raptor food. In sunlight I have no qualms about them. However, here on the cliff in the twilight I grew concerned when three rodents scurried around my shoes. When it got really dark my concern deteriorated into discomfort. I decided my increasingly close and wholly involuntary encounters with rodents were too high a price to pay for a potential look down upon the back of a Black Skimmer. Instead I descended using a path along the pond's southern shore until I came to the east end where I paused.

There I was startled again by the unexpected closeness of wild animals but this time it did not discomfort or even concern me. I found myself standing in front of an adult female Mallard with three

[1]Ken Yasukawa, e-mail message, November 30, 2004.

juveniles. The ducklings were intertwined and snoozing in a heap behind their mother. The female did not flee as I expected her to. On the contrary she held her ground and began making a stream of soft peeping-murmuring vocalizations with which I was familiar from previous encounters. The ducklings awoke to first look at their mother and then at me. I dropped a handful of wild birdseed on the rock where Mother Mallard stood and backed away. She stayed put but unhesitatingly the juveniles rose and rushed over to scrape the seeds off the rock. Meanwhile Mother Mallard continued peeping and murmuring. The pitch and rate of her vocalizations intensified when a duckling moved closer to me. Her stronger peeping-murmuring sounds appeared to prompt the erring duckling to back off. She seemed to be saying, "Come here!" When the duckling moved away Mother Mallard reduced the intensity of her peeps and murmurs but kept up a steady stream of them. When I gave her kids more to eat their enthusiasm affected Mother Mallard. She could not hold out any longer. She joined them but while eating still managed to continuously broadcast vocal instructions to the ducklings. Soon the Black Skimmer made its presence known by passing within three or four feet from the edge of the rock. I would have remained observing the Black Skimmer and the peeping-murmuring Mallard but I received a powerful reminder that I had again been negligent in the application of insect repellent when an uncoordinated but no less effective squadron of mosquitoes assaulted my left knee. I beat a hasty retreat and so have no idea how long the Black Skimmer skimmed or Mother Mallard peeped and murmured.

Except for the scurrying rodents, the mosquito attack, and the return of high humidity this had been an extraordinarily good day in the field. I can keep out of the way of rodents and remember I hope to apply insect repellent, but the subtropical dampness is, for me, a more formidable foe. The Weather Channel predicted high humidity and intermittent thunderstorms will persist for the next three days, but I feel an urgency to be with George as much as I can. It would serve as a fitting finale to see him with his mate and a fledgling before all the Red-winged Blackbirds are gone from the pond. For the remainder of the month only the most severe thunderstorms will keep me away.

Slip Sliding, Oy Vey

This afternoon there was rain, rain, rain and for a change of pace a violent thunderstorm. The Weather Channel predicted this would be coming my way and it had come to pass. On most other occasions I would have been sensible and remained indoors, as thunderstorms are not my forte, but I could not stay away from Central Park. I felt this just might be the day I would see George and Claudia with their offspring. During a lull in the precipitation I put on my American Museum of Natural History cap, the black one with the neon green T. Rex skeleton on the crest often coveted by birders and nonbirders alike, stuffed a folding umbrella, binoculars and a point and shoot camera in my New-York-City-style-messenger-bag and rushed toward the park half believing

Pecking then picking just what he was eating?

that speed would somehow keep me from being caught in a down-pour.

I made it to the park uneventfully and maintaining my frenzied pace I quickly surveyed Morton's Pond. A cursory check was all that was necessary because all I found were three House Sparrows. The majority of usual suspects had the good sense to remain in their shelters. I did not see or hear another bird on the next segments of my walk but as I came to Willow Rock the adult male Northern Cardinal flew out from the nest. I rushed to my observation post behind the tree opposite the site. Through binoculars I could see portions of the nest but despite my high expectations, not the nestlings. When the adult female landed and bent over its rim I was excited because I knew she was feeding her brood but I did not see a recipient of the meal. Mission accomplished she was off again, but soon returned to make another delivery. When she was done feeding the kids she gingerly stepped inside and wiggled down into the nest with them. Likely the nestlings were cold and damp after being uncovered while Mama had been off foraging but they were surely warming up now. All the while her mate perched directly above me keeping up a steady series of soft "chip" calls. The low intensity of those calls reminded me of the quiet "chek" calls I have heard George utter especially the times he and I have been alone on the dock. As Ken Yasukawa has explained George's soft calls were probably an all-is-well signal: he was telling me it was all right for me to be with him and he sensed no danger. I wondered if the male Northern Cardinal was saying something similar. Certainly his calls were meant for his mate to hear, but perhaps he was directing them at me as well, as George had.

I placed a couple of bits of peanut below the male cardinal on a raised flat stone where I thought the food would be easier to find than if I put it in the weeds. The male stared at them but he would not desert his post to come down and get them. He should not have hesitated because the adult female sprang from the nest and was on the food in a heartbeat. Standing on the rock she broke up one piece of peanut in her beak, then another. She conveyed all the broken bits in her beak back to the nest where she fed them to the nestlings. When that was accomplished Mama Cardinal poked her head out from between the leaves to reexamine the flat rock. I was certain she was looking to see if there were more peanuts. I tossed some to her. They fell at the foot of the vine where she dropped straight down to snatch one. It quickly vanished over the rim of the nest. I left while the adults were still comfortable with my presence and pleased with my distribution of peanuts. I did not want to wear out my welcome.

The break in the storm ended as I walked away from Willow Rock. A light rain began to fall but it was not enough to deter me. Instead I splashed along the path to visit the breeding Red-winged Blackbirds at the Lake. I arrived in time to see two tiny beaks reaching up out of their nest in the phragmites one of which greedily received food from its mother's beak. Nearby a male Downy Woodpecker clung to a tall reed and was pecking something too small for me to see. Over the Lake a Barn Swallow and a Northern Rough-winged Swallow zoomed without betraying the slightest hint that the rain, now falling more heavily, interfered with their work. Under them a Mallard-sized bird lifted up from the water's surface. It lumbered along low in my direction. I could not tell what species it was because it came head-on. I could not see its profile or a single identifying characteristic. Ominously as it came closer the bird did not gain altitude and for a moment I thought it was going to crash into the trees or what stood in between them and the water: me. Less than five feet away it veered sharply back toward the middle of the Lake. As it turned I saw its profile and recognized it was a Double-crested Cormorant. I think that it had become heavily weighted down with rainwater and had misjudged how much distance it needed before it could lift itself high enough to get over the trees. The cormorant made two wide circles over the water rising gradually until it had sufficient height to clear the trees and fly on to its destination.

On the outskirts of the Green Heron breeding ground the intensity of the rain overwhelmed the capabilities of my folding umbrella. I sought shelter under the trees. The sound of the rain overwhelmed all noises as completely as it had my umbrella. Not even the expected muffled din of traffic from Central Park West or the dull roar of a passing commercial airliner was perceptible. Under the leafy canopy, safe from its detrimental effects, I truly enjoyed the pelting rain. The sweet smells of the forest were an added bonus. I almost did not want to leave when the storm subsided but I pressed on to complete my mission.

When I looked through my binoculars at one of the Green Heron nests I was confused by what I saw. An unmoving wide gray fuzzy blob protruded vertically from its center. I tried to imagine what this wide gray fuzzy blob might be but I did not have a clue until a small portion of it moved. That small motion was all I needed to understand that the wide gray fuzzy blob was a confluence of gray down-covered Green Heron nestlings standing upright and pressing against one another at the center of the nest. What were they doing? I think they were accomplishing two things. First by pressing together on this cool rainy day they were sharing body heat to keep warm. Second by standing up they minimized contact with rainwater that must have accumulated in their nest. The nest itself is constructed of loosely woven branches with lots of openings for water to escape but I imagine the force of the deluge had temporarily overcome the capacity of the nest's drainage system. The chicks were waiting for the water to leak out of the nest and drip off their bodies before they attempted to lie down and snuggle up again.

I had heard through the grapevine that there were five chicks in this nest. I had first seen three, then four but not a fifth. I was again one chick short or two if I took into account the story about an additional chick having been spotted in the adjacent nest. I had hoped today's sighting would give me a chance to achieve Green Heron chick parity but studying the wide gray fuzzy blob I could neither confirm nor refute a specific number of individuals. In the other nest an adult Green Heron was lying down. I did not see the single nestling reported to be there and there were definitely no wide gray fuzzy blobs in that location.

From the top of the cliff it took an inordinate amount of time for me to locate George. That was because he was in an unexpected place. He was not on either of his high perches but in the center of

the birch tree on his island where he was almost completely covered by the leaves. From this spot he had protection from the rain
while maintaining a reasonable view, if not a panoramic one, of the
nest site and its surroundings. At the base of the cliff his mate Claudia was bent over the rim of the nest. I assumed from her body language that she was feeding nestlings but she in fact was doing
something I had never seen before. Rather than put something in
the nest I saw her take something out of it. The object was white
and large enough to protrude from either side of her beak. She
flew over the water and toward the island holding on to the white
object. I did not see what Claudia did with it but when I saw her
again a few seconds later the white object was gone. Meanwhile
George kept watching Claudia from his leafy sanctuary but one
time, when Claudia made a brief exit, he went alone to the nest. He
had his back to me so I could not see what he was doing but I am
fairly certain he fed the chicks on that visit and had not gone to remove another white object or I certainly would have noticed it.

I was glad to finally arrive at the dock for three reasons. One was
the possibility of an up-close-and-personal visit by George. The second was the leafy Willow Oak at the entrance that could provide
me shelter should another deluge fall. The third reason was satisfied when Ned joined me and I was able to ask him if he could
identify the white object I saw Claudia carry away from her nest. I
asked. He answered. It was a fecal sac. Duh. I had read descriptions
of the fecal sac, baby droppings neatly sealed inside a membrane
for easy disposal, but this was the first time I had actually seen one.
I had not recognized it for what it was in part because the books I
have consulted do not provide illustrations of them. While an illustration would be useful its omission is I think understandable,
don't you? Later I would write on my calendar with some pride,
"Saw my first fecal sac." I expect this story to serve me well at informal social gatherings for some time to come though it will not be
appropriate during meals unless my companions are bird-watchers.

I proceeded alone to the east end to look for the Mallard family
and the Black Skimmer's return. As I climbed onto the rock I
thought about the soft peeping-murmuring sounds the Mallards

made the other night. Out loud I attempted to vocalize my own version. To my ear it did not sound terribly Mallard-ish but there must have been some appealing quality in it because out of the darkness I heard soft peeping-murmuring sounds coming back in reply. I walked toward the voices. As I strained to listen I remember thinking to myself, "The rocks are very slippery. Better be careful." That was when I saw both of my feet rise and float for an instant in front of my face. Then I plummeted toward the rock landing flat on my back. My head bounced once off the rock. I waited to detect severe pain or bleeding or both. To my relief neither came. If I had broken something I figured it would be at least a ten-minute hike to reach an emergency telephone. I have my share of electronic gadgets but I have resisted carrying a cell phone to preserve what remains of my evaporating privacy. A cell phone has great utility in a situation like this and I wondered if I had been foolish not to have one as I continued monitoring my condition. Curiously Paul Simon's song "Slip Sliding Away" began to resonate in my freshly shaken cranium but neither it nor my sense of humor had been damaged in my fall. For the lyrics "slip sliding away" I substituted "slip sliding, oy vey."

A careful inventory of my parts revealed only an inconsequential scrape on my right pinky. I expected when I awoke the next day I would find a few bruises and feel considerable muscle stiffness. Whatever consequences await me this event has provided me another item for my list of things a bird-watcher should never do: do not walk on a slippery rock in the rain, stupid.

Chapter 65 · July 23

Deranged Muppet

Almost immediately upon my arrival at my observation post I saw the red crest on the head of a baby Northern Cardinal poking out of the nest at Willow Rock. I have wanted to see this for so long that I felt as if the emergence of that tiny nestling should have been accompanied by a trumpet fanfare or at least a drumroll, but the muffled sounds of traffic and voices were the only accompaniment. I watched losing track of time while I waited for Mama Cardinal's comings and goings. The sight of one tiny beak

This Green Heron chick is about a month older than those described in this chapter but the photo gives you a good idea of what those birds looked like. The younger birds had considerably more down. With their additional fluff and random openings and closings of their beaks they looked like deranged Muppet puppets.

rising to meet hers was lovely, gratifying and hypnotic. That describes it pretty well I think.

At Morton's Pond another pair of Northern Cardinals captured my attention. Several times the male came close to the female and reached toward her but either the birds were obscured by vegetation or they were turned away from me so I could only surmise what it was they were doing. Any doubts were gone when they faced me and I saw the male cardinal gently place food into the female's beak. Minutes later I saw him pass more food to her. In the next exchange the female gave the male food. That was the second time I have seen a female do this and, if I am not mistaken, these were the same two birds.

As they were arranged yesterday I found the Green Heron chicks standing up and pressed together in their nest, but they were decidedly drier than when I had seen them last. This time they broke ranks and milled around for a while. Three of them climbed outside the nest. These are careful creatures. Their smallest motions were made with great control and consideration. Their caution was understandable. Those undeveloped tiny gray down covered wings could not possibly keep them aloft if they accidentally fell off a branch. These three fidgeted until they were spaced equally along the same bough while the fourth remained in the nest. Then each began to turn their head slowly in different directions while randomly opening and closing their long yellow beaks. If they made any vocalizations I could not detect them. Stray wispy bits of down stuck up from their heads as if raised up by an electric shock. They were adorable and preposterous at the same time. They looked like deranged Muppet puppets.

The fifth chick still eluded me. Sigh. In the other Green Heron nest an adult remained motionless, staring off into the distance, as if in a trance.

Staring straight down the cliff over George's Pond I was anything but in a trance. I imagine I would have appeared quite intense to an independent observer because I leaned over the metal fence as far as I possibly could straining to get the best possible view of the nest site below. I saw Claudia enter her nest while

George watched and called to her from his island perch. He has resumed perching at the top of the birch tree where he has an unencumbered three hundred sixty degree view. My attention was not drawn to him however, but to Claudia, not for what she did but for what she did not do. Though she stood on the rim of the nest she did not lean over to feed or attend to the nestlings that I presumed were inside. Instead she remained there a few seconds and then left. Oh no. Her behavior was not a good sign. Why hadn't she fed the chicks? Were there nestlings in the nest? If not where were they?

Simultaneous with Claudia's exit George dived from the treetop to the ground, hopped up onto a low branch and slipped inside a thick shrub on the south end of the island. Claudia followed and disappeared with him behind the leaves. From inside the bush George began screaming "seer" distress calls and sang out one chorus of his "konk-la-ree" song. I did not know why he and Claudia had gone in there or why George was signaling trouble but it alarmed me. My mind raced through various theories; two seemed plausible. It is possible that one or more chicks had fledged and were hidden in the shrub. A more remote possibility was that there was a second nest located there. In either case if there were offspring involved they were likely to be in danger. I needed more information and got it but there was no way I would have anticipated what it was about.

The shrub into which Claudia and George had disappeared began to shake violently. A few Red-winged Blackbird fledglings and a couple of adults could not have caused so much movement. Even as the bush continued gyrating George and Claudia shot out from it and fled to a spot several feet away. They appeared unscathed by the experience at least superficially but they remained agitated physically and vocally. I trained my binoculars on the spot where the birds exited but was not prepared for what I saw. Two juvenile Common Raccoons were wrestling with each other under the bush. A third relatively sedate raccoon, much larger than the others, was stretched out along the branches above them. My guess was that the relaxed raccoon was the mother of the two brats battling below her. The Red-winged Blackbirds had detected the raccoons, sensed they were a threat and attacked them. Claudia and George had tried to drive them off just as they have Red-tailed Hawks, Great Egrets, Double-crested Cormorants, Common Grackles, European Starlings, Rock Pigeons and Black-crowned Night Herons. The Red-winged Blackbirds had been successful chasing away those creatures but these raccoons showed no indication that they were leaving. I was shocked Claudia and George would have the temerity to attack raccoons but I should not have been. Robert Nero lists mink, crows, and I kid you not, a sheep and a horse among other Red-winged Blackbird targets.[1]

Later, on the dock I shared my Common Raccoon story with other Club George charter members and interested strangers. It was a good yarn but not a complete story. I was missing information about the status of the nest. I did not know if it was intact or had been destroyed. All I knew was that Claudia and George had stopped tending to it and had attacked a family of raccoons. If the chicks had fledged were they safe? Had the raccoons only threatened the nestlings or was the situation much worse? I considered these questions while I waited to see the Black Skimmer.

[1]Robert W. Nero, *Redwings*, p. 75.

Chapter 66 · July 24

One Chick Short Again?

I waited about five minutes in my observation post at Willow Rock for a sign from the Northern Cardinals until I heard a "chip" call. It was very soft and quite close. On the edge of my peripheral vision in my right eye I barely detected a bit of red. I turned to find it was the male adult cardinal. I admired his stealth in sneaking up behind me but I knew he wanted me to find him. Why else had he called out? I tossed a peanut into the brush under him and he unhesitatingly dropped down to get it. I watched him break it up and take it to the nest where he fed it to a nestling. The chick's beak opened sufficiently for me to see it was outlined in yellow and the inside of its mouth was a glowing translucent orange-red. Wow.

George followed Claudia into the shrubs where they both disappeared. Were they seriously courting or merely cavorting?

Later, when I spread word of my sighting through the birders' grapevine I received feedback that others had seen not one but two chicks in the same nest. This news gave me pause. It was not unusual for me to find out I was one chick short, as you know, but somehow this instance was harder to take because this nest was special to me. I had observed it from the first days of its construction and had become personally involved in its fate even as I was promising myself I would not allow myself to do that again. I thought surely that with this particular nest I would get it right from the start and I would account for every nestling. Alas, the truth was otherwise.

When I visited the Green Heron breeding colony I was almost desperate to find that fifth nestling but I still counted only four. In the adjacent nest I saw no chicks but I got a much better look at the adult sitting there. This time the adult was facing me. The bird appeared as emotionless as it was motionless while it stared off into space. Not to be judgmental about it but I got the impression the bird was bored. Maybe it was. How exciting can it be to sit on a clutch of eggs for hours on end, or for that matter on one's end?

When it was getting close to sunset I walked as fast as I could without running so that I might get a look at George's nest before the light was gone. Huffing and puffing from an unaccustomed rapid ascent to the cliff top I rushed to the edge where I could train my binoculars on the spot. Claudia was nowhere near the spot. Neither was George. More revealing was the fact that George was not on lookout duty on the cliff edge or in the birch tree on the island. I had to wonder if this change in behavior was more proof there was no longer a need for the adults to be at the nest at all. I considered again whether the nestlings had fledged and were hidden in the shrubs where Claudia and George had attacked the raccoons. If so had the raccoons done them in or were the fledglings alive? The Red-winged Blackbird's behavior only made it evident that chicks were no longer in the nest. Both adults kept to themselves except for one instance when George made a display flight while slowly gliding behind Claudia. He followed her into the shrubs where they both disappeared. This last action looked like the two were in the midst of courting again but that seemed odd considering that it is far too late in the season for them to try to raise another clutch.

More evidence about the nest was evident when the Great Egret walked along the shore on George's Island where its presence had previously provoked the wrath of George and Claudia. Neither Red-winged Blackbird attempted to drive off the egret. In fact they did not pay the slightest attention to it. If I had any doubts, after seeing this I was certain the nest was empty. What remained uncertain was what happened to the chicks.

The cheerful songs of two Song Sparrows announcing sunset broke the hold of these dark thoughts. From my position high above them I saw that some Club George charter members had gathered on the dock. I decided to join them and the moment I did Julio rushed to tell me his most recent observations of George. In the morning he said George could not be found on either of his high lookout posts but instead roamed around his territory. He had not been in the company of fledglings. Claudia was not seen at the nest or with offspring either. Ruby, his other mate, was not seen at all. However a hopeful bit of news came from a visitor who described what he thought was a baby Red-winged Blackbird that he had seen on the dock a short time before I arrived there. He was convinced that it had been one of George's offspring. If the stranger's observation could be confirmed, as I hoped it would, it was likely that at least one chick from the nest had survived. However the ray of hope dimmed when I questioned the fellow further. I discovered that he was not an experienced birder. He may have easily mistaken an adult female Red-winged Blackbird, or even one of the still singing Song Sparrows, for one of George's fledglings.

While waiting for the Black Skimmer some of the bird-watchers did what they most enjoy doing when they are among other bird-watchers. They shared their sightings for the day with the group. Their descriptions were detailed. They included the location, time, lighting conditions, the names of the species and the quantities of each. I was envious at certain points in the conversation. Bruce had seen four Great Blue Herons flying together. Ned reported seeing two Ospreys. Viviene and Ned spoke of two Northern Cardinal chicks at Willow Rock where I had only seen one and they counted five Green Heron chicks where I counted four. Sigh. I really am sensitive about being reminded about my chick deficit but it made me laugh to talk about it and helped me stop trying to figure out what had happened to George's family.

Viviene had what I thought was the most intriguing news. She had seen all eight members of the Canada Goose family at George's Pond fly north together earlier in the day. Looking around I realized that I had not noticed the geese were not on the pond. I recalled that only four days ago I saw the goslings fly for the first time. I was impressed with how little time it had taken them to gain sufficient skill and strength to leave their breeding ground. I wondered if this family had joined a flock or started on a migration to a winter retreat. Perhaps their parents were merely giving the fledglings a training flight from which they would return soon. I silently hoped on my next visit to George's Pond I would see the six goslings and their parents getting their picture taken with tourists, paddling across the water in their unwavering straight line or hear the clicking of their beaks as they preened themselves on the flat rock before roosting for the night. I am not yet positive they are gone for good but I miss them already. When a Black Skimmer sailed into view the feeling of nostalgia for the geese faded just enough so that I could fully enjoy the moment and the company of my friends, avian and human.

Chapter 67 · July 25

Spearfishing in America

The late afternoon sunlight had been precisely how I favor it. Between openings in the leaves in the Ramble narrow beams of brilliant light cut through the shadows creating dramatic contrasts. I am always looking for an opportunity to photograph these theatrical effects but my choices are limited by circumstance. For

This is an example of my favorite natural lighting effects. A brilliant shaft of light came through an opening in the leaves to dramatically light this Red-bellied Woodpecker and his perch. It takes patience and luck to find just the right conditions for such a composition. Then a quick response is a necessity because the light can change in the blink of an eye.

starters the light does not always illuminate a composition I prefer to record. When it does the conditions are almost always fleeting and require a quick and decisive response.

The first photo possibilities that presented themselves were a troop of foraging House Sparrows. I was distracted by the presence of a redhead among them and lost my opportunity to take advantage of the light. I did not reproach myself that I had allowed this particular redhead to turn my head because it was a House Finch, a bird I do not see often. The House Finch shares a particular distinction other than part of its name with the House Sparrow. Both species have been transplanted. House Sparrows are non-native birds that were imported from England and deliberately released in North America in stages from 1850 through 1867.[1] House Finches, native to the United States' West Coast, were brought east as illegally caged pets. On Long Island, New York, in the 1940s a few escaped to establish a wild population that quickly spread.[2] House Finches, like House Sparrows, have become one of the most abundant North American species ranging from Florida to southern Canada and New York to California.[3]

At Morton's Pond I found more House Sparrows, one of the Blue Jay Brothers, two Northern Cardinals and an unseen number of American Robins calling loudly and frequently. I surmised the robins were making distress calls. I zeroed in on the vocalizations where two other birders were already on the spot, or I should say under the spot. I only had to trace the angle of their gaze to discover the cause of the commotion. A Red-tailed Hawk was perched less than fifteen feet over their heads. The hawk mostly ignored the furious robins and the curious birders but each group got a menacing stare or two. Four passersby joined us. They were not bird-watchers but nonetheless stopped to express their incredulity about having found themselves so near a wild raptor of such impressive size. Their feelings mirrored my own. Even though I have had this experience many times I felt as excited as these first timers

[1]David Allen Sibley, *The Sibley Guide to Bird Life & Behavior*, p. 564.
[2]Ibid., p. 560.
[3]Fred J. Alsop III, *Birds of North America: Eastern Region*, p. 715.

did. The novices' chatter and laughter, the occasional comments from the birders and the demonstrations of the American Robins had no measurable impact on the hawk. This hawk, likely a juvenile product of Lola and Pale Male's union, sat passively, occasionally preening but mostly surveying its surroundings, searching I suspect for an unsuspecting victim. After nearly twenty minutes of nonstop squawking the robins ceased their protests. We birdwatchers laughed joking that the robins were exhausted by the rigor of their vocalizations and were taking a rest before starting up again. As it turned out that was exactly what they were doing. The robins resumed and renewed their protestations after a short interval. Eventually some of us grew weary of looking up at such a sharp angle and decided to quit our hawk watching. Two of the birdwatchers, Betsey and Viviene, and I went to Morton's Pond but we found the usual suspects had cleared out. No doubt the presence of the Red-tailed Hawk persuaded these birds it was wiser to be almost anywhere else but here for a while. With little to see my two fellow bird-watchers expressed their interest in seeing the Willow Rock cardinals' nest so I took them there.

The three of us took up positions in my viewing outpost but we were not terribly inconspicuous because we could not all hide behind the tree and still see the nest site. The Northern Cardinals carried on with their domestic doings, comings and goings without hesitation regardless of what positions we occupied. The male adult sat on a branch fifteen feet from the nest making low-key "chip" calls and looking around in every direction. He was making sure no predators were watching and waiting to follow him to the nest. Convinced no threat was near he made a dash for it. My two companions went "OOOOOH" as the male bent over the nest and three chicks lifted up their beaks. That is right, I said three chicks. You will recall that I had only seen one but had been told there were two. Would you believe that even as my companions were telling me they saw three chicks from my vantage point I could see only two? Once again I found myself inexplicably one chick short. I tried different angles but the result was the same. I could only see two nestlings. Go figure.

When Papa Cardinal left Mama Cardinal almost immediately replaced him. After she deposited food down two of three straining gullets she left. Papa returned lugging a preposterously large chunk of white bread. The tender scene before us turned comical when Papa stuck the entire chunk of bread into one chick's beak. It was larger than the nestling's head, but the determined baby struggled to swallow it. The adult male sized up the situation and decided he would have to make an adjustment. He grabbed the protruding chunk and broke off about a quarter of it and deposited it into another chick's mouth. That left the first chick with a piece still too large to swallow. Papa Cardinal improvised a less subtle but effective solution. He grabbed hold of the chunk of bread and shoved it down the chick's throat. The nestling stretched out its neck and gulped. I worried that the bread was about to be forcefully ejected or worse. There was no need for concern. The bread must have made its way into the digestive tract because the chick immediately reopened its beak to beg for more. This was an entertaining episode but I cannot say I approve of it. Do not under any circumstances try this maneuver with children of any species especially not your own.

I left Betsey and Viviene at Willow Rock and went to the Green Heron nests. I hoped today I would at last see all five chicks. When I arrived the nestlings in the older nest were lying down forming an intertwined mass of gray fluff. They were resting if not snoozing. Now and then a pointy yellowish orangey beak poked out of the mass when a nestling jiggled to get a more comfortable position. I was patient. I found a large rock to sit on and I waited for the chicks to wake. Then I waited some more. Finally one stirred and that set off a chain reaction. One by one they rose to stretch their stubby wings and long legs. Cautiously each exited the nest to walk along the supporting branch. I counted five chicks. Finally I had seen all of them. They slowly moved farther away from each other than I have seen them before as they began to explore adjacent branches. I took some photos, but dense foliage and a setting sun combined to make a decent shot impossible. That was disappointing but I consoled myself knowing I had seen the fifth chick. In the other tree an adult Green Heron was still incubating eggs. This heron was so unrelentingly immobile that it seemed to be more a decoy than the real McCoy. I became certain that the grapevine's talk about a single chick appearing in this nest had been in error. It is possible that an older juvenile Green Heron had been visiting the spot but it was clear there is a family in the making here and not the finished product.

Looking down the cliff at the Red-winged Blackbird nest I saw it was unattended. It looked unkempt with stray twigs protruding from its top and sides that I had not noticed before. For ten or fifteen minutes the only Red-winged Blackbird I saw was Mel, George's neighbor, on his side of the invisible boundary line. Finally George came out of a bush on his island and flew to a high branch on the birch tree where I promptly lost him behind the leaves. I heard him call for several minutes but he remained hidden. There was no trace of his mates or a single fledgling.

WARNING: The following paragraph describes another scene of graphic violence but without the graphics.

From the dock I watched Roger Egret quit the shallows along the northern peninsula to perch on the pillar at the foot of the dock. He came to be near me intentionally. I knew why and I obliged him. I tossed some seeds onto the water below. When a school of minnows began nibbling them Roger stepped gingerly around the pillar to assume a strategic position. For a long while Roger stood poised and ready. When the Great Egret determined conditions were right Roger jumped from the pillar and streaked toward the water thrusting his long yellow beak into the swirling mass of minnows. Roger missed and circled back to the pillar and waited for the next opportunity. The egret struck again and missed again. The big bird missed several more times before finally scoring a palpable hit. Roger had speared a fish. When I say Roger speared a fish that is precisely what I mean. In the past when I have watched Great Egrets catch fish they grasped them between their top and bottom bill, but that technique was not employed in this instance. This fish had been literally skewered. Roger Egret's bottom beak had gone completely through the center of the fish's body. The Great Egret tried to swallow its catch but could not. The fish remained impaled on the end of the blood stained beak. The egret tried vigorous shakes and lunges in an attempt to free the prey. No dice. More strenuous maneuvers followed. It took a prodigious effort but eventually the fish was extricated. Still in its grasp the egret flipped the fish an inch into the air, caught it and swallowed it whole. The prey had been dislodged, dispatched and, presumably by then, was decidedly deceased. It was stirring to watch Roger Egret do his thing, but equally awful to contemplate what the fish experienced. Consider yourself fortunate that I am not subjecting you to a gory photo of the unfortunate fish. I would have, of course, if I had been able to get the picture, but I did not.

Chapter 68 · July 27

Predator Alert Tag Team

A chaotic choir of American Robins, accompanied by a soloing Northern Cardinal, expressed their displeasure in a spot south of Morton's Pond and east of Willow Rock. About half way up a large London Plane Tree calmly surveying the area, ignoring the animated posse that surrounded it, perched a Red-tailed Hawk. It was an adult and most likely Lola or Pale Male. There was too much shadow for me to determine which of the two it was. Lately I have been finding one or the other of the famous Red-tailed Hawk duo in the Ramble and enjoyed these experiences but the location of this particular hawk distressed me. It was less than seventy-five feet away from the Willow Rock Northern Cardinals' nest. My guess was that the lone male Northern Cardinal verbally assaulting the

Green Heron chicks out on a limb.

343

raptor along with the robins was the father of the three Willow
Rock nestlings. For the most part he stayed several yards away from
the hawk but the American Robins came within a few feet. One especially brash robin periodically crashed into and bounced off the
hawk's back, but his target for the most part maintained its composure. Once the raptor lunged at one of its tormentors but it was a
relatively minor effort as Red-tailed Hawk lunges go. Later, I would
receive an eBirds e-mail in which another bird-watcher described
the same scene. The author identified the hawk as Lola's mate,
Pale Male. His version of the happening included an additional
scene I did not witness. In his account Pale Male was seen devour-
ing an ill-fated Gray Catbird. Aren't you glad I missed that photo
opportunity?

I left the Northern Cardinal and American Robins to their
protestations and went to look for the Willow Rock female Northern Cardinal. I situated myself in my personal nest viewing spot
but discovered someone was already there. Instead of keeping
out of Mama Cardinal's way as planned I encountered her standing on a branch at my eye level about four feet away. I froze because I did not want to frighten her. She froze too but I could not
know her motivation. Was she frightened or curious? We stared at
one another for a while. I was reluctant to move thinking my
slightest motion would send her dashing away. After a while the
standoff seemed like it would go on indefinitely. I decided to risk
ending the impasse with a peace offering. Very slowly I reached
into my pocket, took out a bit of food and, making the smallest
motion I could, tossed it to the ground beneath her. Mama Willow Rock dropped headlong toward it. I was convinced she was
going to make a devastating crash-landing but with ease she
righted herself at the last possible moment. I love to watch cardinals do that. She picked up the peanut and broke it up holding
all the pieces in her beak even as she reached down to the ground
to take in larger chunks. No crumbs were left behind when she
raced to the nest where she offered them to the nestlings. Three
nearly translucent heads shot up in response. The chicks shoved
one another out of the way, each trying to get the food before the

others. Two were fed but one, the loser of the shoving contest, was completely shut out of the meal. I was not a loser. I had seen the third chick.

I thought Mama Willow Rock might return for more food but she remained on the edge of the nest facing the direction from which her mate continued to vocally assault the Red-tailed Hawk in the London Plane Tree. Then she sprang into the air toward the source of the calls. Seconds later Papa Willow Rock arrived to take a turn feeding the kids. While watching him with the nestlings I became aware I could still hear Northern Cardinal distress calls coming from the London Plane Tree. Had Mama Willow Rock taken her mate's place and was she now scolding the hawk? I went to investigate. I found the female Northern Cardinal had indeed taken her mate's place. This pair of Northern Cardinals made an effective predator alert tag team while managing to protect and feed their family at the same time.

After finally getting to see all three Northern Cardinal nestlings I relished my good fortune to once again locate the fifth Green Heron chick. All five were cautiously walking along branches either parallel to, above or below their nest. Every day they will venture a little farther away from their home base. In the adjacent nest I saw a Green Heron adult standing up. This might have indicated the bird had just arrived, was just leaving, was getting comfy or was tending to newly hatched chicks. I preferred to believe the last possibility but I did not see nestlings. I would learn from the birder grapevine that there were three newborn Green Herons inside the nest. That was great news. The not so great news was that I had missed all three while others had no trouble finding them. Birdwatching can be a bitter mystery.

When I searched for George I found him within a couple of feet of one of his mates on his island. I believe it was Claudia. I have not seen Ruby and suppose she is gone, but I have been wrong about that before. That was all I would see of the Red-winged Blackbirds on this trip. Even Julio on whom I have come to rely for George-updates had no new information. I asked other Club George charter members as they came and went what they could tell me about George's activities. The few who had seen him did so at a considerable distance and they too had little to report. There were no sightings of Red-winged Blackbird fledglings either.

Mack came by and asked me to bring him up to date about George. Mark asked the same when he arrived. There was little to tell them. Paul and Dotty, two Club George charter members whose acquaintance I was making for the first time, also made inquiries. The only information I had for them was to say that they were about to become recipients of a Club George charter member card. I handed a card to each of them. Dotty said smiling, "This will go up on the refrigerator door as soon as we get home" and by the way she said it I understood that to be the display location of greatest importance in their abode. Paul said that his card was "going to be put in a place of honor in my wallet" and explained his intention to show it with pride to friends and acquaintances. I congratulated myself at being able to identify individuals that would be most appreciative of receiving the cards. Even if I could not find all the chicks in a given nest at least I could tell who George's fans were.

This assemblage of Club George charter members shared expressions of puzzlement about George's behavior. Why had he not been seen on the dock? Why was he keeping such a low profile? What happened to Ruby, his fledglings or the older juveniles from a previous brood? Not only was I frustrated that I had failed to answer these questions but I also had an unshakeable feeling that a major change was about to take place. So did some of the others even if they could not articulate precisely what was making them uncomfortable about the Red-winged Blackbird's status.

The group's spirits were uplifted when the Barn Swallow family swooped into the immediate airspace. They put on a gravity defying aerial show that included an in-flight feeding of two fledglings. That is always a crowd pleaser but there was one act they performed that is a veritable showstopper. Occasionally one of the swallows would shoot down to scoop up a beak full of water and then shoot up ten, twenty or thirty feet to join the others. Each scoop of water elicited a cheer from the audience.

Intermittently two Small Brown Bats flew about us and when they too grabbed a quick drink of water while maintaining their forward motion in flight the crowd of birders displayed admiration for them as well. A good long look at the Black Skimmer was had by one and all about 9:15 PM but our reverie was shattered when a piercing yelp shot up from the island. Someone thought it came from an injured rodent, possibly the victim of a Black-crowned Night Heron. Someone else said it was a sound common to raccoons. I favored the raccoon theory. The location was right. It was where George and Claudia had attacked the two battling baby raccoons and their mother. The group began to break up after hearing that eerie cry.

At the east end of the pond the four female peeping-murmuring Mallards were not at their place on the rock where I hoped to find them but in the water where a dozen of their species were gathered. The adult males and females were hard to tell apart because they are far into their molt and their new plumage is very much alike for both sexes. The easiest way to identify the sexes is from the coloration of their bills. The females' bills are orange with a black center and the males' are yellow. That knowledge was of no use now. In the dark I could not distinguish any colors. Only a few days ago I would most often find the Mallards in distinct clusters. The adult females would be with their offspring in separate groups and the adult males in one large group when they were not off bullying the ladies. These divisions are dissolving as they increasingly congregate into a single flock of both sexes that will persist into the fall. Before long the males and females will start to pair off. Most couples will remain with the flock until it is time for them to start a family. Once the breeding season commences the males will stand by their mates until the eggs are deposited and then they will desert them. The female will incubate, brood and raise her family alone but I have seen a few males go to the assistance of females with chicks in emergencies. By far it will be the mother's responsibility.

Looking at the small flock on the water in front of me I imagined the four peeping-murmuring Mallards were among them and had probably adopted a group mentality. I supposed they would not respond to my own peeping-murmuring vocalizations as they had in the past and they did not. Change was not simply in the air, it was happening.

Chapter 69 · July 28

Bye-bye Birdie

According to my theory about his imminent departure it was likely that George would leave his breeding ground sometime today or tomorrow at the outside. I had an impulse to go at once to George's Pond to find out if he was missing but at the same time I was reluctant to. I did not really want to prove that my theory was correct. Rather than face the music I conveniently rationalized away a direct confrontation with the facts, whatever they might be, and instead decided to follow my usual schedule so as not to miss new developments at my other key spots like Morton's Pond, Willow Rock or the Green Heron breeding ground. The truth was that

How much more successful and fulfilled might I be if I took on every task and responsibility with such dogged determination and unflagging enthusiasm as George does?

I was in denial. I was afraid to go to the pond for fear I would find that George really was gone.

I did make a slight alteration to my routine. I went first to Willow Rock, making no stops along the way, and once there slipped into my observation post off the path ready to be cheered by the sight of the Northern Cardinal family but I found it hard to stand and quietly wait for the birds to appear. My head was filled with uncomfortable thoughts about the Red-winged Blackbirds at George's Pond. When I did focus on my external surroundings there was absolutely no activity in or around the cardinals' nest to observe. Not seeing the Northern Cardinals I substituted worries about them instead of those about the Red-winged Blackbirds. Had something happened to Mama and Papa Willow Rock? Are the cardinal nestlings okay? I waited hoping to find a sliver of evidence, no matter how slight. A single "chip" call or a flash of a red feather would have sufficed but there were no clues, no signs, and no sounds. If I had not been fully aware of it before I could not deny that I had become as emotionally invested in the fate of the Willow Rock Cardinal family as I had in the Red-winged Blackbirds at George's Pond. I was hooked on these particular birds and I knew it.

When the sounds outside my head overpowered my internal conversation I recognized bird distress calls coming from the trees to the north. Not far from Morton's Pond I picked out the voices of two or three American Robins, a Blue Jay and a Northern Cardinal. I traced their location and found Pale Male perched on a low branch preening and ignoring the din produced by the songbirds. The robins and the jay were patently agitated but the male cardinal was positively hysterical. He hopped a short distance over the ground, jerking his upper torso this way then that way before jumping to the next spot where he repeated his jagged body language. Nonstop he yelled his "chip" calls sometimes letting rip with a rapid-fire blast of several in a row. The feathers of his crest appeared to be locked upright and showed no sign that they might descend for a split-second. The robins and the jay were out in the open and physically close to the hawk but no matter how irate the cardinal was he prudently remained under the protective leaves of the shrubs where the predator could not easily get at him. Recently I had witnessed this same scene playing in this area almost on a daily basis. I am sure it has played here in this season for many years. Why was it that I rarely saw it before and see it often now? I owe it to the heightened awareness bestowed upon me by my charter membership in Club George just in case you had not guessed.

Based on the location of the Red-tailed Hawk I guessed the hollering male Northern Cardinal was Papa Willow Rock. This section of the Ramble is what I gather to be the northernmost portion of the Willow Rock Northern Cardinal territory. I came to that conclusion by observing both adults traveling from their nest site, through the trees to the water's edge at Morton's Pond. I have not seen either Willow Rock Cardinal adult cross to the other side of the pond. That is because the southern shore of the pond is the northern border of their territory. Finding only Papa Willow Rock near the pond I went back to the nest site assuming that his mate would be home with the kids while he and his temporary allies tried to dislodge the hawk. Back in my observation post I heard a few soft and widely spaced "chip" calls but frustratingly could not find their source that I assumed to be the female Northern Cardinal. The calls seemed to come from every direction at once. Eventually Mama Willow Rock poked her head out of the leaves in a stand of Japanese Knotweed. She looked left, then right, before moving forward. Cautiously she worked her way to a second location where she paused to reconnoiter and did the same at a third spot before homing in on her nest. The moment she leaned over them the chicks reached up to her. Mama did her duty depositing food in one and then in another whining chick's gaping mouth. What a way to serve dinner.

After she was emptied of cargo Mama Willow Rock left and her mate arrived. Still making distress calls he too took a circuitous route before landing at the nest and feeding chicks. I thought it was curious he bothered to approach so stealthily because his vocalizations gave his position away. What was the logic of using these two seemingly contradictory tactics? I imagined Papa Willow Rock was less concerned with a predator finding him than he was in finding a predator. I think he made those calls as if to say to all potential predators, "You can't catch me. If you're there, show yourself you big zx@#$%&*." In a confrontation with Pale Male, for example, odds are good that the cardinal's small size and relative speed would favor his escape and at the same time lead the hawk away from the nest. Why did he hide at all then? Hiding increased Papa Willow Rock's chances of seeing the predator before it saw him. So, I reasoned, a combination of vocalizations and stealth were a logical strategy after all.

Another Northern Cardinal began making distress calls in the direction of the Red-tailed Hawk while Papa Willow Rock was feeding the chicks. I would bet that Mama Willow Rock had taken her husband's place on the hawk picket line even as he had taken her place on the family buffet line. I did not go to verify that it was a female cardinal scolding the hawk, which would have given further support to my notions about this predator alert tag team behavior because it was time to push on.

Did I go straight to George's Pond and confront the truth? Nope. Instead I counted three newborn chicks in the second Green Heron nest. I will accept that three is the correct number unless the birder grapevine informs me later I got it wrong again. One nestling is considerably larger than the other two, but they all seemed to take equal pleasure sparring playfully with their miniature but menacingly pointy beaks. Several times the gaze of an attending adult Green Heron fell directly on me. It was an impassive stare but the fact of it called my attention to one of its abilities. It was not necessary for this Green Heron to turn its head to the side to focus one eye on me, as many other species, like the Northern Cardinals, might have. Green Herons have a form of stereovision. They can focus both eyes on one point to improve their accuracy when aiming those big beaks at a target.

The time had come when I could no longer put off visiting George's breeding ground. I looked over the breadth and width of the pond from the cliff and the dock. I did not see George, Ruby, Claudia, or their neighbors Mary and Mel. Not making immediate visual contact was not rare so I did not rush to the conclusion that the Red-winged Blackbirds were gone but something else was different that I could not put my finger on until I stopped looking and started listening. It was quiet. It was very quiet. From the very beginning of the breeding season until yesterday the air had been almost constantly filled with Red-winged Blackbird songs or calls. I did not hear them now. I strained to hear something, anything. I heard the breeze. I heard a commercial jet and a muffled voice of a softball player far off on the Great Lawn. I knew then the moment I had anticipated and dreaded had come. The Red-winged Blackbird colony was gone.

"Weather-wise it's such a lovely day," the old popular song says and it certainly fit. The temperature was eighty-one degrees and the humidity was low. We were experiencing a taste of typically early June New York City weather in late July. It crossed my mind that the day offered optimum flying conditions for migrating birds but such perfect traveling weather seemed imperfect for a farewell. I wanted this to be a cloudy, rainy, miserable day not a gorgeous one. Rather than mirroring my feelings, as I illogically wanted it to, nature seemed to be contrarily celebratory. "George is gone," nature seemed to be saying. "Long live George." I appreciated the sunny sentiment but my internal environment was decidedly gray and rainy.

I had obsessed about George's departure for a long time. All right, I admit it, for too long. I had read into every change and perceived inconsistency of his behavior, real or imagined, not only trying to predict his departure date but searching for reasons why it might be postponed. Finally I had clung to the hope that George's final nest of the season would delay his departure. George would remain with the chicks, I told myself, until they were able to leave the pond and care for themselves. I had continued looking for fledglings because I did not want to believe that they had perished even though there was circumstantial evidence to conclude that they had. The truth was that despite my intellectual and psychological preparation I was not ready to accept that George had left very close to the time I had anticipated all along. I sat on a bench staring at the pond but not seeing or hearing anything except my own silent self-talk. To other birders I might have resembled the nesting Green Heron adult staring unemotionally at an indefinite point but inwardly I was flooded with memories of the events leading up to this moment. Gradually I came to acknowledge that the Red-winged Blackbirds had quit their breeding ground sometime during the prior twenty-four hours.

Where had the Red-winged Blackbirds gone? From what I have read I assume that George and the other adults in his colony would first complete their molt before traveling a great distance. They may congregate in a staging area before joining other groups heading south. Where they might be during this process I do not know but when they are through the Red-winged Blackbirds will eventually gather in sexually segregated flocks. Some flocks will wait from one to three months before migrating. The farther north they are the earlier each group begins to move. I have no knowledge of where large flocks of Red-winged Blackbirds congregate in this region. If they did so in Central Park I would have heard about it. The birder's grapevine would be positively buzzing with a story like that. By the time they reach their winter territories their flocks will number in the tens or hundreds of thousands. A million or more is not inconceivable.

A relatively few individuals of their species may remain in this region throughout the winter. Last winter, for example, there was a flock of ten male Red-winged Blackbirds that roosted in the phragmites near Bank Rock Bridge and could be seen foraging almost daily at or near the bird feeders in the Ramble. Had George been one of them? I do not believe so. None of those males exhibited George's character traits and none had a droopy wing that would have distinguished him from the others.

The Red-winged Blackbirds can stay only if there is an adequate food supply but in this region that can be problematic. So why would some male Red-winged Blackbirds risk possible starvation and harsh winter weather? Ornithologists theorize that males who remain on or close to breeding grounds have an advantage over those that migrate because they will be in a better position to claim a piece of turf before the returning migrant males can. Doing so does not guarantee success. Keeping territories after their original owners return to reclaim them will not be easy. Studies prove the odds are that the former resident will retake his turf unless he is ill, weak, or, of course, fails to return.

I will remain inordinately fond of George wherever he may be. Why? I cannot accurately describe him as a pet. Surely he is too wild and unpredictable to fit that description. He is not a friend or companion in the sense that the family dog, cat or bird can be. His interactions are a treat but I will not claim they constitute a form of affection though I will argue they do convey a measure of trust. His energy, antics, song, adaptability and the zest with which he lives his Red-winged Blackbird life are as entertaining as they are inspiring to me. How much more successful and fulfilled might I be if I took on every task and responsibility in my life with such dogged determination and unflagging enthusiasm?

There had been relatively few people visiting the dock. I was aware that some came and went but I took little notice of them. I was lost in my thoughts about how I had been changed by my very first encounter with George. I could pinpoint the place and time on a brilliantly sunny Sunday in June when my interests and awareness of the natural world were altered forever as George literally sang and danced his way into my life.

In the evening some people gathered to watch for the Black Skimmer. Betsey, Margaret and Julio came one by one. Betsey had news for me. She told me that a bird-watcher whose skills were well respected had corrected my count of Willow Rock Cardinal nestlings. She said five chicks had been seen in the nest, not three. Could it really be that I was two chicks short? Of course it could. Why did I even question it? No doubt I am doomed to suffer a continual chick deficit far into the future but that prospect is truly insignificant and trivial compared to the thought that my next bird-watching session will not include a visit with George.

Gradually, I had been gently nudged out of my reverie by the arrival of a series of Club George charter members and Betsey's update about the status of my personal chick deficit in particular. At first I had been loathe to tell the others that George was gone but at one point in the conservation I could not hold back any longer and I announced that all the Red-winged Blackbirds had left the pond. Julio was beside himself. "Are you sure George is gone?" he asked several times hoping, I assume, that I might reconsider and change my reply to one of his queries. Margaret had a difficult time explaining to her son Stanley that he was not going to have his usual visit with George. I was comforted knowing I was not alone in my emotional reaction. The entire Club George charter membership would be seeking comfort once word spread through the birdwatchers' grapevine that George was gone.

Chapter 70 · July 30

Unidentified Just Started Flying Object

When I arrived at George's Pond, it was too quiet. I expected to hear much less now that George, his mates, children and neighbors were gone but I felt this silence was greater than their absence could explain. I found the reason perched at the highest point on the castle. It was a Red-tailed Hawk with a prominent dark band across its belly. I believe this was a juvenile, very probably one of Lola and Pale Male's children. All the usual suspects were lying low and out of sight except for one. A small dark bird plunged into the Red-tailed Hawk's back five or six times before giving up and flying off. I could not identify what species the attacker was. The backlighting robbed the image of detail and all I could see was its silhouette. I was

Several Club George charter members came looking for George. They did not find him.

filled with the hope that the bold little bird might have been George but I could find no clue to this bird's identity before it disappeared.

Several Club George charter members came looking for George. They did not find him. Julio arrived and said he had continued to look for George hoping I had been mistaken but he had not seen him. I read a curious e-mail report later that said a female Red-winged Blackbird was seen on George's Island, but no one else I know could confirm that sighting. No one could have wanted to find evidence that the Red-winged Blackbirds were still on the pond more than I did, but I was not finding any.

I had more disappointing news that I could not help but feel very personally. Yesterday the Willow Rock Cardinal nest appeared to have been deserted. From the bird-watcher grapevine I heard that Pale Male, the Red-tailed Hawk, had very likely raided the nest and devoured its contents. However there was no eyewitness account, only circumstantial evidence strung together to create a plausible explanation for the cardinals' apparent absence. Pale Male, I recalled, had been stalking prey in the neighborhood in recent days and I had been very concerned about his proximity to the Willow Rock nest myself. It was with a great degree of trepidation that I approached the site of what was now said to be the "former cardinal's nest." My discovery of this nest had raised my spirits when they had been sinking in direct proportion to the approach of George's departure. In the process of observing the cardinals I had become fond of them and the knowledge that I would be able to observe them long after the Red-winged Blackbirds had gone had given me a lot to look forward to. Instead the thought of having to face another sad story, and one with such serious consequences, made me feel awful.

I approached Willow Rock with mixed emotions. I feared the story would prove to be true but I hoped I would discover it was mistaken. Feeling ambivalent I did not bother taking up my position in my usual observation post thinking it probably no longer mattered if I tried to keep a low profile or not. I stared at the nest and saw nothing. My heart sank. But then from behind the Wisteria vine leaves, about a foot or two away from the "former cardinal's nest," I heard an adult Northern Cardinal softly and repeatedly calling "chip." Another voice, much different from the first, seemed to be responding a short distance away. I recognized these new vocalizations as being similar to the begging calls of fledglings of other species that I have heard before. I wondered if I was listening to a fledgling cardinal asking to be fed. As I felt excitement begin to flow through me I scanned the Wisteria vine with my binoculars. I found a tiny gray ball of down with pinkish legs and only the merest hint of a tail. I could not see its head. This was a fledgling but it did not look to me like a Northern Cardinal. Female and male cardinal juveniles are very similar to the adult females in appearance. They are a warm light brown with dark bills, have a little bit of red on their wings and tails but none on their crests. This babe looked to me to have the wrong colors. It was not until later that evening after I pored through my reference books that I found a description in *Sibley's Guide to Bird Life & Behavior* of hatchlings in the *Cardinalidae* family that solved the mystery for me. These hatchlings are covered, if sparsely, in down that ranges in color from white to gray. Gray! That was all I needed to know. At least one Northern Cardinal nestling had survived. The gray baby I saw hiding in the vine was a newly fledged cardinal so young it was still clad in gray down.

Knowing with certainty that this was so was a great relief. The disappointments of George's nest disaster, his vanished juveniles, his departure followed by the apparent demise of the Willow Rock Northern Cardinal nestlings were wiped away by my discovery that one cardinal fledgling was alive. There were three lessons in this experience that I should have learned a long time ago but had not. The first was that bird-watching inevitably reveals triumph as well as tragedy. The second was that whenever the bird-watcher invests her or his emotions in the fate of a wild creature she or he must be prepared for the consequences, no matter how disagreeable they may be. The third was to remember that even the bird-watcher's grapevine can be wrong.

The beginning bird-watcher can avoid the type of emotional wear and tear I endured by deliberately remaining unattached to the animals he or she observes. That is easier said than done and in my case does not seem to be a viable option does it? If this is not an issue for you then you are probably lucky. If you do not know how you feel about it I assure you, after you spend sufficient time in the field, you will find out when the situation arises, as it surely will.

I had a special mission to fulfill before I went on to the Green Heron nests and George's Pond. That was to find out if other Red-winged Blackbirds had left their territories as George's colony had. The breeding colony on the northwestern side of the Bow Bridge was the most logical place to look as I had some familiarity with it. I was sorry now that I never made the effort to count the number of individual Red-winged Blackbirds here but I thought it would have taken a commitment of time I could not afford if I were to follow up on the creatures already on my itinerary. The Red-wing Blackbirds had divided up the reeds on the shore and on a tiny adjacent island into micro-breeding territories. The birds seemed to be jammed in here and did not have the luxurious amount of space George and Mel commanded. At Bow Bridge I had long known there was a minimum of four adult males and at least twice as many adult females. This season there were at least three nests that I know produced offspring. I am told by other bird-watchers that Red-winged Blackbirds have returned to breed in these phragmites and cattails for years. It was not until I became a charter member of Club George that I became aware of them but of course you won't be surprised for me to say that.

Heading toward Bow Bridge I began to hear the voices of those Red-winged Blackbirds at about one hundred feet away from their headquarters. Walking into my favorite viewing position there I at once saw two juveniles, one adult female and three adult males moving along the reeds at the island's edge. Behind these birds came additional Red-winged Blackbird voices and the rustling leaves gave away the position of even more individuals but I cannot say how many. Here were two more adult males, there a female and over here three more juveniles. My first impression was that this colony of Central Park's Red-winged Blackbird population had not left the breeding ground. My second impression was that my first impression had been pretty goofy. There were many more Red-winged Blackbirds here than I could recall seeing in the past.

The more I considered the sight of Red-winged Blackbird juve-

niles and adults of both sexes mingling together the more provocative the scene became. Why? If breeding season were not "officially"
over I would expect to find each adult male defending his piece of
territory within the colony. I should find clear divisions between
families but that was not the case. Today it looked as if all of the individual territory boundaries had broken down. Adult males not
only tolerated one another, they perched together. Adult females
and juveniles came and went with such rapidity and confusion I
could not identify separate family units. I became really excited to
think I was actually witnessing how breeding colonies break apart
and how the initial stage of flock formation begins. It was beyond
my sophistication to interpret with absolute certainty, but I believed this group was made up of many Red-winged Blackbirds that
had quit other breeding territories and had come together in this
spot to prepare for the fall migration. Might George have been
among them? Maybe, but I found no evidence that he was. Sigh.

A new mystery presented itself to me in the Green Heron breeding ground. I could not locate the five juvenile Green Herons from
the earlier nest. I scoured every opening in the leaves of their nesting tree and the adjacent trees but I could not find them. Maybe
they had fledged and were exploring areas farther from their home
base or had they dispersed permanently? I will make inquiries to
find out what the bird-watcher's grapevine has to say about them
but there was no mystery about the three Green Heron chicks in
the other nest: they were cuddled up and fast asleep.

There were other attractions around Bank Rock Bridge. Four Gray
Catbirds came out of the brush to cautiously encircle and investigate
me. There were three American Robins and one male Northern Cardinal perched in the same tree as the sleeping baby Green Herons.
Fifty feet to the south came the "chek" calls of more Red-winged Blackbirds. They were in another thick patch of phragmites and cattails
where this small swampy cove opens onto the Lake. Red-winged Blackbirds habitually breed in this territory too but I know very little about
their colony. Hearing the sound of their voices signalled they had
not left their breeding territory, but I could not determine if another
gathering of their species was underway here as it was at Bow Bridge.

Chapter 71

Tail's End

The environment of Central Park is an artful blend of the artificial and natural. Within its borders a surprising number of birds make their home. They have learned to overcome the obstacles this urbanized civilization puts in their way and have adapted to successfully live alongside people or, as some might say, in spite of them. The bird friendly management philosophy of the New York City Parks Department, the Central Park Conservancy and a few dedicated individuals has so far ensured that this 843 acre oasis continues to provide shelter, food, water, and a variety of habitats to support twenty-four year-round resident species and the dozens more that pass through during the spring and fall migrations.

I think this picture of George speaks for itself. See you next year, George.

My story about George is in part about how the close proximity between birds and humans in the park can lead to an entertaining and provocative interaction between the species, an interaction that can be mutually beneficial.

Sandra Blakeslee reporting in the *New York Times* summarized the conclusions of a meeting of twenty-nine avian experts from six countries who met to discuss their study of bird intelligence that took seven years to complete. Blakeslee contends that there is a growing consensus that birds in general are a lot smarter than scientists had supposed and that the pejorative appellation "birdbrain" is a misnomer.

Today, in the journal *Nature Neuroscience Reviews,* an international group of avian experts is issuing what amounts to a manifesto. Nearly everything written in anatomy textbooks about the brains of birds is wrong, they say. The avian brain is as complex, flexible and inventive as any mammalian brain, they argue, and it is time to adopt a more accurate nomenclature that reflects a new understanding of the anatomies of bird and mammal brains. . . .

Scientists have come to agree that birds are indeed smart, but those who study avian intelligence differ on how birds got that way. Experts, including those in the consortium, are split into two warring camps. One holds that birds' brains make the same kinds of internal connections as do mammalian brains and that intelligence in both groups arises from these connections. The other holds that bird intelligence evolved through expanding an old part of the mammal brain and using it in new ways, and it questions how developed that intelligence is. . . .

The reanalysis of avian brains gives new credibility to many behaviors that seem odd coming from presumably dumb birds. Crows not only make hooks and spears of small sticks to carry on foraging expeditions, some have learned to put walnuts on roads for cars to crack. African gray parrots not only talk, they have a sense of humor and make up new words. Baby songbirds babble like human infants, using the left sides of their brains.[1]

While I never encountered tool-wielding crows or talking parrots with a sense of humor in Central Park I believe that my narrative supports similar conclusions about a generally underrated level of avian intelligence. However it may not be as easy for other bird-watchers to have the same kind of up-close-and-personal experiences as I did.

I would be irresponsible if I gave you the impression that the species I have written about are likely to permit everyone to observe them as directly as I have been privileged to. In your local park, your neighborhood, a national forest or along a beach the birds are not as likely to be as accommodating. I advise the beginning bird-watcher not to approach a Red-winged Blackbird nest, for example, believing you can do so with impunity. The odds are overwhelming that you will be the target of one or more angrily screeching dive-bombing blackbirds.

I have written about my hand-feeding of birds and how many of them had come to trust me and come physically close to me to varying degrees. I must stress that I never forced the birds into any of these situations, though I surely used food to bribe them, but that was the limit to my direct contact with them. I make no claim to have a special skill or talent that attracts birds to me. The environment in which these episodes occurred had an enormous influence that I cannot overemphasize. There are not many places I can think of where so many birds and so many people come into contact with each other routinely. These conditions predisposed the birds to tolerate my being among them, and keep in mind, I was with them quite often. *Club George* roughly covers a four-month period during which I was in the company of certain birds, some like George, almost daily for the entire period. The familiarity this created between this observer and the objects of his observations

[1]Sandra Blakeslee, "Minds of Their Own: Birds Gain Respect," *New York Times*, February 1, 2005, www.nytimes.com.

tremendously influenced the results. I do not believe I could have witnessed many of the events I described if individual birds had not become comfortable in my presence. Why do I stress this? You should understand that your experiences in the field will depend on many factors not the least of which is how familiar you are to the birds you chose to study. It can make a difference.

Whatever your frequency of visits may be you must keep your well-being and that of the animals you observe as top priorities. Above all the beginning birder has to be sensitive to recognize when his or her interaction borders on intervention. Even the most well-intentioned bird-watchers can sometimes do the wrong thing. My advice is to study individual birds' behaviors in the literature and in the field in order to understand how closely you can or should approach them. Never force yourself upon wild birds. When you move toward them do it quietly, cautiously and respectfully. As much as you may come to adore them they are not pets and should never be. Their freedom to go about the business of life is not only what sustains them but our interest in them.

Your personal safety must never be overlooked. It may sound simpleminded but one of the most important bits of wisdom I can pass on to you is to remember to watch where you are walking. It is easy to trip or fall while looking at a bird instead of the terrain in front of you. Also when an opportunity presents itself to you to be physically close to a wild animal, especially those farther up the food chain, consider the wisdom of doing so before you act. Inadvertently you, the animal or both may be injured. Dangerous predators play a small part in my urban birding experience but I do not need to be an expert to know that in wild environments it's possible to encounter creatures representing a far greater potential danger than the occasional Snapping Turtle or Common Raccoon I may meet. Use common sense in the field. Keep a considerable distance away from bears, coyotes, mountain lions, badgers, rattlesnakes, leeches, and wasps to name a few and any other creatures that move erratically and make menacing noises. This last category may be applicable to errant members of our own species as well.

Now is the time for you to accept your own Club George charter membership. Get off the sofa, turn off the TV, gather your gear, making certain it does not include open-toed shoes, and get out of doors. The birds will enlighten and entertain you if you will only let them.

Bibliography

Alsop III, Fred J. *Birds of North America: Eastern Region.* Smithsonian Handbooks. New York: DK Publishing, 2001.

Beletsky, Les. *The Red-winged Blackbird: The Biology of a Strongly Polygynous Songbird.* San Diego: Academic Press, 1996.

Blakeslee, Sandra. "Minds of Their Own: Birds Gain Respect." *New York Times,* February 1, 2005. www.nytimes.com

Brown, Robert M., Sheila Buff, Tim Gallagher, and Kristi Streiffert. *Where the Birds Are: The 100 Best Birdwatching Spots in North America.* National Wildlife Federation. New York: Dorling Kindersley Publishing, Inc., 2001.

Butcher, Greg. "The State of the Birds Report," *Audubon* October 19, 2004. *www.audubon.org/bird/stateofthebirds.*

Central Park Conservancy website www.centralparknyc.org.

Chesapeakbay.net. *Common Snapping Turtle: Chelydra Serpentina Serpentina,* October 19, 2004. Chesapeake Bay Program, 2003.

Chipley, Robert M., George H. Fenwick, Michael J. Parr, and David N. Pashley. *The American Bird Conservancy Guide to the 500 Most Important Bird Areas in the United States: Key Sites for Birds and Birding in All 50 States.* New York: Random House Trade Paperbacks, 2003.

Cogger, Harold G., Joseph Forshaw, Edwin Gould, George McKay and Richard G. Zweifel. *Encyclopedia of Animals.* Illustrated by David Kirshner. New York: Barnes & Noble, 2002.

Coombes, Allen J. *Smithsonian Handbooks, Trees.* 2nd ed. Smithsonian Handbooks. New York: Dorling Kindersley, Inc., 2002.

Drilling, Nancy, Rodger Titman, Frank McKinney, *Mallard.* The Birds of North America, ed. A. Poole and F. Gill, no. 658. Philadelphia: The Birds of North America Inc., 2002.

Forshaw, Joseph, Steve Howell, Terence Lindsey, and Rich Stallcup. *A Guide to Birding.* Consultant editor Terence Lindsey. San Francisco: Fog City Press, 2002.

Grubb, T. C., and V. V. Pravosudov. *Tufted Titmouse.* The Birds of North America, ed. A. Poole and F. Gill, no. 86. Philadelphia: The Academy of Natural Sciences; Washington, D.C.: The American Ornithologists' Union, 1994.

Halkin, Sylvia L. and Susan U. Linville, *Northern Cardinal.* The Birds of North

America, ed. A. Poole and F. Gill, no. 440. Philadelphia: The Birds of North America, Inc., 1999.

Hallowell, Christopher, and Walter Levy (eds.). *Listening to Earth.* New York: Pearson Longman, 2005.

Heinrich, Bernd. "Hibernation, Insulation and Caffeination." *New York Times,* January 31, 2004. Op-ed page.

————. *One Man's Owl by Bernd Heinrich.* With drawings and photographs by the author. Abridged and revised by Alice Calaprice. New Jersey: Princeton University Press, 1993.

Jackson, Jerome and Henri R. Ouellet, *Downy Woodpecker.* The Birds of North America, ed. A. Poole and F. Gill, no 613. Philadelphia: The Birds of North America, Inc., 2002.

Kaufman Kenn. *Birds of North America.* With the collaboration of Rick and Nora Bowers and Lynn Hassler. Kaufman Focus Guides. New York: Houghton Mifflin Company, 2000.

Kroodsma, Donald. *The Singing Life of Birds: The Art and Science of Listening to Birdsong.* New York: Houghton Mifflin, 2005.

La Rouche, Genevieve Pullis. *Birding in the United States: A Demographic and Economic Analysis.* Addendum to the 2001 National Survey of Fishing, Hunting and Wildlife-Associated Recreation, Report 2001–1. Washington D.C.: 2003.

Lowther, Peter E. and Calvin L. Cink, *House Sparrow,* ed. A. Poole and F. Gill, No. 12, 1992, Philadelphia: The Academy of Natural Sciences; Washington, D.C.: The American Ornithologists' Union, 1992.

Mowbray, Thomas B., Craig R. Ely, James S. Sedinger, and Robert E. Trost, *Canada Goose.* The Birds of North America, ed. A. Poole and F. Gill, no. 682. Philadelphia: The Birds of North America, Inc., 1994.

Nero, Robert W. *Redwings.* Washington, D.C.: Smithsonian Institution Press, 1984.

Peterson, Roger Tory, and Virginia Marie Peterson. *A Field Guide to the Birds of Eastern and Central North America.* 5th ed. New York: Houghton Mifflin, 2002.

Reid, George K., *Pond Life: A Guide to Common Plants and Animals of North American Ponds and Lakes.* Edited by Herbert S. Zim and George S. Fichter. A Golden Guide. Revised and updated. New York: Saint Martin's Press, 2001.

Robbins, Chandler S., Betel Brunn, and Herbert S. Zim. *Birds of North America.* Revised by Jonathan P. Latimer, Karen Stray Nolting, and James Coe. Illus. Arthur Singer. A Golden Field Guide. New York: St. Martin's Press, 2001.

Shackelford, Clifford E., Raymond E. Brown and Richard N. Conner. *Red-bellied Woodpecker*. The Birds of North America, ed. A. Poole and F. Gill, No. 500. Philadelphia: The Birds of North America, Inc., 2000.

Shaw, John. *John Shaw's Nature Photography Field Guide*. New York: Amphoto Books, 2000.

Sibley, David Allen, *National Audubon Society The Sibley Guide to Birds*. 1st ed. Illustrated by David Allen Sibley. New York: Knopf, 2001.

———. *National Audubon Society The Sibley Guide to Bird Life & Behavior*. Illustrated by David Allen Sibley. New York: Knopf, 2001.

———. *The Sibley Field Guide to Birds of Eastern North America*. Illustrated by David Allen Sibley. New York: Knopf, 2003.

———. *Sibley's Birding Basics*. Illustrated by David Allen Sibley. New York: Knopf, 2002.

Stokes, Donald, and Lillian Stokes. *Stokes Field Guide to Birds: Eastern Region*. 1st ed. Boston, New York, London: Little, Brown and Company, 1996.

Swift Instruments, *How to Care for Your Binoculars by Swift* (Japan: Swift Instruments, 2001), pamphlet.

Tarvin, Keith A., Glen E. Woolfenden. *Blue Jay*. The Birds of North America, ed. A. Poole and F. Gill, no 469. Philadelphia: The Birds of North America, Inc., 1999.

Wells, Diana. *100 Birds and How They Got Their Names*. Illustrated by Lauren Jarrett. Chapel Hill: Algonquin Books of Chapel Hill, a Division of Workman Publishing, 2002.

Winn, Marie. *Red-Tails in Love*. New York: Vintage, 1998.

Yasukawa, Ken, and William A. Searcy. *Red-winged Blackbird*. The Birds of North America, ed. A. Poole and F. Gill, no. 184. Philadelphia: The Academy of Natural Sciences; Washington, D.C.: The American Ornithologists' Union, 1995.